PLAN**SIMPLE** *Meals*

Get More Energy, Raise Healthy Kids, and Enjoy Family Dinner

50+ GLUTEN-FREE & PLANT-CENTERED MEALS INCLUDED

by Mia Moran

For my husband. You are the light of my life, my most patient partner, and my #1 cooking teacher. Without you, there would be no book. Thank you!

CONTENTS

CREATE YOUR HAPPY HEALTHY FAMILY

Introduction	7
Step 1: Set your intention	11
Step 2: Find "your" food	27
Step 3: Set a rhythm	39
Step 4: Plan for good meals	91
Step 5: Build your village	135
Step 6: Celebrate	221
Step 7: Tell your new story	253

CHANGE YOUR FOOD ONE MEAL AT A TIME

Breakfast	47
Lunch	103
Dinner	145
Snacks	231
THANK YOU! THANK YOU!	260
RESOURCES	262

Introduction

Six years ago I lost 65 pounds, and though it sounds pretty incredible when I say it out loud, it's the least important part of all of the information that I want to share in this book.

In changing my food to lose weight, my whole understanding of health care changed. I always thought "something" happens to your body, you go to the doctor, the doctor gives you medicine, and you get better. It never dawned on me that it was weird that the same things happened to me over and over, or that perhaps I could avoid the doctor altogether. In the heyday of $10 co-pays, I almost looked for reasons to go to a physician. I don't think I am alone.

It's no exaggeration when I say that changing my food changed my life. I will delve into the astonishing details of that transformation throughout this book, but here are the highlights.

Three days after changing my food, I got a period without taking hormone medicine, which I had taken my whole adult life.

Two weeks after changing my food, I noticed that I could sit in a room with a cat without running for the door or the medicine cabinet.

Three weeks after changing my food, I had no coffee in my system, yet felt boundless energy — a huge change from someone who six weeks prior existed on six or seven cups a day, only to feel utterly exhausted.

A year after changing my food, I enjoyed the first year of my life without a significant ear infection or antibiotics, and my dentist was shocked by how much my teeth improved.

After a year of reaping so many benefits of healthy food, I was able to help my daughter too. At three years old, she was a royal mess with eczema, constipation and a cranky attitude. Once I used food to heal her instead of laxatives, she became a brighter and happier little girl, and even her schoolwork improved.

I never anticipated any of this when I set out to lose some weight. My goal was simply to be a mom who could sport skinny jeans. But once I transformed my family followed suit. We did it one step at a time. My kids were not born loving spinach, but today, my daughter actually craves salads, and my son asks for sautéed greens all of the time.

As a family, enjoying healthy food has made us happier people. It is a lifestyle, and we choose it every day. On this journey I have encountered many people who have felt better once switching to a gluten and dairy-free diet, and I have yet to meet a person, including myself, who wouldn't benefit from more veggies. For this reason, all the recipes in this book are plant-based and gluten-free. It isn't my goal to insist everyone eat this way, but I do hope that learning these tools gives you many new healthy alternatives. While many beautiful cookbooks full of delicious gluten-free and dairy-free recipes exist, my goal is to go deeper. There are many pieces to the puzzle of creating a happy and healthy family, and that is why I wrote this book.

A healthy lifestyle is not just about food, but also how you're eating and functioning as a family. Because if you're only eating healthy food, you're missing the bigger picture. Lifestyle changes are less about ingredients and more about managing your busy schedule, day to day parenting, and teaching your kids healthy habits in the long term. Neither choosing food nor parenting are topics that are taught much formally, but in my opinion, they are the most important jobs.

Before I dive into the specifics, I really want to be clear about three things: 1. No one is perfect. 2. Parenting is a journey, and 3. Food is a daily practice.

I am a work in progress. I am far from perfect. I have good days and bad days, as do my kids and husband — and they don't always overlap. We have been putting food first as a family for about six years now, and while we have come so far, I still have goals in mind to make my life even healthier and more vibrant.

Remember that change takes time, consistent action, and patience. Take it day by day. Acknowledge the practice. I know what it feels like to pick up a nine-year-old girl from school who just falls into your arms after having a really tough day. I know what it feels like to just think that the best thing to do for her at that moment is to comfort her with the nurturing smell of a neighborhood bakery and to buy her a cupcake. We've all had those days as parents, but I invite you to look at food in a new way. To find better solutions that will be just as sweet.

This book may help you lose the baby weight that still weighs you down even though you have a five-year-old, or it may help you feed a picky eater with food allergies. This book is really about considering the role that food plays in our lives as people, and our role as parents to pass valuable information to our children. Between parenting and food, we're literally building our future kids day by day. No matter what we think in the moment, these things are more important than making club soccer, art class, or getting the perfect score on the SATs.

And I know that it's not always easy to make good food choices in the modern world we live in. Fast-paced lives often mean a world of fast food options. But it doesn't have to be that way for you and your family. I invite you to create a life consisting of less choices, less ingredients, and more healthy habits that are going to serve your families for generations to come.

When it comes to food, I've found that if I lead by example, others follow naturally. Throughout my journey, I've watched my healthy changes effortlessly trickle to my parents, siblings and friends — not because I am special but because it is the way humans learn. I have learned so much of what I pass on to you from my husband, mother-in-law, and friends who were curious about cooking or health before I ever was. Over the past six years, this amazing ripple effect was created. I'm totally humbled by how that expansion has now grown into writing this book, and even bigger, you reading with a curious mind. Community is the key to lasting change that will eventually change the world and the way we see food forever. Let's do it – and let's do it together.

HOW THIS BOOK WORKS

I have created the **7-Step Plan Simple Meals System** that looks like this:

1. Set your intention
2. Find "your" food
3. Set a rhythm
4. Plan for good meals
5. Build your village
6. Celebrate
7. Tell your new story

This 7-step system is how my family and I, and all the families who have gone through our programs, are making lasting changes.

Throughout the book I will dance between stories, strategies for your family, and food formulas.

Each chapter is then divided into three parts:

1. You
2. Your Family
3. The Food

With every change you choose to tackle, my hope is that you start with yourself and extend the positive change to your family – always learning, upgrading, and having fun in the process!

9 PLAN SIMPLE MEALS

STEP ONE
Set an Intention

"To accomplish great things, we must not only act, but also dream; not only plan, but also believe."

– Anatole France

LETTING A STRONG "WHY" PULL YOU FORWARD

I remember a cold winter day in January when everything changed. My third child was about to be a one-year-old, and somehow that gave me permission to take care of myself after five years of pregnancies and nursing. Don't get me wrong, I loved every inch of my kids, but in the process of working and caring so deeply for the rest of my family, I had lost myself.

I was 65 pounds heavier than I had ever been. In my head, I thought if could just lose weight, I would be happier. But I wasn't quite sure how to achieve this. I had followed diets in my past — Weight Watchers, Bagels, South Beach to name a few, but ultimately nothing kept the pounds from creeping on over the last few years.

I have not always been a "foodie." In fact, at this point in time, I was not sure how to cook an egg or even what kale looked like. Food was an overwhelming and emotionally loaded topic for me. I was not sure what to do, but it was a new year, and my resolution was to try hot yoga. The owner of the studio was teaching class on a particularly cold winter day, and afterward, I introduced myself and spent some time telling her my story, including my struggles with food. She ended up giving me exactly what I was looking for regarding my diet and more — and it's the more that was particularly powerful and new. While she helped me examine what I was eating, the bigger thing she did was to make me examine why I wanted to change. She encouraged me to make daily affirmations as though I was already healthy, thin, and filled with energy. I learned that in order to make big changes last, I needed a strong reason to push me forward.

Every day, I wrote on a card in the present tense: "I am full of energy. I am great mom. I am really happy and at my ideal weight." I wrote it down and read it aloud every single day, sometimes five times a day if needed. Through reading and repeating, I started believing. Through affirmation, I could visualize my present reality in its ideal form.

There is power in the present tense. I started to act "as if" my three statements were true. Reading them over and over allowed me to eventually believe what I was saying, and once I believed my affirmations, my actions followed suit. For example, if I was my ideal weight would I get upset and eat an entire pizza? No. Would I maybe wake up a little early and go for a walk instead? Yes. Affirmations started changing the way I made decisions, little by little.

In the same vein, I started to observe the negative stories I was telling myself. I noticed that when I told others that chocolate is my weakness, I felt bad when I ate chocolate. Or if I said I am really bad at drinking water, I would forget to drink it all day. Affirmations changed these negatives around. When any unhelpful stories came up in my mind, I would consciously turn them around and create a new positive story that could pull me forward.

My story began with a strong desire to lose weight. Then that desire transformed into a big motivation to learn how to cook. Somewhere in there, I was desperate to help my daughter feel well. Next, I wanted to help my whole family eat better. Finally, I knew I had to share healthy eating with friends and my community. In each of these stages, I had a really strong intention that kept me in the present, moving forward and making great decisions.

WHAT IS YOUR WHY?

What is your goal? What's the drive that's going to pull you forward every day? Let your goal be your new story.

Pause for a moment and think about why you're here. Why did you get this book? Why are you opening the pages? Why do you want to learn about eating better? Is it because you are unhappy in some way?

Discontent is a great place to start because negative experiences can be so powerful in turning us toward a positive future. Maybe you feel overweight, overwhelmed or tired. Maybe you or your kids are battling a behavioral or health issue that you believe can be improved with food. Maybe you are curious about eliminating gluten or dairy and you have absolutely no idea how to start. Maybe you just hate your role of chef that you inherited when you became a mom.

With food, often stories become embedded in our minds which we blindly believe without question. We hear very compelling stories our whole lives from commercials, books, our parents, our doctors, and maybe even our hairdresser. We believe what we hear because it is told to us with passion and love, but really, food is personal. Only you know how food makes you feel.

Let's turn the negative stories around. What would it feel like to realize a negative story you often tell yourself was untrue? What would be different in your daily life? Instead of being a spectator of your life, take the initiative to tell your new story. Write it in the present tense. Make it your intention. Put it in a place where you can read it every day. Let that story start to be your new truth. Let it pull you forward.

My story was, "I am fat, exhausted and overwhelmed." I turned it into, "I am my ideal weight and have endless energy to be a great mom, wife, and business woman."

> "If you don't like something, change it.
> If you can't change it, change your attitude."
> — Maya Angelou

When you have a strong "why," and put yourself first from time to time, then you are truly able to start making good decisions for your healthy future. And leading by clear example is the best way to teach our kids. We can tell our children to eat their broccoli and finish their plate repeatedly and get nowhere, but when we quietly demonstrate it for them, without giving them other contradicting options, they eventually follow suit.

BRINGING FAMILY ALONG FOR THE RIDE

As food started to completely transform my life, I began to feel pretty successful in the kitchen. But the truth is only two out of our family of five were reaping the positive benefits. I discovered the real joy begin to flow once I started preparing healthy meals for everyone. That way, we could bond and move forward in our healthy lifestyle as a family.

The one tool that felt most accessible to me was the nightly tradition of family dinner. I had grown up in that routine as long as I could remember. While not always healthy (TV dinners and microwaves were all the rage in the '80s) family dinner connected me to my family as a child and young adult.

The funny thing is, before I experimented with food 7 years ago, family dinners always occurred in our house, but never with much intention. After a full work day, I realized I was more pooped than relaxed by the time I got to the table. Because my husband didn't always make it home in time, I would pick at the food when the kids ate and then pick at the same food again with my husband – or worse, eat a full meal with both. I was pretty emotionally checked out by the time I sat down at the table. In hindsight, I had no idea how meaningful dinner could be until I changed it.

The transition wasn't all rainbows, but once again, I started small. I made a list of things we all liked and were healthy, and started building meals around that. I also made a list of things that were not OK to have anymore and kept that list handy for times when my willpower was low (like at the supermarket at 4:30 pm with three cranky kids).

I struggled with my kids popping up from the table after I spent a long time preparing a nice meal. This got me super frustrated. Then one day I noticed that I wasn't sitting either. I was popping up to get someone more food, fill cups with water, or to tend to one child. I figured out simple things to keep us all sitting, like serving from bowls on the table instead of the stove, and filling a pitcher of water ahead of time. I made it clear to everyone that we all sit until everyone is done.

Little tricks kept me sitting there, and pretty soon we would have peaceful, hour-long meals. I'm not saying that everybody would always eat everything that I put on the table. But having me there, eating my healthy food

FROM THE FAMILYDINNERPROJECT.ORG

Our belief in the "magic" of family dinners is grounded in research on the physical, mental and emotional benefits of regular family meals. Some of the specific benefits of family dinners are:

- Better academic performance
- Higher self-esteem
- Greater sense of resilience
- Lower risk of substance abuse
- Lower risk of teen pregnancy
- Lower risk of depression
- Lower likelihood of developing eating disorders
- Lower rates of obesity

in front of them, definitely influenced them over time.

I also started setting an intention to have as many family members present as possible for dinner. At the time, my husband and I were rarely both home in the evenings together due to work schedules and switching childcare duties. So we started making small changes. We cleared our weekends to accommodate at least four family meals. We started saying no to extracurricular activities on weekends. Over time, we added a weeknight when we could all be together and eventually started focusing on valuable conversation.

I highly encourage everyone to adopt a family dinner practice. I truly believe those 45 minutes together are so optimal for family transformation, especially as they are perfectly timed after a busy day and before a restful night.

YOUR FAMILY BRAND

If you have kids you know that every age brings a new stage: The "no" phase, the "why?" times, and much later (and I think I am nearing it) the "you are so dumb" stage. There's always something. And it usually comes out full force around meals.

Dinner is an amazing tool for sharing both food and values, but what are your values as a family? Where do they originate? And even if you know them, are they crystal clear for every family member? Are they practiced daily?

I would like to offer you a tool — a tool that has served corporations for years: Your Family Brand.

Five years ago it dawned on me, in the midst of business training, that much of what I do for design clients is also something that could be translated to my growing family. While I was distracted by choosing which hospital, which stroller, and which baby clothes, I forgot to carefully choose our values. I assumed that values would just come naturally. I had no idea how crucial strong values would become or how often they would be tested.

Every good business develops a strong brand identity. It serves to define them among others and distinguish their unique set of values. Some even have a mission statement or a manifesto to outline their intentions as a company. They usually come to these conclusions by asking lots of valuable questions and considering all the facts. I realized this could also work in establishing a family.

A Family Brand could simply be ten words written on a piece of paper, or carefully laid out on a poster with definitions to be more visual. This document outlines the top values that your family stands for. You can make them into sentences, or just use simple words. If you use words, map them to where they intersect with food.

The ideas are endless. Maybe your Family Brand commits you to having at least five family dinners a week. Or maybe it calls for friends to gather once a week or forbids the unhealthy snacks at Little League. By first deciding your values, you create an entire series of "whys" for your family as a whole.

I recommend you choose 7-10 values, and be sure to discuss them as a family so that everyone knows what they mean. Younger kids could benefit from simple explanations, visuals, or rhymes, while older kids can help by being collaborators and voicing what's important to them. Write them down. Sit with them. Change them as you evolve.

As you come to specify the values that you stand for as a family, discipline will make more sense to your children as it will no longer seem arbitrary. You will also have a marketing plan that has a chance of rivaling soda, blue yogurt, and donuts.

In the not so distant past, I felt like my husband and I were often picking fights in the kitchen. It went something like this: I was cooking, and he was going through the trash, moving anything that should be composted or recycled to the appropriate bin.

"Really?" I would think. I was never a detail person. I mean well for the planet, but I have mistakenly thrown banana peels in the trash on multiple occasions, and I didn't understand why he took it so seriously.

Then I realized the banana peels were part of my husband's "why." To him, they weren't just details. He rides his bike to work even though driving is easier, always separates the trash from the recycling, has our heat programmed, and to my dismay, has had the same backpack for 20 years. He strives to leave the most minimal footprint he can on our planet. While I am not opposed to any of this (except for maybe the backpack), I didn't fully understand them until I understood his "why." Now creating minimal waste is a part of our family brand, and we all feel empowered to commit to that as a team.

I am a big believer in the airplane directive to put on your own oxygen mask before your child's. That is what we do when we set our own intention and start our journey with healthy food. The family brand gives that same sense of direction and purpose to move forward as a group.

APPROACHING FOOD: ONE DOABLE CHANGE AT A TIME

Throughout the book, you will get inspired, prompted, and excited to make some changes about what you eat. Or at least that is my intention in writing this book. I recommend that you ease into this transition for the maximum benefit. Find a reasonable place to start so that the changes work for you. In the next chapter, we're going to dive into some of the food that you can consider living without. But to start off, I just want to share a few doable changes that might serve you — small things that you could start with to shift your perspective and your relationship with food. If you want to kick start your health transformation today by making one small change, here are some easy suggestions to start you on your way:

1. Upgrade the food you love to eat. Consider avoiding food that comes from a box, the deli, or the frozen isle. Don't buy food without knowing what's in it. Read labels. Ask lots of questions. You may not change everything at once, but you will start to pay attention. A good way to get your feet wet is to commit to making one new thing a week that you usually buy, like veggie burgers, French fries or burritos.

2. Plan your meals. Making a plan for what food you're going to eat makes a huge difference in the choices that you make throughout the week. Remember, we are human. Often it's hard to make good choices when hungry. Nine times out of ten, we won't make the healthy choice if we are starving and don't have a plan. Planning ahead will even prevent you from getting too hungry in the first place, and when you do, you'll be prepared with strategies to make the best choice possible.

3. Acknowledge when your body is full. This is a great skill to cultivate because so many times we overeat when food is in front of us, or because we think it's polite, or because it's 6 pm and it's time for dinner and we think we're supposed to be eating. There are many reasons that we overeat, but paying better attention to hunger cues can help minimize mindless grazing.

4. Drink enough water. This sounds really basic but actually can be life-changing. Try to get those eight glasses that you hear you're supposed to drink. Try to drink them every day and create a system that enables you to do so.

5. Substitute homemade treats for processed ones that still make it in your kitchen. Start with items your kids are always asking for — muffins in the morning or homemade cookies instead of packaged ones. Use the recipes in this book and pack them with nutrients. Even in moments when you're not substituting homemade, simply taking treats out of their packages and displaying them nicely makes a difference. Put cereal and crackers in Ball jars. It will help your kids start to shift their perspective—maybe food doesn't come out of a box all the time.

6. Make family dinner a priority. One of the simplest and most effective changes you can implement is just to take the time to enjoy food together every night. Watch how it changes your dynamic as a family and makes everything a bit more harmonious. If you have them once a week, try to have them twice a week. If you have it every night, work on making the conversation more meaningful.

7. Serve raw fruits and vegetables for snacks. We eat so many unnecessary empty calories between meals. We feed our toddlers Cheerios, our athletes Gatorade, and our school children donuts. These are all empty calories that can make us sick. Put carrot sticks on the table with hummus. Put the fruit bowl where everyone grabs for it.

8. Drink smoothies. Smoothies are a great way to incorporate fruits and vegetables and they're loved by most. Just putting two fruits and water in a blender makes a smoothie, like banana and strawberry and water. You don't need yogurt, milk, or sugar. If you need it sweeter, you can always add dates. If you need it creamier, you can always add cashews.

9. Add vegetables to every dish. This is a great way to supplement your existing routine with a healthy boost. Even a sweet cake could house some shredded zucchini, but I'm really thinking more savory dishes. If you're making meatballs, for instance, try adding some chopped veggies. If you're making tuna fish salad, instead of just tuna and mayonnaise, consider adding radishes, pickles or cucumbers.

Getting healthy with food can be a drastic lifestyle change, depending on your current habits. But no matter how insurmountable it may feel, focusing on one doable change can help you take small steps toward your goal. Some changes take an hour and others may take weeks, but the important thing is that you know what is right for you, and you commit.

I'm a person who does very well with structure. I like rules, and my willpower with food is close to none. You may be more of a "fly by the seat of your pants" kind of person. You may detest structure and rules, and have a healthy sense of willpower. Whatever your style, don't underestimate the small changes, like an improved cookie recipe or less sugar in your coffee. Small steps will really add up when practiced habitually over time.

Let's talk chocolate — something I personally love! Gretchen Rubin was featured on one of my favorite podcasts, "Glambition Radio" hosted by Ali Brown. Gretchen explained two ways a person might cut back on chocolate, which I found fascinating. For some people, the easiest way to reduce their chocolate is to allow themselves one little square of chocolate a day and savor it. But to others, that one little square might as well be torture. One small taste just makes them want 100 more bars and so for them, just eliminating chocolate altogether is the best bet. Think of this example when considering your own food choices. Can you indulge in a small amount? Personally, I have never been very good at moderation, but that has definitely changed over time. Now, there are definitely things that I savor in small amounts when the time is right, but it started with a lot of structure.

As you're going through the content in this book and all the new information, don't get overwhelmed. Focus on what your next doable change is and hold close to that. You are going to change the way you and your family eat; sometimes that has to do with the actual food, and sometimes you will change the stuff around the food.

TOOLS THAT WILL HELP MAKE THE FOOD CHANGES EASIER

There are certainly some tools that make healthy cooking easier. Some of them are little things and some are big investments. I highly recommend cleaning out your cabinets first. Too much clutter in the kitchen can get in the way of what would otherwise be a simple, doable change.

Sell or give away kitchen items you aren't using, and then evaluate what you need. If your first doable change is about smoothies, a new blender makes sense — save the pressure cooker purchase for when you take on soups. It is a good goal that everything is your kitchen is useful and in good working order.

HERE'S A GLIMPSE OF MY MOST USEFUL AND HEALTHY KITCHEN APPLIANCES.

Vitamix

This is the first thing I would recommend to any busy person who wants to get healthier. I use mine about five times a day for smoothies, nut milk, salad dressing, dips, sauces, and soups. I have had it for over six years and it is still going strong. It makes eating healthy at home easy and convenient. If you are overwhelmed by the cost, start saving a little each day. Think of it as an investment in your health that lasts long after your kids are out of a stroller! Remember the cost of that? I recommend a refurbished 5200. They are good as new (only used in demonstrations), have a warranty, and save you a bunch of bucks.

Pressure Cooker

We eat a lot of beans in our house. In a pressure cooker, dried beans that are soaked overnight take 12 minutes, vs. 3-4 hours in a big soup pot. I also use it to make super-quick veggie soups.

Food Processor

I consider my food processor a crucial tool in our healthy house. I mostly use it to make nuts and dried fruit, or veggie burgers out of seeds and veggies. Adding an attachment to shred carrots, beets, and turnips for quick salads saves loads of time.

Good Knives

Good knives make a huge difference. I use three knives – a 3.5" paring knife, a 6" utility knife, and an 8" chef's knife – plus cooking scissors. My husband makes sure the knives are always sharp using the hone and we have them professionally sharpened once a year.

A Fruit Bowl

Making room for fruit on an otherwise clear counter is one of my favorite healthy eating tips. It can be like a sculpture in your kitchen. And if you or your kids see a beautiful pear or ripe plum before you open the pantry and dig for snacks, that is what you will grab!

Salad Bowls

Eating more greens was the single most important strategy I embraced on my journey to a healthy weight, so green smoothies and regular salads are an important part of my repertoire. I have a salad every day for lunch and it is the centerpiece of our family dinner. Having a salad twice a day does not have to be monotonous. There are endless veggie combos and delicious dressings to explore and enjoy. Check the blog for interesting variations!

Cutting Boards

I love interesting cutting boards and would love to have a collection, but for practical purposes I suggest having two at a minimum — one for fruit and one for veggies, so your apples don't taste like garlic! I love our collection of mini cutting boards that I use to both cut and present a carrot or an apple – and the kids love snacking off of their own individual board!

Pyrex Containers

Pyrex containers cost a little more than plastic but are better for you as they are made of glass. The great thing about a set is that they stack well in the fridge. I frequently use them for leftovers, but also to store fresh-cut veggies, cooked beans, and healthy grains that I prepare on Sundays, so we have easy meals during the week.

Mixing Bowls
Good nesting mixing bowls are essential in my life! I use them for muffins and to divvy up salad among lunchboxes in the morning. I use a particular set which is stainless and has a matching top for each bowl. I also use them for soaking nuts and beans.

Silicone Muffin Molds
I use these to make gluten-free muffins for the kids' breakfast and snacks at least twice a week in the colder months. They are great for gluten-free baking that can be crumblier than wheat flour recipes. They are also fabulous for travel – compact, flexible, and light. I just place them on a cookie sheet to bake.

Citrus Juicer
My go-to dressing is lemon, sea salt and olive oil. A citrus juicer is really useful to make a large jar of lemon juice once to use throughout the week.

Ball Jars
Ball jars are the best! I have them in a variety of sizes. You can usually get them at your local hardware store. I use them for smoothies on the go; water throughout the day; to store nuts grains, and beans; for my salad in a jar; to can tomato sauce and jam in the summer; and as pretty vases.

Microplane
A Microplane, which is a small coarse grater, is perfect for lemon and lime zest, but its true genius is with ginger. Freeze ginger, and use the Microplane to grate it into soups, sauces and smoothies. I used to avoid ginger because it was hard to clean the grater, but I just rinse my Microplane and put it away!

Nut Milk Bag

This is such a simple shift that you can use to make your own delicious nut milks. They taste amazing and fresh, and also teach your kids where their food comes from. A nut milk bag is the modern-day version of getting a cow for your family!

Spiralizer

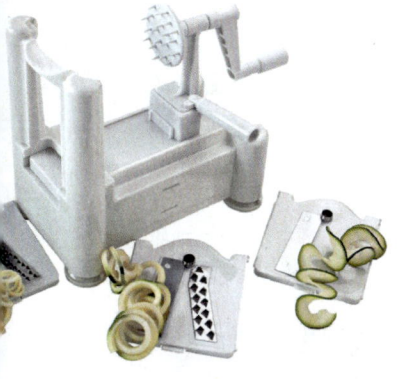

This low-cost tool is something I highly recommend! I use it for one thing: to make zucchini pasta. So it is not something I use all year, but I enjoy it during the season. This is also a good way to involve kids in the food preparation which helps them become more adventurous eaters. It has a blade, so I supervise, but my kids are always amazed to see a zucchini become pasta. And though zucchini is not their favorite, they are always more curious about a dish when then helped make it!

Dehydrator

This is not the first thing I would purchase if you are just transitioning to healthy eating, but it takes it to the next level — allowing you to dry your own local produce, make your own cheesy kale chips, make fruit leather for the kids, and prepare seeds and nuts more nutritiously than store-bought.

Mandoline

I think I have this because it was listed on our wedding registry years ago. Now I use it at least four times a week. It neatly slices radish or cucumber salads that my whole family devours. I also use it for raw beet and turnip slices that can be used as "crackers" for a dip. I also cut sweet potatoes and bake them as round thins on a cookie sheet once or twice a week — they are a family favorite!

(Go to plansimplemealsbook.com for the latest promotions.)

Doable Changes

At the end of each step, I want to offer up a few doable changes. A really fun way to think about doable changes is to play with a new one each week. Don't think too much — choose one that feels great and experiment this week.

1. Know why you want to get healthier, and write it down.
2. Repeat affirmations every morning.
3. Meditate for ten minutes a day.
4. Create your family brand.
5. Write a list of habits you want to kick and something to do instead.
6. Commit to eating food that counts. Tell five people.
7. Get yourself a high-speed blender like the Vitamix.
8. Clean out the pantry of food you know doesn't serve you.
9. Invest in sharp knives. Keep them sharp.
10. Get a pressure cooker to prepare beans and soups.
11. Get rid of your microwave. It does not serve healthy behaviors in the long run.
12. Invest in new serving dishes.
13. Buy Pyrex storage containers and ditch your old plastic variations that don't all have tops.
14. Create a system for fruit and veggie waste, like compost.

STEP TWO
Finding Your Food

"As parents, we want what is best for our children. We would never intentionally harm them — in fact, we make sure to get them the best possible care, read to them, play with them, and ensure their safety at home, at school and at play. But when it comes to feeding them, somehow we don't know what's best. Our kids seem finicky and eat nothing but cheese or pasta or chicken fingers or milk and cookies, and we let them. At the same time, we notice that they are frequently ill — they suffer from recurring ear infections, runny noses, stomach aches, and headaches… We assume, because we also see it happening with friends and family, that it is the par for course when bringing up children. It doesn't have to be so."

— Joel Fuhrman, M.D., from *Disease-Proof Your Child*

We don't always realize how often what we eat is chosen for us: Thanksgiving turkey, decadent birthday cakes, cereal for breakfast, eggs and bacon for brunch, cookies with milk. Who decided these combinations of foods and events? Somehow, at restaurants all over the US, kids still choose between the same disappointing selection of chicken fingers, French fries and macaroni & cheese. Food has become an automatic thing that we don't always think about or choose carefully. What if we decided to choose for ourselves?

When I changed my food, I eliminated gluten, dairy, animal protein, caffeine, and alcohol. The cool thing is that I did not restrict myself. I ate as much fruits and greens as I needed. I learned how to make smoothies, use nuts as cream, and add in foods like nori, kelp, and sauerkraut.

Over the years, I have added some foods back. I have had times where coffee is the perfect start to a day, and I have certainly enjoyed a glass of red wine, or two. I have experimented adding back in fish when my body craves it, and I noticed that I still feel OK, though I still choose to leave out animal protein most of the time. Dairy and gluten, on the other hand, send my stomach to another planet and my energy plummeting — but that's just my personal reaction, yours may differ.

YOU: THE DETECTIVE

I invite you to start asking questions when it comes to food. Examine your meals more closely. What are you eating and why? Is the food contributing to your best self? Is every bite making you healthier?

Let go of any blame and instead, focus on the positive changes that are possible through your new awareness.

Food, like stories and heirlooms, get passed down from generation to generation and eventually become ingrained our culture. Sometimes media takes a particular food and convinces us it is good. And an actual chemical addiction can also be responsible for our powerful, not always healthy food cravings.

Study after study has shown that if you put a rat in a cage with a choice between cocaine and sugar, the rat always goes after the sugar. Sugar is in everything. It's in all these processed foods that we feed our kids, and it's super addictive. It is hard to say no to sugar. There's no question about that.

So many of our ideas about food are conditioned, either by the media, or advertising, or from our grandmother, or sometimes just from the grocery store strategically placing a product. We get information about what we should eat from all these places, and we assemble it together in our heads in a very unconscious way.

But we are not going to do this anymore.

Right?

Instead of accepting automatically the food that is offered to you at work, at a friend's house, or at the grocery store, ask yourself one simple question. "Will this help my future self?" This does not mean you will only say yes to broccoli. You may very well say yes to a cookie because you have checked in, and you are certain that it will make you happy, and that will cause you to do a better job of parenting later. But if you are grabbing it to be polite, because you are bored or out of a nervous habit, say "no thanks," and simply observe the effects of your decision.

If you said yes to something unhealthy, like the cookie, then later, not in the moment, consider why you thought it would bring you happiness. My guess is that cookies are associated with a memory that brings you joy. When you are not hungry, and you are in your kitchen with some time, consider how you might rework that recipe to serve both your happiness and your body.

One of my happy foods is brownies. Brownies were something that my grandmother mastered — they were probably 90% butter and sugar, super chocolaty, and perfectly undercooked. She kept them in a gold tin in the freezer, and I can still remember the sound of the pop. You did not say "no" when my grandmother offered you a brownie. They were a source of great pride for her, and she would visibly take offense if they were refused. So, when she looked at me and said, "Please have a brownie" I couldn't say no.... and many times I would sneak back for more.

Of course, my grandmother did not intentionally shape my ideas of food with her brownies, but these are the kind of associations that we inherit through the daily ritual of coming together and eating.

Though family is hugely responsible for how we see food, the media may be even bigger. Milk is a clear example of how strongly advertising can affect our thinking. Over the last few decades, milk has been advertised to us consistently as the thing that will make us healthy and strong. How many of those commercials do you remember? Now data overwhelmingly shows that Americans consume too much dairy. Many studies show that dairy isn't necessary at all. Yet still, just three weeks ago, my pediatrician asked if my kids were drinking their milk.

MIA'S BROWNIE MAKEOVER

INGREDIENTS

1 cup raw walnuts

1 cup raw pecans

3/4 cup raw cacao powder

1 cup Medjool dates,
  pitted and firmly packed

DIRECTIONS

1. Pulse walnuts and pecans in a food processor, with S-blade, until nuts are finely ground.

2. Add dates and cacao. Process until mixture begins to stick together.

3. Press dough into a loaf pan that is lined with parchment paper.

    Refrigerate until you are ready to eat.

    (Pictured with almond milk)

Though I'm not claiming all pediatricians share this view, I also doubt mine is the only one who does.

It's hard to reconsider what has been handed to us through years of conditioning. It's especially difficult as parents who just want the best for our children. It takes a little extra curiosity and awareness to start choosing the foods that actually make you and your children feel good and thrive, and perhaps separating that from the dozens of stories and messages you've been inundated with subconsciously. The cool thing is that you get to decide the new stories you tell your family. You support them in creating healthy choices and lives that will eventually be passed along to their own children. We can use conditioning and learned behavior to our advantage, instead of being a victim of it.

TAKE STOCK, MOVE FORWARD.

Take stock of where you are today — make a list. What foods do you crave or eat out of habit? What foods do you want to let go of? What foods are you excited to integrate into your diet? What is one step you can take tomorrow to go towards the direction you want?

FAMILY: BRINGING GOOD FOOD TO EVERYONE

My second "doable step" was bringing my middle daughter, who was four at the time, along for the healthy eating ride. My intuition and a lot of tantrums told me on several occasions that she wasn't thriving the way she could be.

I thoroughly examined her diet, starting at the beginning. When she was little, and I was nursing her, I had to eliminate soy and dairy because she had so many digestive problems. When she turned 18 months, her doctor decided her indigestion was just a phase and approved yogurt. Of course, once introduced, yogurt became her favorite food, but it never seemed to make her feel good.

I always had weird inkling that she was in a little bit of pain. Even though she was old enough to speak, at age four, I suspected that she didn't use words to express her pain because she was so young and didn't know anything different. I decided to eliminate dairy.

I kid you not, two days later, I got a call from the teacher saying, "What happened?" I didn't quite remember at first. "What do you mean?" I asked. Her teacher was overjoyed. "Orly followed all the instructions perfectly today. She was like a different person!" I couldn't believe how such a seemingly insignificant change could affect my daughter so much, but then, of course, I had my own healing experience through food.

Orly suffered from awful eczema. Her hands, especially, were so swollen that some days that they were nearly three times their normal size. It was obviously painful for her. She also had bumps all over her body due to eczema. For a while, we had been trying creams. Since we live in New England, winter can be especially cold, and Orly's skin would dry out. Though we were furiously slathering her with creams, nothing seemed to really help.

In three weeks off dairy, it all went away, and she hasn't had any symptoms since. Although it took a little extra patience and awareness to get to the source of her issues, it has been so worth the investment in her childhood!

It was a year later when we tried eliminating gluten to help her with too-often tummy pains.

After cleaning up our diets and reaping the positive effects, I felt compelled to focus on our family as a whole and to find what worked for us as a group. At this point, I was a bit more like a line cook than a mom making dinner. I read many books, took classes and gathered all the information I could about eliminating common food allergens in children and adults. Though my other two children did not seem as affected by dairy and gluten, I still speculated that they could benefit from more fruits and veggies and less gluten, dairy and sugar.

We will get into exactly what we eat in chapters to come, but I would like to share the tool that made the biggest difference — announcing when food makes us feel good.

PRAISE FOOD

Think about holidays. If you're somebody who really loves holidays like Thanksgiving and Christmas, you probably associate them with happy times and togetherness in your childhood. Maybe you loved unwrapping gifts, or that moment in the morning when you woke up early to see the stockings, or maybe you cherished the fact that both grandparents traveled far for Thanksgiving dinner. In those moments when family is gathered together to celebrate, food is inevitable. Smell and taste are senses that cause us to remember things, but if you really look at the stories we tell during the holidays, it's easy to see how happiness and over-indulgence get connected. Like, "Oh my God, I was so full after that meal. I feel so tired. I just need to take a nap," or "That was so good and now my stomach hurts so much."

Over time, we start to associate the good moments with feeling bad soon after, when really that isn't what food is supposed to do to us at all. We inherit the idea that it's normal for food to make us feel bad. It doesn't have to be this way. Once you figure out how to eat a meal filled with nourishing food in portion sizes that work for you, it's important to share it aloud so that your family hears. Maybe you stand up from dinner and you say, "Oh my gosh, I feel so great" or "I loved eating that salad, it made me feel so good," or "I ate just the right amount, I could have eaten that whole extra bowl but I'll save that for lunch tomorrow."

You're not trying to preach or to say something negative; you are simply sharing how good you feel after you eat. Then all those people around you start thinking at the back of their heads, "Oh I'm supposed to feel good after I eat." Little by little you start to open the door for conversations about food and wellness, and the connection between the two.

BE MINDFUL OF WHAT YOU BRING HOME

Willpower is a pretty unreliable trait to depend on for the long haul. I will explain how to develop systems and rhythms to depend on instead, but a really simple tip is not to bring food into the house that you don't want your family to eat. Examine the snack drawer or shelf you've assigned for snacks in your home. Decide what is really serving you. Once you've identified those few things, eliminate the rest.

If there are a few processed brands that pass your test, take them out of the package and keep them in clear airtight containers. This way, food becomes less about exciting boxes and more about the food.

Ideally, the designated snack area in your home should be sparse and maybe only contain some nuts and some dried fruit, not packages of candy and cookies. Snacks are a great starting point for identifying what truly serves our bodies, because a lot of times we snack all day long, especially with kids — Saturday sports games, after-school scout meetings or a ride to Aunt Sarah's house. Going from place to place may make you feel like you are accomplishing many things, but just take notice of how many activities involve food to keep children engaged. Do you really need that extra cupcake or cookie that's being offered? Will the kids starve if they don't have something to munch on while you travel? Eliminating excess snacks are a really great place to start because, for the most part, we don't need them.

FOR PARENTS OF KIDS WITH FOOD ALLERGIES OR OTHER HEALTH ISSUES THAT HAVE CAUSED YOU TO RE-EVALUATE FOOD...

One of the things that I've noticed in my life is that often children just want to fit in, especially at school. That's been one of the prime challenges surrounding my daughter and her allergies. In our journey, we found the right foods that made her feel the best and empowered her to make choices for herself. In doing this, she was able to let go of the opinions of others. At some point, she learned to own her uniqueness instead of feeling self-conscious about it. She had enough episodes of eating the wrong thing and feeling sick that she didn't even miss the cake and the candy when other children were eating it. Even as a mom and a healthy food advocate, there were times I felt guilty that she wasn't enjoying the same things everyone else around her was. I already knew that I didn't want her to have those foods, but I wanted her to be happy.

The thing about food and children is that we often use treats to soothe bad emotions. Even in my childhood, I remember that a cookie, or my grandmother's brownie, or a lollipop would always help me feel better on bad days. Now that I'm a mother the roles have switched. I know how it feels to scoop up my daughter when she's upset after a bad day and just want to do anything in the world to make her feel better. I know that food sometimes feels like the programmed response.

FOOD: CLEARING YOUR CANVAS

Now, I'd like to share an elimination program that could help identify what foods best serve you.

While there's no need to choose a specific timeframe, 21 days is an optimal timeframe to reap the benefits and create lasting habits. But decide what is really doable for you. Even just a few days can help you experience a fresh perspective with food. Set your intention, knowing that whatever you choose is fabulous.

The idea is to eliminate gluten, dairy, meat, alcohol and caffeine for the time period you choose. If 21 days seems way out of your comfort zone, then do it for a week, and have fun with it. Use the tools we've discussed in this step to heighten your awareness of how food makes you feel and make sure to sprinkle some extra self-care into these days.

Again, see how you feel and what your body is telling you. Notice the difference in your energy levels when you aren't pumping yourself full of coffee or knocking yourself out with wine.

Don't worry about how much you eat. Focus more on what you are eating rather than how much. You want to feel satisfied, not hungry, so eat as much as you need to stay on plan.

Though sometimes changing your food will hit hard in the beginning, and you may experience somewhat of a detox period. If you were eating lots of sugar, gluten and dairy daily, you might actually experience headaches and low energy in the beginning. But the second you get over that hump, the lasting benefits are far worth the shaky start you may feel... Promise!

Please note, if you are nursing or pregnant, consult a doctor. This is a week of detoxifying, and you can come back to this exact formula when the time is right.

FOR EVERY DAY YOU DECIDE TO DETOX, FOLLOW THIS FORMULA

When you wake up:

- Drink 16 oz of water first thing. Then fill eight glasses or bottles, so you drink all day long!

- Plan when you can fit in 15 minutes of exercise — go for a brisk walk, do some yoga, or download a fitness app. You need to sweat for at least 15 minutes each day!

Breakfast:

- Start with a green smoothie or two. (pages 50-53).

- If you still feel hungry, and it is not yet noon, eat as much fruit as you want until lunch.

Lunch:

- Start with a huge salad. Do not add gluten, meat, or dairy to your salad. Make it about the wide assortment of raw, steamed, or roasted veggies available to you over a large bed of leafy greens. Avocado, nuts and lentils make a salad heartier.

- Enjoy an amazing healthy dessert or smoothie (pages 236–39, 242, or 247).

- At 2:00 pm, call it quits to eating, and take a break until dinner. If this is day one, it is totally possible that you have now been eating all day! This is an OK time to catch up on water and enjoy a cup of herbal tea.

Dinner:

- Dinner should be gluten-free and vegan and you should not eat much after 6pm. It may be a bowl of veggie soup (page 201), a bed of greens with warm lentils, a sweet potato and salad, or quinoa with sautéed kale and avocado. (Note these are all things your whole family can eat too!)

- You have had a nourishing day! Commit to no food after dinner. Brush your teeth with your kids after dinner. Drink more water. Enjoy time reading, taking a bath, relaxing with your husband...

{You can download a daily checklist at www.plansimplemealsbook.com/hub}

Doable Changes

At the end of each step, I want to offer up a few doable changes. A really fun way to think about doable changes is to play with a new one each week. Don't think too much — choose one that feels great and experiment this week.

1. Eat a minimum of 3 cups dark leafy greens a day.
2. Try yoga. Already go? Add one extra class a week.
3. Always have a beautiful fruit bowl out where everyone can see it.
4. Try a one-day juice cleanse and see how you feel.
5. Tell your kids how good you feel after eating the right amount.
6. Reinvent an old family recipe so it is gluten-free and dairy-free.
7. Drink a green smoothie every day for a week.
8. Drink eight glasses of water for one full day. Fill a pitcher or 8 glasses in the morning and work backward.
9. Ditch coffee for a week.
10. Find three regular times that you can exercise each week.
11. Make a list of 15 exercise routines you can do when your kids are around.
12. Read three new labels at the store.
13. Omit dairy for a week.
14. Clean out one drawer that you are always searching through.
15. Start a food journal.
16. Try an elimination experiment.

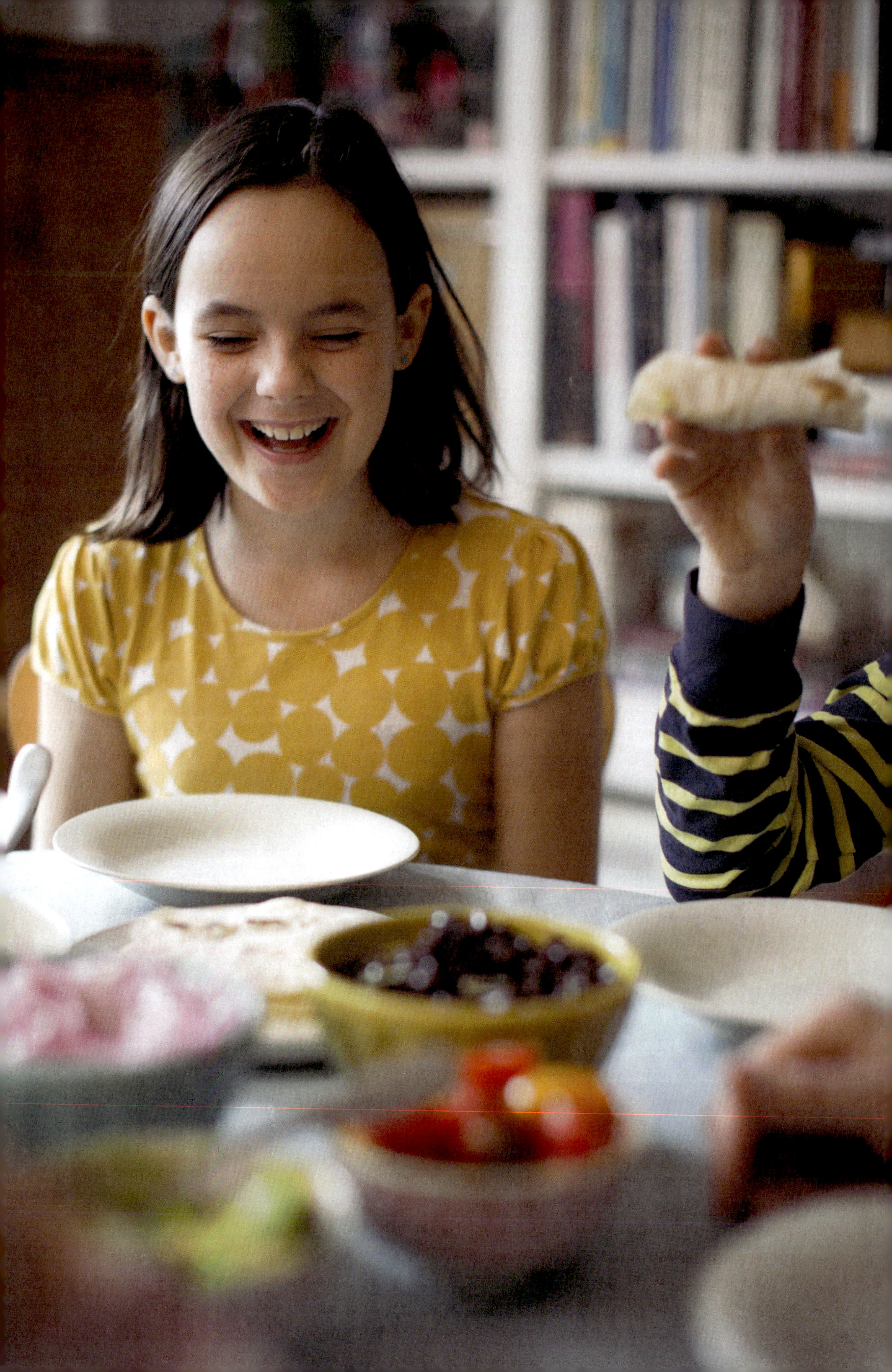

STEP THREE
Setting a Rhythm

"In the tapestry of childhood, what stands out is not the splashy, blow-out trips to Disneyland but the common threads that run throughout and repeat: the family dinners, nature walks, reading together at bedtime, Saturday morning pancakes."

– Kim John Payne, *Simplicity Parenting*

Rhythm is the most important component of lasting change. I like to think of rhythm as "routine with love and flow," or a "series of practical rituals." Rhythm is something that can expand or contract, so it fits into your life at any given moment.

This is in stark contrast to a schedule which is made up of blocks of time. With kids, it is easy to get off schedule and feel delayed. When we operate from this place of rigidity, it is very easy to fall behind when we have a hundred more tasks left in the day.

Let me share a story about how I've seen rhythm work with food and children: All three of my kids cycled through the same kindergarten class at a Waldorf school. Waldorf philosophy puts a strong emphasis on rhythm with its students. In kindergarten, all three of my students were in Ms. Leah's class, who created a different healthy snack each day of the week. Monday is bake bread day. Tuesday is porridge day. And the day that had a huge impact on my family was Thursday — vegetable day.

With all three of my kids, I watched as vegetables became a topic of conversation. Through the rhythm of vegetable day, a natural curiosity and interest in healthy food was created. And, through the course of their years in kindergarten, my kids each started getting a little bit more adventurous when it came to food.

Each of my children reacted a little differently to vegetable day, and it was fun to witness their respective journeys. I will never forget the day that my son, our first kindergartener, requested sautéed spinach with "brown sauce" for dinner one evening. It was even before my healthy transformation, so not only could I not believe my ears, but also I had no idea how to make it. To this day, seven years later, he asks regularly for sautéed greens.

My daughter, who was second to experience vegetable day, had a different experience. I don't know that she's ever loved her sautéed greens, but she became very smitten with pickled vegetables. Interestingly, she's my pickiest eater, but she just loved the pickled garlic and green beans.

At a farmer's market recently, my kids were delighted to find a woman selling pickled food. All three of my kids started jumping for joy after picking up jar after jar. My son grabbed a jar of pickled asparagus. My daughter a jar of pickled green beans. My youngest rejoiced over the pickled garlic. The looks of the people around them were priceless. I wish I could've had a picture of their faces, seeing these three little kids so excited about pickled vegetables.

Watching the kindergarten students navigate Ms. Leah's snacks was fascinating. At the beginning of the year, some kids pick at the food or simply move it around their plates. At some point, either boredom or curiosity or acceptance causes them to try the new dish they resisted at first. By the end of the year, it really is a rare case of a child who doesn't love at least one new thing. The rhythm around snacks gives kids the permission to ease into new foods without letting them off the hook. While each of my children had a unique experience in Ms. Leah's class, I observed them collectively begin to embrace nutrient-rich, unprocessed, sugar-free foods by the year's end.

I took careful note. Create a rhythm. Stick to it. Show up each day with a smile and hold consistent to your food "why."

YOU: ROUTINES AND RITUALS

How often have you felt overwhelmed by the time you've gathered the kids for school in the morning? I am talking 8 am. Most days start off with the best of intentions — you wake up on time, make breakfast, and pack lunches— yet everybody's scrambling to get out the door and causing chaos. So many mornings, by the time you're in the car, you're furious and gritting your teeth.

But what would happen if you applied the same principles to your morning as the ones Ms. Leah applied to snack time?

RITUAL: a series of actions or type of behavior regularly and invariably followed by someone.

The amazing thing about using rhythm to create change is that your new habits will fit into your life with ease. The most important mindset shift most of us have to make is letting go of the clock, and the anxiety it so often creates.

Instead of thinking I have to do this at this time and that at that time, instead build your day around the key rituals you have already committed to: your meals.

And, here is the thing I want you to hear again and again. Getting out the door in the morning has a lot more to do with you than you might think. It is not about your daughter who would rather sleep in, or the child who can never decide what to wear. It is not about your son who seems always to be tripping over himself as he gathers his stuff to get out the door or the one who hits his sister when you just need him to get in the car.

My guess is that from the time you wake up in the morning to the time you manage to get out the door and start your day, you've forgotten the needs of the most important person — you.

So let's change that.

I can promise you that if you feel nurtured by the time you are in the car, your energy will be 100% different than it would've been if you hadn't nurtured yourself.

If there are parts of your morning that trigger your anger or take away from your peaceful attitude, try to shift those. For example, if your daughter takes too long to choose her clothes, make picking out an outfit part of the evening rhythm. If you are all forgetting to brush teeth, then do it as a family. If you are always running up and down the stairs between food prep and helping a child, see how you can make that process better — maybe it is as simple as a hug ritual, so your child feels attended to, or maybe she can get dressed downstairs while you prep breakfast. You can also just decide to change your attitude about a task, like packing lunches or washing dishes. Instead of seeing these things as chores, see them as your means to a healthy lifestyle. If it is fun for you, someday, your kids will want to take over that job!

As kids get older, they become more self-sufficient and can support you more. They also might need a little less sleep. They might also be more aware of the food that they need in the morning. Once you have written self-care into your rhythm, then we can move into creating a rhythm that serves your whole family.

MAMA'S ROUTINE EXERCISE

Write down all those things that you, as a grown up, need to get accomplished from the time you wake up to the time your kids get out the door. Don't make it all about packing lunches and doing stuff for the kids — list those things but also list the things you have always wanted to do or used to do for yourself. Don't worry about how you will accomplish these things — let yourself dream.

If you have always wanted to meditate, write that down. If exercise is important, maybe you figure out a way to sneak out of the house and go for a quick walk before you're in the kitchen making breakfast. Other ideas include: brush your teeth, take a shower, get dressed in non-yoga clothes, make a green smoothie, drink water, pack your own lunch, kiss your spouse, hug your kids, take a supplement, breathe, write in a journal, take care of your skin… the list could go on!

Write them all down. Then look at the list. Cross off anything that is not necessary. Circle the things that family members could help you with. Put a heart next to the one thing that is popping off the page as something that will light you up each morning. Put everything in order. Lead up to breakfast and then lead out the door. Post it on the fridge as you get used to your new rhythm.

Now take the same idea and make a nighttime rhythm that starts with walking in the door, leads to dinner and ends when you go to sleep. It could include any of the ideas above: read a book, leave your electronics downstairs, light a candle, take a bath, connect with your spouse, call your mom, prepare food for another day, wash dishes, say a prayer, read with the kids, stretch.

Make sure to check in with your list from time to time to see if it needs amendments. After all, you are a different person at 30 than at 40, and your needs change. I can't speak past that, but I'm sure things are different at 50 too. Likewise, our kids' rhythms change.

{You can download the worksheet at www.plansimplemealsbook.com/hub}

FAMILY: FINDING THE RHYTHM THAT WORKS

One of the ways that we can add rhythm into our family mealtimes is by doing exactly what I explained in that story of the kindergarten class, where each meal was labeled by theme. Food themes can be assigned to each day of the week and each meal. I have found that food themes are a fabulous place to start in really changing how you eat.

THE FOOD IDEAS IN THIS BOOK WILL BE ORGANIZED BY THESE THEMES:

Breakfast	**Lunch**	**Dinner**
Porridge Day	Pasta Day	Bean Day
Granola Day	Leftover Day	Wrap Night
Fruit Day	Salad Day	Kids Cook Day
Muffin Day	Wrap Day	Pasta Day
Fruit and Fancy Drink Day	Dip Day	Rice Bowl Day
Smoothie and Toast Day	Unsandwich Day	Soup Day
"Yogurt" Day	Soup Day	Farm-to-Table Day
Pancake Day		Cookbook Day
		Clean out the Fridge Day

The amazing thing about this system is it makes life easier for us parents as well as for kids. How often have you panicked at 5:00 pm thinking, "S***! What's for dinner?" Without rhythm, a few unhealthy things begin to happen. We tend to cook the same things over and over. We make compromised choices on what foods we are eating. We give into what kids think they want and like very easily because at that moment our energy is low and our willpower is weak — we just want to get dinner done.

The beauty of daily food themes is that they are flexible enough to provide a variety of dishes that utilize the season we are in. Themes also create a structure that quells the daily anxiety that sometimes comes with meals and new foods — both for the cook and the kids.

When kids protest about a meal, it is usually just a way for them to test control. Sometimes when they say no, it's not even that they don't really want what's in front of them, but more that they want to take charge over that moment. As a child grows, he or she will naturally push back on boundaries just to see what happens when they do. Sticking to meal themes is a really effective way of eliminating that by offering consistency.

Take soup day for example. While every child might not love soup, if it appears rhythmically throughout the week, say every Wednesday, there's a higher chance that a child will warm up to it over time. Then, as the weeks carry on, maybe the soup changes and includes new ingredients, vegetables, broths or spices. Generally, my children have become more adventurous using this technique, though of course some meals are still more liked than others.

RHYTHM STRATEGY

Try consistent food themes for three weeks and just observe how it changes your level of organization as a parent and also how your kids show up to a meal.

RHYTHM PLANNING EXERCISE

Think of the natural course your week takes and notice the ebbs and flows. Pay attention to which days feel busy and which days have some space. Get out a piece of paper and write it all down, organized by days. Then look at the themes provided or make your own and mark ones that feel easy and ones that feel challenging. If you have older kids, Kids Cook Day might be a way to get you off the hook on a busy day while if your kids are little, Kids Cook Day might feel totally draining. This is a very personal process.

(Get the rhythm planning template at http://www.PlanSimpleMealsBook.com/hub)

Don't forget that some meals can be made in advance pretty easily. And know that every day does not have to be different. You can have two soup nights, or oatmeal three days a week. I highly recommend moms having a big salad every day for lunch, so that would be the same every day!

You might have to revisit this at different times of the year— one system for when the kids are in school and one for when they're out. Seasons play a part in our sense of rhythm too, so for now focus on the one you are in.

So often we revert to feeding kids what we know they will eat after a tantrum because really, we just want them to eat. We start to think less about what they're eating out of necessity and desperation. But because it is soup day, I stand on firm ground and serve it with way more confidence than I would have on an unplanned day. I think kids pick up on our strengths and our weaknesses. When we aren't fully confident behind a meal we serve, kids sense that and test us.

In his book, *Simplicity Parenting*, Kim John Payne mentions how it takes a child seven times to like a food. Yet how often have we given up after one tantrum, if not two? Seven times is a lot. But, when you have benchmarks and consistency around food and mealtime, along with a formulaic approach to incorporating the new, then seven times feels a lot more doable.

To allow these themed meals to create a rhythm in your house, it's helpful first to observe the natural way your life already flows. That way, you can begin to insert the rhythm of food with harmony, instead of forcing new habits that work against you. For example, if Tuesday nights are busy with after-school activities, or a time when you often have to work late, then it is best to keep Tuesday's dinner simple. Do something easy, like pasta day or soup (that you have made over the weekend) day. On the flip side, when you're looking at your schedule and notice there's a day that perhaps the kids get out of school early or your workload is lighter, then push yourself. One of my favorite challenges during my week is Cookbook Day when I decide to conquer a new recipe with my kids. It's fun, but definitely takes a bit more time and patience, so it happens on a quieter day — when there is less school, work, or outside activities.

RHYTHM IS LIKE GOLD FOR PARENTS — CONSISTENCY HELPS PARENTS MAKE AND PREPARE FOOD WITH EASE, WHILE CHILDREN FEEL THE SAFETY OF REPETITION AND PREDICTABILITY.

As you begin to fit good food into your rhythm, you will naturally want to optimize the rhythms already happening around you. Then the steady passing of time becomes something you savor as a family. Maybe your family enjoys outdoor meals, farmer's markets, or hikes during the summer and hot tea and board games in the winter. Maybe you learn to love prepping healthy meals on the weekend, helping hands with the dishes, and the extra time to snuggle up and read with your kids in front of a fire.

Look at your schedule. Look at what you have said yes to. Are there too many things that are fighting with your healthy lifestyle? Have you said yes to being class parent, babysitting someone else's child on Saturdays, or extra hours at work with your boss? Have you said yes to everything your child wants to do and added some extra activities yourself to make him more well-rounded? I am here to tell you that a quiet afternoon at home may make your child smarter and more resilient, and it will make space for good food, rest, and exercise!

MAKING SPACE

While time can feel constraining, rhythm flows naturally. Create a rhythm to your meals that fits your life, and then consider how you can shift the activities in your life to make more room for food.

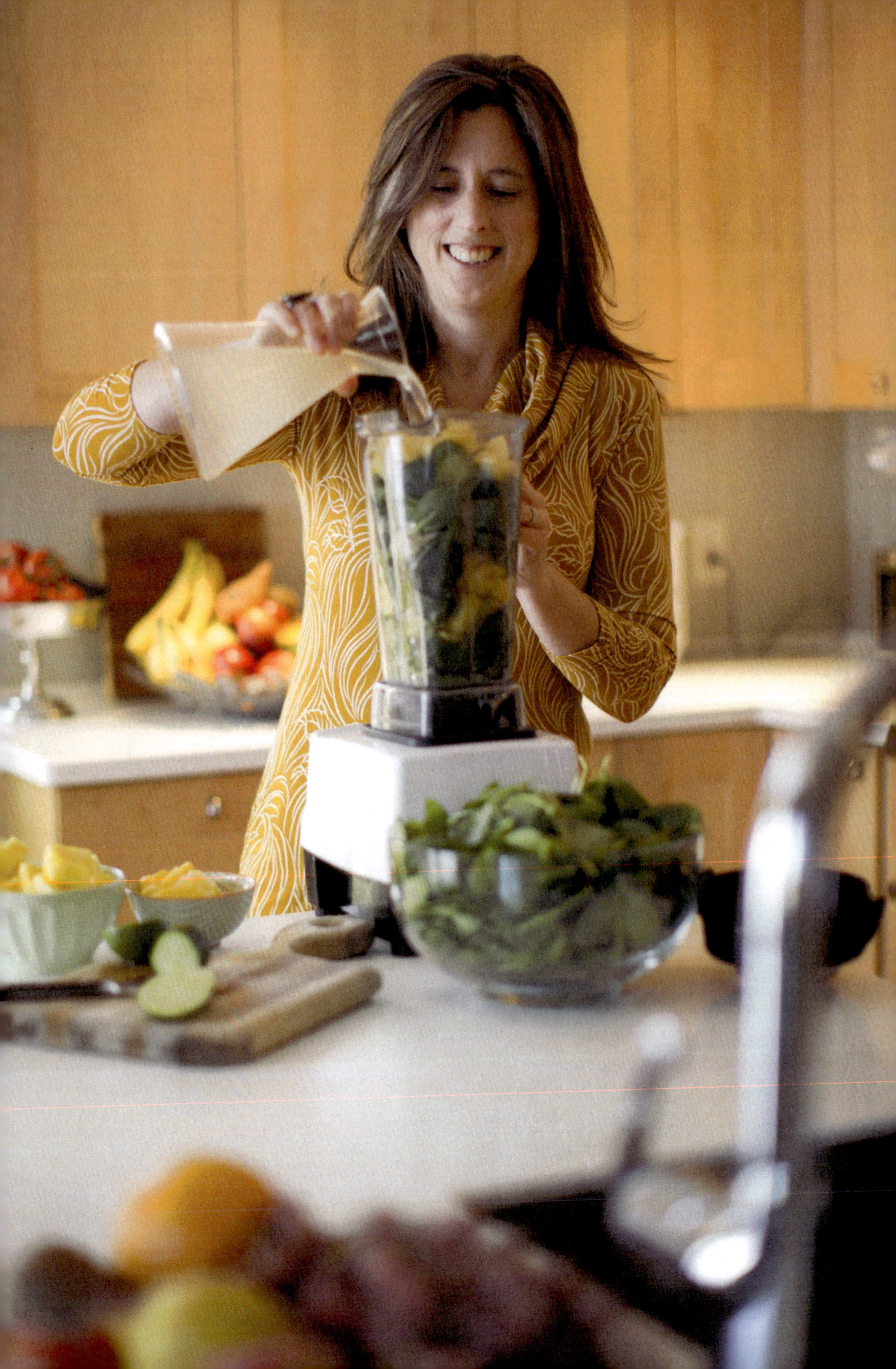

Food: Breakfast

"To eat is a necessity, but to eat intelligently is an art."

— François de La Rochefoucauld

Let's dive into breakfast.

If you consider the word "breakfast," it literally means "to break the fast." Usually, we have eaten dinner the night before, had a sufficient restful sleep of eight hours (hopefully) and woken up fresh with empty stomachs. Breakfast is the perfect opportunity to be deliberate about how you are fueling yourself and your kids, and to set a positive tone for the day to come.

Unfortunately, many of today's breakfast products and the choices reflected in the Standard American Diet do little to optimize nutrition and energize us sustainably. Morning is a time to ramp us up for the day and begin to fire our internal engines. High-sugar cereals, which describes most on the supermarket shelves today, are not the best choices. Highly processed carbohydrates combined with sugar will only cause a sharp spike in blood sugar and a dramatic crash soon after. Eggs and bacon, another all-American breakfast, contains more protein and fat, but may be too heavy first thing in the morning.

This is meant to be a template and some ideas to consider. I sincerely want you to find the foods that work best for your body. I mention cereal and eggs because these are things that are so programmed into our minds, but keep in mind the wisdom you have received from your body while considering what you eat in Step 2.

If your child is not thriving in school, breakfast may be a good place to start experimenting and seeing if it has an effect. It might be that he or she is experiencing a spike in energy from food and then a crash

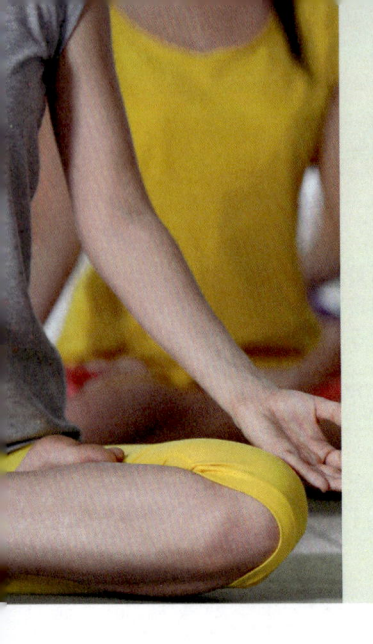

MONTH AT-A-GLANCE

Mark time on the first of every month to look at the month ahead.

Are there mornings you or your spouse will be away? Is there a morning you want to exercise? Is there a morning event at school? Mark them on the calendar.

What worked and what didn't last month? Look at what foods your kids loved and what you want to work on them loving. How is your morning routine going? What is one thing you can work on this month?

{Download Goals Sheet at www.plansimplemealsbook.com/hub}

during the two hardest classes in school. If you often feel tired by midmorning and reach for a second or third cup of coffee by noon, maybe instead consider what you are eating for breakfast. The right foods—that is—the tastiest, simplest, and most nutritious, will leave you energized enough to maybe cut coffee altogether, or opt for tea instead.

Breakfast in a minivan is definitely not ideal, for kids or adults. Neither is standing at the counter of your kitchen, nor eating on a bus or subway. Taking the time, however brief, to center yourself and your family in the morning will have lasting benefits throughout the day. If you are always eating breakfast on the go, see if you can move things around in your morning rhythm and connect with your family before you all part ways. If you can figure out how to assemble everyone together for just a few moments in the morning, breakfast takes on a peaceful, ritualistic calm, which feeds into the calm of getting out the door and starting the day.

SO WHAT ARE YOU SERVING FOR BREAKFAST?

The number one way to create healthy eaters is to eat with your kids and model how delicious and fun healthy eating can be. This is why at dinner, I recommend your goal is for the whole family to eat the same things – no more different meals for kids and parents, everyone eats one meal as a group! At breakfast, I have a different take. Each day you are going to create a totally healthy breakfast for your family based on a rhythm you create. But each morning, you will enjoy a green smoothie. You can offer a smoothie to your kids too, but don't feel like you have to push it. You get to model the smoothie, and they enjoy one with you one morning each week if that is part of the rhythm you create. Drinking a green smoothie every morning will change your world! And eventually, one day your practice will be contagious!

SMOOTHIES

If we go back to the idea of breakfast setting the tone for the day, it's great to get greens in as early as you can, so my smoothie is almost always green though sometimes chocolate plays a role as well.

WEEKLY WELLNESS CHALLENGE

Try having a green smoothie every morning for seven days. See how this doable change transforms your day.

Morning green smoothies are fabulous for busy parents who need nutrition on the go. Invest in a reusable cup with a straw, so if you don't finish before you walk out the door, you can bring your drink along for the ride!

SMOOTHIE HACKS

If your smoothie doesn't quite do it for you, a little extra lemon or a banana usually helps with taste. Ice also helps in warmer weather with texture.

You'll find more recipes in the Snack Section for afternoon smoothies that include nut milk and are more like shakes. If you're hesitant about trying a green smoothie, maybe start with my afternoon smoothies instead, as they are heavier and sweeter. These are great for transitioning toward healthy food for kids, and when you are craving something sweet in the morning.

But eventually, work your way to a greener smoothie to start your day!

Many people tell me they think green smoothies are gross, and I usually I find that is for one of three reasons: 1. There is no citrus to offset the sweet; 2. There is not enough liquid; or 3. Their blender in not strong enough to make a smooth, creamy texture. (The Vitamix is the blender that I recommend.)

49 PLAN SIMPLE MEALS: GET MORE ENERGY, RAISE HEALTHY KIDS AND ENJOY FAMILY DINNER

5-INGREDIENT FORMULA TO MAKE YOUR OWN GREEN SMOOTHIES

FILL YOU BLENDER IN THIS ORDER FROM THE BOTTOM TO THE TOP.

Water or Coconut Water
To desired thickness

A Handful of an Herb
A Handful of an Herb: Parsley, Cilantro, Basil

1 Part Light Green
Cucumber, Celery, Bok Choy, Avocado

1–2 Parts Sweet Fruit:
Banana, Mango, Pineapple, Apple, Pear, Peach, Papaya, Melon, Berries *(Note: berries shift the color from green)*

2 Parts Dark Leafy Greens
Kale, Chard, Spinach, Collards

1 Part Citrus
Lemon, Lime, Grapefruit, Orange

PLAN SIMPLE MEALS: GET MORE ENERGY, RAISE HEALTHY KIDS AND ENJOY FAMILY DINNER

FRUIT TIP

Frozen berries are actually better than the fresh ones at the supermarket that are out of season, because they have not been sprayed with something to keep them from molding. In the summer or when fruit is getting old, freeze it yourself so you enjoy them throughout the year.

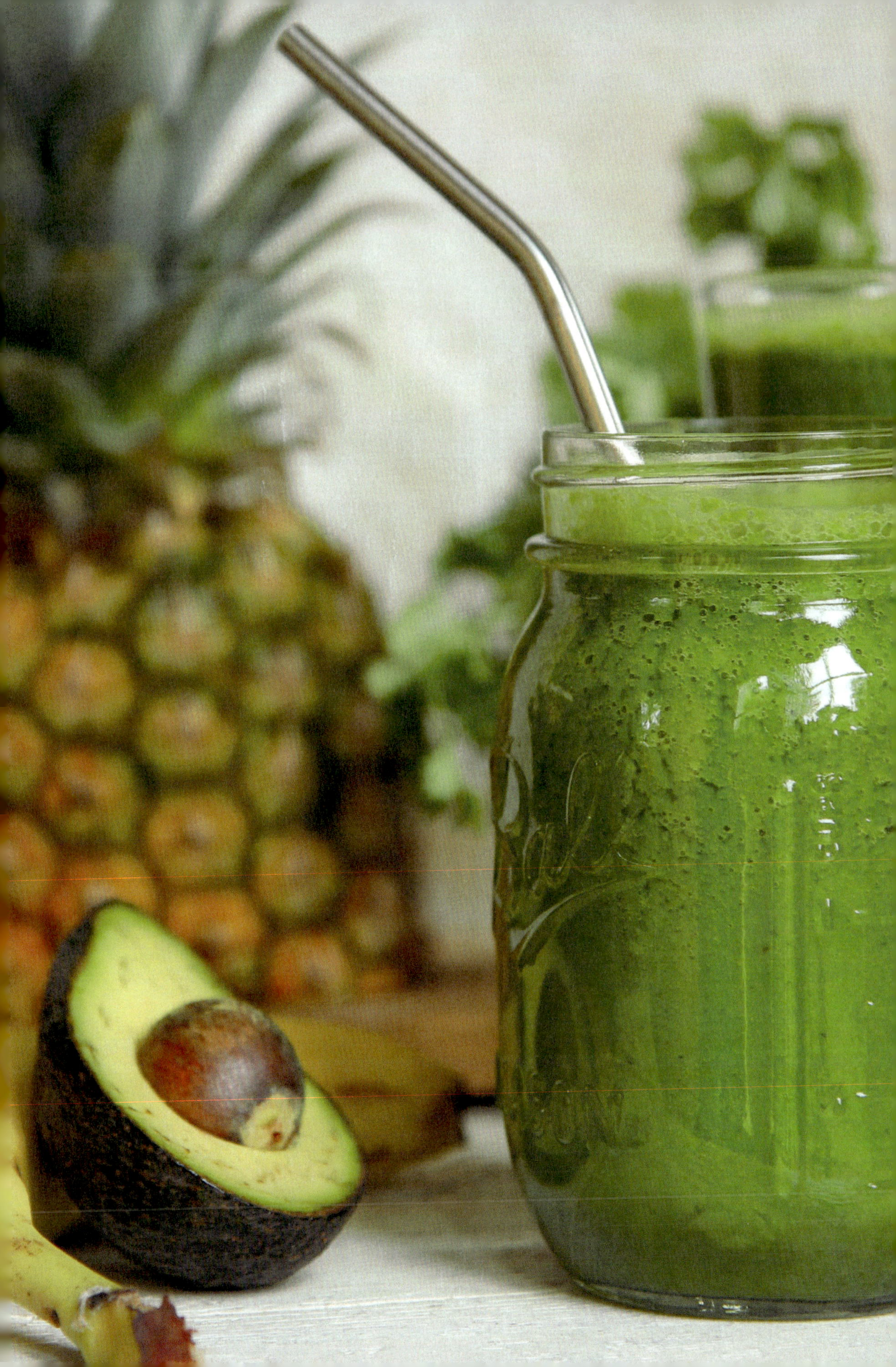

SMOOTHIE FORMULA IN ACTION

GREEN APPLE SMOOTHIE

INGREDIENTS

2 cups kale leaves, without stems
1 small cucumber
1 lime
1 green apple
1 ripe pear (or banana)
A handful of parsley
3 cups water (more for thinner)

DIRECTIONS

Blend in a high-speed blender.

TROPICAL SPINACH

INGREDIENTS

2 cups spinach
1/4 cup cilantro or parsley
1 cup pineapple
½ cup frozen mango
½ avocado
1 banana
1 lime
2-3 cups water

DIRECTIONS

Blend in a high-speed blender.

ORANGE AND GREEN SMOOTHIE

INGREDIENTS

10 clementines
2 cups chard leaves without stem
1 banana
½ cucumber
2 cups fresh squeezed orange juice
1 cup water

DIRECTIONS

Blend in high-speed blender.

BREAKFAST RHYTHM
PORRIDGE DAY

I used to call this oatmeal day, but really it is so much more than oats. In the fall and winter, the warmth of a hot bowl of porridge is delicious. You may regularly pick oats, but you can also use quinoa, brown rice, corn, millet, and amaranth, which you will see on the following pages. In the summer, oats can be chilled, and dishes like Chia pudding can replace warm whole oats.

CHOOSE A GRAIN OR SEED

Gluten-free Oats

Millet

Quinoa

Quinoa Flakes

Buckwheat

Cornmeal

Chia

SELECT 1-3 TOPPINGS

Chopped fresh fruit, such as Apple, Pear, Banana, or Berries

Chopped dried fruit, such as Dates, Figs, Apricots, Mango

Raisins

Walnuts

Sunflower Seeds

Sesame Seeds

Hemp Seeds

Spirulina

Maca

Maple Syrup

Raw Honey

ADD SOME EXTRA MOISTURE

Almond milk

Coconut Oil

Rice Milk

Cashew Cream (page 65)

Yogurt (We love coconut milk yogurt)

PORRIDGE FORMULA IN ACTION

MAMA MORNINGS

I find that despite the fact that the muffins and pancakes we make are super healthy and yummy, my "mama" body feels much better starting my day with a smoothie. My exception is sometimes porridge day. You will see, I have even found a way to make it green thanks to my good friend Jen!

COCONUT QUINOA

INGREDIENTS

2 cups quinoa, thoroughly rinsed
2 cups coconut milk
2 cups of water
3 teaspoons flax meal
1 tablespoon vanilla extract
½ teaspoon cardamom

DIRECTIONS

1. Bring coconut milk and water to a boil.
2. Add quinoa, flax seeds, vanilla extract and cardamom.
3. Turn down heat and cook, stirring occasionally, until all liquid is absorbed and quinoa is cooked through, about 15 minutes.

You may want to add more coconut milk to finish.

BRAZIL NUT OATS

INGREDIENTS

1 cup Brazil nuts
4 cups water
A pinch of sea salt
2 tablespoons maple syrup
1 tablespoon cinnamon
1½ cups steel-cut oats
2 bananas, mashed

DIRECTIONS

1. Put Brazil nuts, water, sea salt, maple syrup, and cinnamon in a blender and blend until smooth.
2. Pour the milk (with pulp) into a pot.
3. Add oatmeal and mashed banana to pot and cook according to directions, stirring frequently.

MILLET PORRIDGE

INGREDIENTS

1 ½ cups millet

2 teaspoons coconut oil

3 ½ cups unsweetened almonds

1 ½ cups water

DIRECTIONS

1. Pulse millet in your dry blender or food processor.
2. Melt the coconut oil in a small pot on medium heat.
3. Once hot, add the millet and stir for two minutes. Slowly pour in the almond milk and water and stir.
4. Bring to a simmer stirring occasionally.
5. Reduce heat to low/simmer and place a tight fitting lid on top. Simmer for 8-10 minutes.
6. Remove the lid and stir. You can add more liquid and toppings at this time.

BUCKWHEAT PORRIDGE

INGREDIENTS

1½ cups roasted buckwheat oats

5 tablespoons chia seed or flaxseed

3 cups nut milk

3 cups water (see notes)

3 teaspoons vanilla

A pinch of cinnamon

DIRECTIONS

1. Combine the buckwheat, chia, milk, vanilla and cinnamon into a pot. Let sit overnight in the fridge (or on stove if cool at night).
2. In the morning cook over low heat for 5 minutes until thick and creamy. Add more water or milk if needed.

JEN MAZER'S GREEN OATS

INGREDIENTS

2 cups gluten-free oats
Spirulina
Raisins
Blueberries
Cinnamon
Almond Milk
Maple Syrup
Almonds or Pecans
Hemp Seeds, Chia Seeds, or Flax Seeds

DIRECTIONS

1. Place in bowls and add spirulina (or green powder): one baby spoonful for children, and half a tablespoon for adults.

2. Add as many nutritious toppings as you wish! We suggest a handful of fresh blueberries or raisins, a few dashes of cinnamon, a big splash of almond-coconut milk (unsweetened), a bit of grade B maple syrup for a little sweetness, and a sprinkle of hemp seeds, ground flax seeds, and chia seeds. Stir it all together and the oatmeal will turn a gorgeous shade of green.

(Note: It's important to stir it before eating. Otherwise, you'll get a mouthful of spirulina, and you won't be happy!)

OVERNIGHT CHIA PUDDING

INGREDIENTS

¼ cup chia seeds
1 cup raw cashews, soaked for 1-3 hours
3 cups water
3 dates
1 tablespoon vanilla extract
1 teaspoon cinnamon
A pinch of sea salt

DIRECTIONS

1. Place the chia seeds in a mason jar (big enough for 4.5 cups of liquid).

2. Place the rest of the ingredients in a high-speed blender (such as Vitamix) and blend on highest speed until smooth.

3. Pour the cashew mixture into the jar and shake very well, so no seeds are sticking to the jar.

4. Place in the refrigerator overnight.

5. Serve with fruit.

BREAKFAST RHYTHM
GRANOLA DAY

Most cereal is not so good for us. Granola is a great way to eat whole grains and nuts, and get that "cereal" feel. Granola is something you can make once a month in big batches and store. And for times when I am not in Granola-making mode, I'm grateful there are some terrific brands that are making healthy granola.

HAVE GRANOLA ON HAND

Make granola once a month in batches or buy granola that is made of great ingredients. I like granolas that are honey or maple sweetened. Granola that is labeled raw or paleo usually fits the bill too.

CHOOSE THE MOISTURE

Almond Milk

Rice Milk

Hemp Milk

Brazil Nut Milk

Soy Milk

Cashew Cream

Smoothie

Apple Sauce

CONSIDER A FRUIT TOPPING

Berries

Banana

Raisins

Shredded Coconut

GRANOLA FORMULA IN ACTION

HOMEMADE GRANOLA

Homemade granola is super easy to make, saves you money, and you can make sure it is free of sugar and preservatives!

You could commit to making a few batches to store for the coming weeks.

SHIFTING AWAY FROM SUGARY CEREALS

This is a transition that may take some effort. Cereal is one of the foods most heavily marketed to kids. Think about the cereal aisle!

Some ideas to make the transition easier are to make an old favorite a snack once a week as you phase it out. When any cereal comes in the house, put it in another container, so the packaging is out of the equation. I recommend just avoiding the cereal aisle — out of sight, out of mind.

DITCHING DAIRY

We give you many alternatives to dairy on these pages. If you feel you or your child needs milk or yogurt, make sure it is organic and has no added sugar.

And if anyone in your family gets a cold, definitely ditch the dairy until the sniffles are gone.

NO-COOK MÜESLI

INGREDIENTS

Toasted Buckwheat Groats
Almonds, chopped
Sunflower Seeds
Raisins
Dates, chopped
Coconut, shredded
Hempseed
Banana, chopped
Apple, chopped

DIRECTIONS

Mix the ingredients in a bowl and serve with Nut Cream.

HOMEMADE OAT GRANOLA

INGREDIENTS

5 cups oats
2 cups coarsely chopped almonds
1 cup pumpkin seeds
¾ cup sesame seeds
2 teaspoons cinnamon
1 teaspoon sea salt
1½ cups mixed dried fruit
¾ cup maple syrup
2 tablespoons canola or other vegetable oil

DIRECTIONS

1. Preheat the oven to 350°.
2. Put all the dry ingredients in a large mixing bowl.
3. Mix the wet ingredients in a separate bowl.
4. Slowly mix the wet ingredients into the dry ingredients.
5. Spread mixture on cookie sheets lined with wax paper and bake for 30-40 minutes, checking and tossing every 10 minutes.

GRANOLA WITH MILK

You can buy nut milk, but please promise to read labels. The best alternative milks have the fewest ingredients.

- If there are more than three ingredients you don't understand, consider not buying it.
- It is best not to buy it if it has carrageenan or sugar.
- Rice milk is also a great non-dairy alternative.

MAKE YOUR OWN NUT MILK

INGREDIENTS

1 cup nuts (cashews, almonds, Brazil nuts)
4 cups water
1 pinch sea salt
1 pitted date
1 teaspoon vanilla

DIRECTIONS

Blend in high-speed blender.

NOTES

- If you have used almonds or you don't want any pulp, pour through a nut milk bag or strainer.
- If you have used a softer nut like cashew, macadamia or even Brazil, you may not need to strain it.
- Good for three days in the fridge.

CASHEW CREAM PARFAITS

INGREDIENTS

CREAM

3½ cups soaked cashews

1½ cups coconut water

2 tablespoons raw honey

1-2 tablespoons of vanilla

A dash of nutmeg

PARFAIT

Granola

Berries

DIRECTIONS

1. Blend cream ingredients in a high-speed blender (such as Vitamix) to make Cashew Cream.

2. Create parfaits with alternating layers of granola, cream and fruit in a cup or jar.

NOTES

- Coconut, macadamia and almonds also make great creams. You could also use a coconut, almond or dairy (if you drink it) yogurt here.

- You can add a touch of fruit to color the cream.

- You can use a variety of fruits and any granola and make parfaits. We use Ball jars and pack them for picnics or snacks at school and work.

CHRISTINA'S GRANOLA FRUIT BOWLS

The idea behind a fruit bowl is that you enjoy granola with a fruit purée.

You can easily make homemade warm apple sauce in the winter by steaming apples and pears, blending them and serving it warm with granola and some diced apple for added crunch.

My girls love what they call ice cream bowls. For these, we simply take a bag of mixed frozen organic berries, half a banana, and the tiniest bit of liquid (almond milk or water), and blend with a plunger. (If you don't have a Vitamix or Blendtec, this may be better done in a food processor.

We put a bit of the "ice cream" at the bottom of a bowl, then some granola, then a bit more ice cream and top with goji berries.

BREAKFAST RHYTHM
MUFFIN DAY

Baking from scratch is a key component to clean eating. It does not need to mean that you quit your day job and move into the kitchen, but it does mean you pick one time a week when you show yourself and your kids what it means to eat a muffin.
With Starbucks and ready-made mixes, many of our kids don't understand the components of what they are eating or have an appreciation of the process.
And to be honest, I did not either, until Muffin Day.

EGGS OR NO EGGS?

All the recipes on the following pages can be made with or without eggs. They are all dairy and gluten-free.

I have chosen to stick to being strictly vegan myself — not so much for the label, but it is the best way to describe what my body loves. But in an effort to raise healthy eaters who don't rebel later, and who also understand the connection of food to their bodies, I have chosen to include some very well-sourced animal protein for my kids. This includes the purchase of one dozen eggs from a farm that I trust (when they are available). These eggs sometimes land in muffins for the kids.

Muffins made without eggs are absolutely amazing when warm, but do get denser on day two. They are not bad by any means, just different.

SILICONE MUFFIN HOLDERS ARE A MUST-HAVE KITCHEN ITEM.

MUFFIN RECIPES

Alas, baking does not lend itself to a formula, so for this day, you get some recipes. You can certainly add other berries when a recipe calls for blueberries, and top muffins with nuts, seeds and grain sweetened chocolate chips.

RASPBERRY MUFFINS

INGREDIENTS

1 cup brown rice flour
½ cup quinoa flour
½ cup almond flour
1 tablespoon baking powder
½ teaspoon sea salt
½ teaspoon cinnamon
2 large eggs (or Flax egg*)
1 cup almond milk
2/3 cup maple syrup
½ cup coconut oil
1 tablespoon vanilla
1 cup frozen organic raspberries

DIRECTIONS

1. Preheat the oven to 400°
2. Place 12-16 silicone liners on a cookie sheet or in a muffin tin.
3. In a large bowl, whisk together and thoroughly combine the flours, baking powder, salt, and cinnamon.
4. In another bowl, whisk together the eggs, almond milk, maple syrup, melted coconut oil, and vanilla. *Note: If the coconut oil is solid because it is cold, just heat it up by placing the glass jar in a pan of hot water on the stove.
5. Add the dry ingredients to the wet ingredients and mix together.
6. Add the raspberries last. You may consider taking the bag of frozen raspberries and crushing them in the bag. Smaller bits in the muffins appeals to some kids.
7. Divide the batter among the muffin cups.
8. Bake until a toothpick inserted in 1 or 2 of the muffins comes out clean, about 12 to 18 minutes depending on how big the muffins are.

CHOCOLATE ZUCCHINI MUFFINS

INGREDIENTS

½ cup buckwheat flour
½ cup brown rice flour
½ cup Amaranth Flour
½ teaspoon baking soda
½ teaspoon salt
½ teaspoon cinnamon
½ cup maple syrup
½ cup apple sauce
1 cup zucchini, grated
½ cup coconut oil
1 teaspoon apple cider vinegar
2 teaspoons vanilla
½ cup vegan chocolate chips

DIRECTIONS

1. In a small mixing bowl, combine dry ingredients.
2. Put zucchini between paper towels to dry.
3. In a large mixing bowl, combine wet ingredients, including zucchini. Coconut oil needs to be warmed to its liquid state (you may place the jar in a pan of hot water).
4. Add the wet ingredients to the dry ingredients and mix with a rubber spatula until smooth.
5. Fold in chocolate chips, and scoop into greased muffin tin or reusable silicone muffin cups lined up on cookie sheet.

* **A FLAX EGG** is 1 tablespoon flax meal left to sit in 4 tablespoons of warm water for 10 minutes.

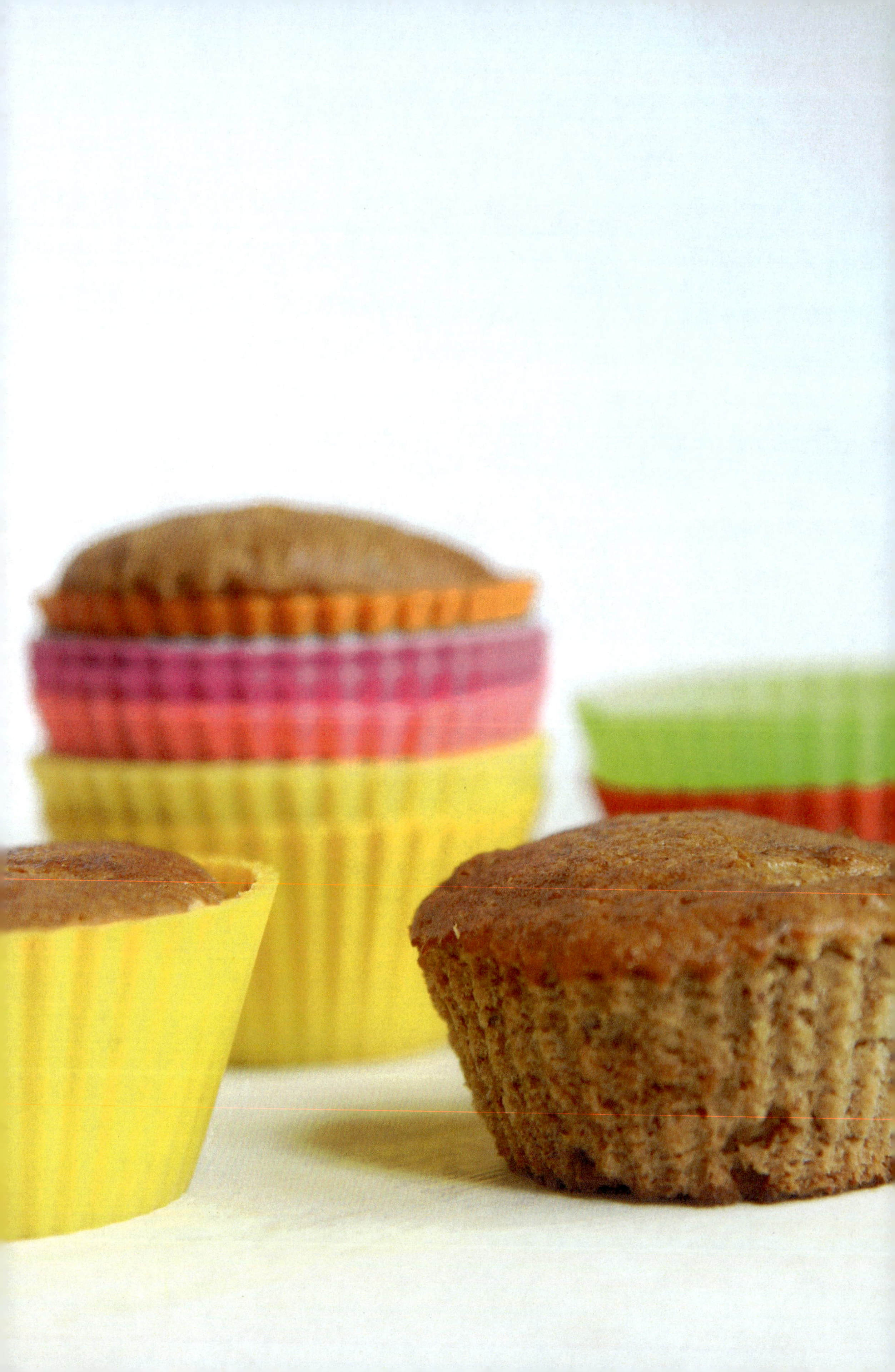

BANANA MUFFINS

INGREDIENTS

1 cup brown rice flour
1/3 cup hazelnut flour
¾ teaspoon salt
½ teaspoon baking soda
¼ teaspoon baking powder
1¾ cups super-ripe, mashed banana
5 1/3 tablespoons coconut oil
¼ cup maple syrup

DIRECTIONS

1. Mix dry ingredients in a bowl.
2. Mix banana, coconut oil and maple syrup in a blender, so the mixture gets fluffy.
3. Add mixture to dry ingredients.
4. Pour in cupcake tins greased with coconut oil. (I like mini cupcakes)
5. Bake for 35 to 50 minutes at 350° depending on size.

Note: The hazelnut flour is to add a nutty flavor. Almond flour/meal could be used instead. Or if you need a nut-free version, use oat flour.

CHOCOLATE VARIATION

Same recipe, but add a half cup of Cacao Powder to the dry mix. If you want them extra chocolaty, add a half cup of Grain Sweetened Chocolate Chips to the batter.

PUMPKIN VARIATION

Instead of banana, add the same quantity of baked pumpkin. Sweet potato and squash also work. Canned pumpkin will also work if you are in a pinch. These will not be as sweet, so you could also do part pumpkin, part banana or add a little extra maple syrup. Adding a teaspoon of pumpkin pie spice or cinnamon also tastes fabulous.

SOFT STAR ELF APPLE MUFFINS

INGREDIENTS

1 cup millet flour
½ cup almond meal
½ cup + 2 tablespoons rice flour
1 teaspoon baking soda
½ teaspoon sea salt
2 teaspoons cinnamon
1 cup almond milk
½ cup applesauce
½ cup maple syrup
1 tablespoon flax meal
3 tablespoons warm water
1 apple, peeled, cored and finely diced

DIRECTIONS

1. Place flax meal and warm water in a blender, swish around and let sit for 3-5 minutes.
2. Add dry ingredients to a bowl.
3. Preheat the oven to 350°.
4. Put silicone muffin holders on a cookie sheet or grease muffin tins. (Recipe makes 12)
5. Add the rest of the wet ingredients to the blender and blend (do not add the apples).
6. Add the blended mixture to the dry ingredients and stir with a rubber spatula until just combined.
7. Fold in the apples.
8. Pour into muffin tin or forms.
9. Cook for approximately 18 minutes.

(For additional recipes by some of our favorite chefs, visit plansimplemeals.com)

BREAKFAST RHYTHM
FRUIT AND FANCY DRINK DAY

Fruit is an overlooked food group or at least one that we feel the need to complement with something more. I know that I have thought, "What can I add to that apple to make it a more filling snack?" or "What should I serve with melon for breakfast?" The truth is, fruit is full of the vitamins and fiber we need, and is a winning food all on its own. And if you are still hungry after a piece of fruit, you can have another! So one day a week, try having fruit for breakfast.

CHOOSE 1-3 FRUITS THAT ARE IN SEASON, IF POSSIBLE.

FALL
Apples
Pears
Raspberries
Grapes
Plums
Passion Fruit
Pomegranate

WINTER
Apples
Pears
Grapefruit
Oranges
Kiwi
Pomegranate

SPRING
Pineapple
Grapefruit
Oranges
Kiwi
Mango

SUMMER
Strawberries
Peaches
Apricots
Cantaloupe
Watermelon
Honeydew Melon
Cherries
Plums
Mulberries
Tomatoes
Blackberries

ALL YEAR (SOMEWHERE)
Avocado
Banana
Coconut
Dried Fruits
Frozen Fruits
Papaya

MAKE IT BEAUTIFUL.

A pleasing aesthetic speaks to everyone. Display your fruit in a lovely bowl or dish prominently in your kitchen

CUT WITH CARE.

Consider the small hands that are grabbing the fruit and chop accordingly. Good knives make this a breeze.

STILL HUNGRY AFTER FRUIT?

Add a fancy drink, something warm and nourishing.

73 PLAN SIMPLE MEALS: GET MORE ENERGY, RAISE HEALTHY KIDS AND ENJOY FAMILY DINNER

FRUIT BOWL FORMULA IN ACTION

A VARIETY OF FRUITS

There are so many options with fruit. Don't forget that there is variety in each fruit type. Think of how many different kinds of apples and oranges there are... Try them all!

This is a great meal to get your kids involved with at the grocery store or farmers market. Teach them how to choose ripe fruit that's in season. Let them find exotic fruits they think may be "cool" to try. Show them all six kinds of pears.

If fruit is in season, take a trip to a local farm and pick it with your kids, so they can experience where it comes from.

MELON BOWLS

INGREDIENTS

2 cantaloupes

DIRECTIONS

1. Cut cantaloupes in half and remove seeds with a spoon.
2. You can put banana or berries in the "melon bowl" or other favorite fruits. Kids enjoy scooping out the cantaloupe.

BANANA COINS WITH DICED MANGO, KIWI AND BLUEBERRIES

INGREDIENTS

4 bananas, sliced
2 mangoes, diced
2 kiwis, diced
1 cup blueberries

DIRECTIONS

1. Cut fruits into similar bite-sized pieces.
2. Place each fruit in its own bowl, and let children serve themselves; or create bowls of mixed fruits for your kids, and have them ready when they come to eat, whatever fits in with your morning routine.

   Sit down with your kids for breakfast and talk about the fruits' colors, flavors, and textures.

WARMING CINNAMON APPLES

INGREDIENTS
5 apples
2 tablespoon cinnamon
1 teaspoon coconut oil

DIRECTIONS

1. Peel and dice apples.
2. Place coconut oil in a skillet and turn on at medium heat, add apples and cinnamon.
3. Toss apples so they are coated in the cinnamon.
4. Add a tablespoon of water and warm the apple for a few minutes.

CINNAMON MILK

INGREDIENTS

Almond or Rice Milk
Cinnamon
Vanilla
Honey

This recipe has no specific amounts because I want you to play with proportions here!

Experiment with the different flavors and adjust to your taste.

Ask your kids to help you measure or add ingredients to encourage them to help you in the kitchen. Little ones can also be taste-testers!

DIRECTIONS

1. Warm all ingredients on your stove, stirring frequently.
2. Serve in a mug.

ALMOND MILK HOT CHOCOLATE

INGREDIENTS

Almond Milk
Honey
Cocoa Powder (no sugar added)

DIRECTIONS

Make hot chocolate by following the directions on the cocoa powder canister, using almond milk instead of cow's milk, and honey instead of sugar.

AVENA

INGREDIENTS

3 cups hemp milk
3 tablespoons maple syrup
1 tablespoon cinnamon
1 tablespoon vanilla
1 cup cooked oats
(Ice in the summer)

DIRECTIONS

Blend in high-speed blender.

BREAKFAST RHYTHM
HEALTHY TOAST & SMOOTHIES

One of my children will often drink a green smoothie with me daily. One of my kids knows to ask for green juice when sick. One is not a big fan, but will drink it on Green Smoothie Day.

My rule with kids' green smoothies is that they must include a serving of dark leafy greens, but are generally sweeter than the ones I crave each morning (heavier in fruit). Sometimes I'll add almond milk or other nuts for creaminess.

To top the toast, I strive to introduce non-dairy alternatives to butter, but it's a constant work in progress. I buy Earth Balance for my dairy-free girl while my husband and two other kids love butter, so we still enjoy it from time to time. As for bread, I'm always really aiming to make that piece of toast really count towards their health.

FIND A HEALTHY BREAD THAT SATISFIES YOUR DIETARY NEEDS.

Bread is a great product to teach label reading. There is so much extra stuff in the average loaf of commercial bread!

When reading the label, ask yourself these questions: Is there sugar in the first three ingredients? Are there more than 20 ingredients? Do some of the ingredients sound like chemicals? Is there dairy? Is there egg? What are the grains?

Of course, you can choose to make your own bread instead!

I check the freezer aisle regularly for new gluten-free breads because new brands appear each month. We often get Udi's brand, but I am always on the lookout for breads with fewer ingredients and no eggs. See if you have a local gluten-free bakery in your area.

For the non-gluten-free variety, I recommend Ezekiel brand.

PICK SOME HEALTHY TOPPINGS TO SPREAD OVER YOUR TOAST.

Avocado with a dash of Herbamare (a vegan seasoning)

Fresh tomatoes sprinkled with salt

Homemade (un) cream cheese made out of cashews

Almond butter or cashew butter drizzled with honey

Bananas, apples, pears on top of nut butter

Homemade Nutella (see recipe)

Coconut butter

Homemade jams in a blender

SPRINKLE ON SOME SUPER CRUNCH

Chia seeds

Sprouts

Hemp seeds

Sesame seeds

Sunflower seeds

Slivered almonds

TOAST FORMULA IN ACTION

AVOCADO TOAST

INGREDIENTS

Bread of your choice
Avocado
Sea salt

DIRECTIONS

Spread avocado on toast and sprinkle with sea salt.

TOMATO TOAST

INGREDIENTS

Bread of your choice
Tomato
Olive Oil
Sea Salt

DIRECTIONS

1. Slice tomatoes and place on toast.
2. Drizzle with olive oil and sprinkle with salt.
3. You can warm this in the winter for a breakfast pizza.

TOAST WITH ALMOND BUTTER, HONEY AND BANANA

INGREDIENTS

Your favorite gluten-free bread
Almond butter
2 bananas cut into thin slices
Raw honey

DIRECTIONS

1. Toast bread
2. Spread organic almond butter on toast.
3. Lay banana slices on top of almond butter.
4. Drizzle honey over the whole thing.

OLIVIA'S HEALTHY "NUTELLA"

INGREDIENTS

1 cup raw hazelnuts
½ – 1 cup cacao powder
8 Medjool dates
2/3 cups water (or nut milk)
Pinch of sea salt
2 tablespoons coconut oil, melted
1 teaspoon vanilla extract

DIRECTIONS

Blend in a Vitamix (with plunger) or a food processor until smooth.

Enjoy on a gluten-free bagel, or on a slice of apple or banana!

CINNAMON TOAST

INGREDIENTS

Bread of your choice
Coconut butter
Honey
Cinnamon

DIRECTIONS

1. Take one part coconut butter, one part honey and one part cinnamon and mix together in a small bowl.
2. Toast bread with the mixture spread on top, so it soaks in.

TOAST WITH CREAM CHEEZE

INGREDIENTS

1½ cups raw cashews, soaked for 12 hours
2 tablespoons raw apple cider vinegar
2 tablespoons fresh lemon juice
2 tablespoons water

DIRECTIONS

1. Drain and rinse the soaked cashews.
2. Put cashews in a blender with remaining ingredients.
3. Blend until the mixture is completely smooth. (You can add a tiny bit of salt and herbs at this point for herbed cream cheeze.)

GREEN APPLE SMOOTHIE

INGREDIENTS

2 cups chopped kale (stems removed)
2 bananas
1 cup apple juice
½ cup green grapes
2 tablespoons lemon juice
½ cup ice

DIRECTIONS

Blend in high-speed blender.

NOT-SO-GREEN GREEN SMOOTHIE

INGREDIENTS

2 cups spinach
1 banana
2 cups frozen raspberries
1 cup frozen blackberries
1 cup frozen blueberries
2 dates
4-6 cups of water

DIRECTIONS

Blend in high-speed blender.

KID'S GREEN SMOOTHIE FORMULA

**Choose 2 fruits
(They can be frozen for sure)**

Banana
Strawberries
Blueberries
Blackberries
Raspberries
Mango
Peaches
Oranges

Add a handful or 2 of spinach.
You can ease into the greens. Once they love spinach, try adding kale or chard.

Use almond milk for the liquid to desired consistency.

If you need it sweeter add a date.

Add protein if that speaks to you.
My favorite protein powder is Complete by Juice Plus because it's made of whole food vegan protein, plant-based and super delicious.

A FEW TIPS FOR KIDS WHO ARE PICKY AND SEEM CLOSED TO A GREEN SMOOTHIE…

- Add ice and make it like ice cream. Frozen fruit also has the same effect.

- Just add a bit of spinach to a very fruity smoothie. I love a banana shake with some spinach. Let them taste the before and after. They will see there is no difference.

- You can always tell the story of Popeye, whose daily spinach habit gave him super strength!

BREAKFAST RHYTHM
"YOGURT" DAY

"Yogurt" Day (in quotation marks because you may choose to eliminate dairy) happens about mid-week in our house. But again, consider what works for you and best serves your family.

CHOOSE YOUR YOGURT

There are so many options for yogurts these days, and you can also experiment with making your own. If you go the dairy route, definitely opt for organic, and consider goat milk yogurt. There are also lots of non dairy options these days.

Just always be sure to read the label and make sure it's a plain, no sugar added variety. That way, you can supplement the plain flavor with healthier choices, such as honey or fruit.

Cashew cream is a great alternative to yogurt.

You can sprinkle a leftover amount of granola from Granola Day. Also, muffins that have gone a bit stale, and are too hard to eat sink nicely into dairy-free yogurt.

MAKE IT YUMMY

You can sprinkle a leftover amount of granola from Granola Day.

Also, muffins that have gone a bit stale, and are too hard to eat sink nicely into yogurt.

To mimic a fruity yogurt just blend in fresh fruit and dates, honey or maple syrup for sweetness.

Try a good old parfait. Everybody likes a good layered dish!

BREAKFAST RHYTHM
PANCAKE DAY

Pancake Day is really one of my kids' favorites. I almost want to call it Papa's Pancake Day, because one day a week, it's good to shift who's doing the cooking. I find that sometimes this is a great thing to happen on the weekends, especially if I've been cooking all week long. (If you are a dad who cooks, then mom can take over the weekend!) It just brings a sort of novelty and excitement to a weekend meal. Pancake Day is a tradition that we love and look forward to.

PANCAKES

INGREDIENTS

1 tablespoon flax meal + 2 tablespoons water
2 tablespoons coconut oil
1 teaspoon vanilla
¼ cup of unsweetened applesauce (or one banana)
1½ cups almond milk
½ cup brown rice flour
½ cup buckwheat flour
¼ cup GF oats (not steel cut)
2 teaspoons baking powder
1 tablespoon cinnamon
¼ teaspoon sea salt
Coconut oil for pan

DIRECTIONS

1. Put flax meal and water in your blender, give it one pulse and then let it sit for five minutes.
2. Add the rest of the wet ingredients to the blender and blend.
3. Put dry ingredients in a bowl.
4. Add wet ingredients to bowl and mix well.
5. On a greased, heated pan use ¼ cup of batter to make each pancake.
6. Flip the pancake when you see little bubbles forming on top.

FRENCH TOAST

INGREDIENTS

8 pieces sliced gluten-free bread
1 tablespoon chia (You can use 2 eggs instead)
1 cup almond milk
1 tablespoon cinnamon
1 tablespoon vanilla
Coconut oil

DIRECTIONS

1. Beat chia, almond milk, cinnamon, and vanilla with whisk. Let sit for a few minutes.
2. Meanwhile, lightly toast your bread to dry it out.
3. Soak bread in mixture.
4. Add pieces of French toast to a skillet that is warm and has some melted coconut oil.
5. Cook in a skillet over medium-low heat until browned on both sides.
6. Serve with fresh berries or other sweet chopped fruits.

WEEKENDS

I have learned to love weekends! I very clearly remember a time when they felt so overwhelming that I counted the days until Monday. And though that still happens from time to time, in general we have created a very nourishing weekend rhythm.

Saturday is usually Pancake Day (or French toast). It is also the day Mama is guaranteed yoga. This means that breakfast is with Papa, and he has become an expert pancake and waffle maker!

Sunday is about cleaning out the fridge and preparing for the week to come. This may mean eating extra oatmeal, or figuring out a creative way to use it. Or it may mean baking muffins for the following week while also enjoying some for breakfast.

Doable Changes

At the end of each step, I want to offer up a few doable changes. A really fun way to think about doable changes is to play with a new one each week. Don't think too much — choose one that feels great and experiment this week.

1. Try juicing.
2. Teach your kids how to make smoothies.
3. Make your own nut milk.
4. Ditch boxed cereals.
5. Create a rhythm for your meals.
6. Learn how to make muffins from scratch.
7. Drink green smoothies every morning for seven days.
8. Try making granola from scratch.
9. Sit down and construct your month-at-a-glance.
10. Create a schedule of meal themes that work for you.
11. Create your self-care regimen for the mornings.

WEEKLY RITUALS
One of my weekly rituals is soaking beans on Sunday, so there are always two types of cooked beans around during the busy week.

STEP FOUR
Plan for Good Meals

"A goal without a plan is just a wish."

– Antoine de Saint-Exupéry

Let me tell you about Carmen. She was a super-excited member of the Plan Simple Meals community. She was particularly excited at the prospect that her son might eat something that is not white or beige someday.

Carmen worked really hard at her career and never seemed to be home before 6 pm, and felt like she was spending a lot of time on the road. To make up for her time away, she enrolled her son in soccer, cello, Russian math, and a Lego robotics class.

Now let me tell you about Charlotte. She decided not to go back to work after her second child was born, and then she had a third. Her goal was to be the best mom ever, but she was first to admit that was not what she imagined before kids. She loves her kids, but in order not to feel like the crazy housewife, she made sure they were busy with play dates and activities. She was also super involved in their schools. When one of her children was diagnosed with Celiac Disease, she decided she had to consider food more seriously.

Carmen and Charlotte arrived at healthy eating from totally different places, but they both had one major problem in common when came to actually getting healthy—their schedules simply did not have space for good food.

I get this. I was there. Before I started on my healthy journey, I felt so bad about not loving every second of parenting that I figured if I stayed busy, all would be well. I worked all day, took the kids to the grocery in the afternoons, went out for food often, visited many parks, went to a myriad of museums every weekend, and basically held my breath knowing Monday, and a babysitter, would come to our rescue soon.

What I didn't know was that if I just stood still, my kids would entertain themselves for chunks of time, even at ages three and five. I had no idea that they were getting over-stimulated too late and too often, and that actually caused tantrums rather than prevented them. I had no idea how easy it

SCHEDULING

Try scheduling some time to "just be" on your calendar. Or if that feels too strange, maybe schedule a quiet activity like reading, relaxing outdoors, or completing a jigsaw puzzle. Sometimes we just want to fill all the space in our calendar, so if you set aside a chunk of downtime, you are less likely to schedule something in its place. Begin to observe the changes in behavior you see in your family as the home becomes a more habitual place of calm. Whether you keep an electronic or paper calendar, use a relaxing pastel color so you can feel the energy of these blocks of time.

could all be if I just took control of food. But I realized controlling food took some patience and time, something sorely lacking in the overly-hectic life I was leading.

So many of the concepts in this book evolved after reading and implementing what I learned in the book Simplicity Parenting by Kim John Payne. If you have not read it yet, please do. I read it precisely when I decided to change my food. It gave me permission and encouraged me to let go of all the activity. It let me off the hook of the constant enrichment I was trying to give my "smart" boy. It ended up he did not need the noisy Museum of Science every time it rained. He needed time to think, time to play. I also learned about owning fewer things and simplifying our spaces. Cleaning out the playroom and clothes drawers alone made cooking easier because I didn't have to clean up as much.

It ends up that Carmen and Charlotte had more in common than I even realized when I met them. Basically, they had to let go of some limiting beliefs and start creating more time in their busy days. Carmen quit two of the after-school activities she committed to, as she realized they no longer served her peaceful weeknight rhythm. She learned how to be super clear with her boss about leaving work when they had both agreed and no later. When her son was in activities, she spent time exercising and getting food organized. Charlotte discovered some tricks for making more time, getting happier in the kitchen and finding her food. Eventually, she started to really get behind the big change.

What would your life feel like if you had more time?

YOU: RECONSIDERING TIME

When I say planning, what I mean is writing down and documenting what you are going to do. This does two things. First, it clears brain space to think about other things. You do not have to remember what you intend to cook in four days or the ten things you need from the grocery store. Second, it gets you moving in the direction of your goal by visualizing it on paper first.

Allow the planning that you do to support your rhythm, and the rhythm to support your planning. That way, your days may expand or contract, but there is always a sense of flow. The fast-paced world we live in often forces us to interact with some kind of calendar system to keep our time organized. Whether it be electronic or old-fashioned pen and paper, find the best one to work for you and notice how your natural rhythms begin to occur effortlessly. My favorite is Google Calendar because I can share it and that, as you'll see in the next chapter, might be an important step in enlisting help from others.

Let's dive into planning the year as a whole. Regularly set a time aside to visualize the months to come. Maybe this happens once every six months, or even more often if you're a busy mom and life changes frequently. I love reconsidering rhythms in August before school starts, on New Year's Day, and at some point in June before summer break — this helps me in the transition.

We are talking food here, but you can also think about vacations, camps, after-school activities, date weekends, some solo time, etc. Ask yourself things like: When is seasonal food available? When are the best times to buy certain things? When can you get food locally? Is there a farmer's market that is convenient to you? When is it open? What about signing up for a farm share? Record these things on your calendar so you'll remember that every Wednesday the farmer's market is open, or February is when you need to sign up for your farm share. Maybe there's a farm that's actually near you that has "pick your own berries" on a certain weekend. Begin to track those things so you know where you can get healthy food and when.

Start to pay attention to the changing of the seasons around you so that you can make the best possible food choices and begin to relish the delicious variety that Mother Nature is offering around you. Take grapes for example. Where I live, grapes are only in season three months of the year. During that time, they're super fresh, and you can always find them organic, which is important for grapes. With this information, I've stopped buying grapes at other times of year, and I've noticed a difference in how they taste. It also gives my family and me something to look forward to and reminds us to take pleasure in the steady passing of time. Google will likely give you a list of when fruits and veggies are in season in your area. It is confusing how much is available every day at the grocery store, so researching what's truly in season is something valuable to pass onto our kids.

On the other hand, know that some fruits and vegetables will never be locally in season in your area. For instance, the Northeast doesn't provide the right climate for tropical fruits like oranges and mangoes to be grown locally. That means they're usually shipped in from Florida or farther, but are still better (and cheaper!) when they are in season in the place it is coming from. Do a little research to find where your produce comes from, and when it's the best time to buy.

After sketching out your year, start the practice of considering each month. Schedule one day a month that you will do this — the last day or the first day of a month is easy to remember. Go through and understand your month. Are there vacations that your family is expecting, or time off from school? That seems to have a different impact on how you make food and who's around. Is there a holiday during this month? How is that going to affect your meals? Are you traveling? That's a big one. What do you need to do to prepare for that? What kind of research needs to be done to ensure that you can make healthy choices away from home?

When planning your month—think about food shopping and what you can order ahead of time to make the buying and getting of food easier. Many online retailers now offer monthly groceries delivered to your doorstep. So what can you order that you know you'll need throughout the month? That will simplify things. There's no need, for example, to rush to the store for last minute quinoa or rice. Those are the things you could either buy in bulk locally or order online. That way, you are always full stocked with beans, grains, flours, and super foods. You can walk to the grocery or to the farmer's market to get your vegetables, fruit and other fresh goodies. This can streamline your food shopping process.

Then consider each individual week of the month to come. Spend time every Friday or Saturday morning—or Thursday evening would work too — and plan the next week of meals. You can stick to the rhythm of meals you created but start figuring out what soup you are making on soup day and what you want in your tacos. Make sure that your rhythm still fits into your week, and move things around if it is getting too hectic. Make it a date for yourself. Maybe go to a coffee shop and treat yourself to an almond milk latte or berry smoothie. Maybe sit in the sun or on a park bench, do whatever you can do to make your time planning to feel special. Bring along your gear: a planner, binder, electronic device, whatever it is, and indulge in planning the next week of meals for your family.

Keep a few things in mind when planning your week: First, try visualizing your week as a whole, not just with food. Take note of which days are busy, and which have less going on. Obviously, you don't want extra cooking and fussing with food on the days that are already occupied with other things. Use the quieter days to maybe incorporate your children into the process of cooking, because that will certainly require more time. Or maybe push yourself to try something new from a cookbook on more leisurely days. If you plan accordingly, you're less likely to get frustrated in the kitchen. If you anticipate a few busy days in a row, you can always make healthy options ahead of time so you'll have something on hand.

What if every day is busy? If you're someone whose calendar is packed to the brim, don't worry. The best thing you can do is start with small, doable changes. Begin by designating a weekend day or evening that stays clear. Then move toward lightening your week. Maybe ask your boss if you can work remotely one day a week, or evaluate what single after-school activity is best for your kids, and scrap the rest.

Each week, decide the best days to do your shopping so you don't have to constantly make runs to the store. Maybe you already have a day that works best for grocery shopping, like Sunday, but just be sure that if you have a busy week, you're only making one or two trips a week, not a day! Or if you're the kind of person who likes visiting the store every day, just make sure that going to the store works in your rhythm.

Once you have a shopping schedule, consider involving the children in your grocery flow. I love the idea of bringing kids shopping. Being present with them in the store can be huge teaching tool for their future as healthy eaters. On the other hand, it can also work to their detriment, considering the situation. If I know that I'm going to be preoccupied during the store run, like on a phone call and that they are going to just be looking at all the advertising that's being thrown their way, maybe it's best to exclude them from those trips. Many times I've taken kids under these named circumstances, and it only ends badly. Too often if I'm distracted while shopping, my child ends up crying because I won't buy them the gummy bunnies they're begging for. Then I'm so frenzied that I've forgotten three items that I've needed for dinner. Meanwhile, they're crying so much in the checkout that I go ahead and get them the gummies anyway and then feel crummy that I can't keep my word. We've all had those moments, but we want to eliminate them as much as possible.

Next, plan what days you can use to prepare food for the week. My favorite thing to do is pick a weekend evening, usually Sunday night, and spend it mindfully preparing meals for the week to come. This might mean chopping fresh veggies, or lovingly baking the homemade cookies and muffins to replace the packaged goods that you might have bought otherwise. It might mean that you make a whole meal that you can warm up later in the week. Sunday food preparation is going to have a variety of meanings on different weeks. If you follow my rhythm somewhat, then Monday means Bean Day, so Sunday is always spent soaking beans. Though it seems small, the moments you can take advantage and prepare for what's ahead will make a difference in your busy day, and ensure healthy choices throughout the week.

SHOPPING TIPS

Go shopping. Make it an experience you enjoy. If you want to spend time with a child, bring them along; if you need a little alone time, see if they can stay home, go to a friend's house, or go to Grandma's.

Unpack the groceries as soon as you get home. Prep anything you can right away. For example, you can wash the spinach, wrap it in paper towels and put it in the fridge (you can do the same with lettuce). You can take the leaves off of radishes, wash the radishes, cut off any stems, and store them in an airtight container.

Remember, it's helpful to write this all down until it is habit and part of your natural rhythm. In the beginning, it may be too much new information to hold in your head.

(You can get planning worksheets at www.plansimplemealsbook.com/hub)

POST-IT STRATEGY

If you want to feel more liberated in the kitchen, that's ok. Remember my definition of planning is not necessarily about becoming a slave to a calendar. For many of us, using the calendar helps us develop our rhythm. But if everything calendar seems daunting, try the Post-it strategy and the Move Food Forward strategy or the Daily Sheet. They also work wonders for planning.

Every morning, take a moment and write what's for dinner on a sticky note. Alternatively, you can make a memo with your smartphone, or whatever's handy for you. Just write out dinner and place it somewhere prominent. This will ensure that what you're having still works, and you can enjoy the small victory that your planning is serving you. This will psychologically pump you up. Also, the note you write will be a helpful reminder for you to check that you have all the ingredients that are needed. I don't know about your house, but in mine sometimes ingredients seem to just disappear. The Post-it is the first step in getting dinner in motion, so you are ahead at breakfast.

MOVE FOOD FORWARD STRATEGY

Another practice that helps me stay on top of meals is to take some time in the morning to "move food forward." In other words, what can you do to streamline 6 pm dinner at 6 am? After you've written dinner down and posted it on the fridge, take a second to get it started. That way, when you come home after a busy day, you're already a small step ahead. Perhaps that means just chopping some veggies and placing them in individual containers. Maybe just taking out the key ingredients, organizing them in the fridge, or marinating something will make dinner that much easier. While different meals require different steps, many things can be done in advance. You'll be amazed how a small moment of moving food forward can save you the stress of dinner later on.

PLAN SIMPLE MEALS: GET MORE ENERGY, RAISE HEALTHY KIDS AND ENJOY FAMILY DINNER

THE DAILY SHEET

I have always loved calendars, but there was a time when I would eagerly get a new one, fill it in for week one and do everything, fill it in for week two and ignore everything, and then not bother for week three. When I first started my food journey, someone gave me an inspirational quote of the day notepad. It was sort of like a planner because it had space for your intention then the hours of the day, each with a line next to it. But it did not have the date. This was fantastic for me because each day I could make my list, and each night I could recycle my list.

Many days I got it done, but when I didn't there was no guilt and no quitting due to a blank week. Over the years I have fine-tuned the practice, and this is what is on my blank sheet each day now: 1. What I am grateful for; 2. Three tasks I will do for work that moves my mission forward; 3. Three emails or calls that will take 15 minutes; 4. What we will eat and what I can do to move that forward throughout the day; 5. How I will take care of myself; 6. Three 15-minute tasks I can do around the house.

TIME

Besides using your daily planner to schedule free time, there are some other ways in which you can use calendaring to better achieve a simple family life. If you are someone who benefits from scheduling meals at certain times, be sure you allow enough time to indulge in the process of cooking, eating and cleaning up. Give yourself adequate buffers surrounding meals to ramp up and ramp down. Even if you don't actually sit at the table for longer than 20 minutes, which is probably true if you have young children, be sure to schedule dinner longer than that. Ignore all the advertising you see in the grocery store and television that boasts meals that can be made in five or ten minutes. That expectation will only prove to be frustrating in the end. The only meal that takes five minutes is not something you'd want to be serving to your family anyway. It's important to make enough time in your week to start feeding your family well. If it seems time-consuming, which it might at first, take solace in knowing that you are investing in your family's health and future, and really, what could be more important than that?

PLAN SIMPLE MEALS: GET MORE ENERGY, RAISE HEALTHY KIDS AND ENJOY FAMILY DINNER

FAMILY: MINI ROUTINES

It's clear that how adults show up at the table for meals has a lot to do with how the meal goes. When we are tired and flustered, we get tired and flustered dinner guests. When we show up present, happy, and relaxed, we can expect good eaters and happy banter. And if for some reason one child is off, we don't let it get under our skin and it helps our child recuperate.

Learn the power of mini-routines. While small at first, simple things that are practiced daily can yield a huge transformation over time. Just like with music, you learn to play the piano by beginning with simple exercises. In general, you don't just sit down and perform Bach. Instead, you start small by practicing one chord at a time. The same is true with mini-routines. They encourage you to start small and work towards bigger goals. Once you practice small changes, they become habitual and no longer require conscious effort to accomplish. Green smoothies have proved this concept in my life. When I first started this new food story for myself six years ago, smoothies were an important mini-routine. I promised to start each new day with greens, either juice or blended into a smoothie. It was difficult initially, but today, I barely put any thought behind greens first thing in the morning. It happens out of pure habit because I've consistently practiced the routine.

Before green smoothies, I barely made any time for myself in the morning. I would rush to get the kids where they needed to go first, then grab coffee and a sugary muffin on my way to the office. Then I would get to work, sit in front of my morning e-mails, and mindlessly devour. Once I discovered green smoothies, my morning routine changed drastically. First, I empowered myself by knowing what I was putting in my body instead of choosing something processed or premade. After a few weeks, I noticed how great the smoothies made me feel. Though it was an effort at first to learn a new behavior, the effort was well worth it as I continuously reap the mental and physical benefits of this daily practice. Now I make green smoothies every day without even thinking about it. Even if I'm rushing in the morning, or taking care of a child, somehow my smoothie still happens. Either my husband will step in, or I'll make it in advance and keep it in the fridge. That's how automatic and ingrained a habit can become through the power of a mini-routine.

AUTOMATIC CHOICES EXERCISE

How do we make healthy choices automatic? First, take out a piece of paper and draw a line in the middle. In the left column, write a list of all the things that you need to accomplish in one day. Think through your daily tasks, morning to night. These are the things you already do 85% of the time. Don't worry yet about adding new things. Include all the things you do like brushing teeth and taking a shower— nothing is too small. Don't forget to include all your children's needs too, like getting them dressed and making lunch. If you have older children, maybe you have to help them with homework or drive them to an activity. Put all those things down on the piece of paper.

Then in the other column, write down some of the things you are wanting to upgrade or change. Maybe you pull from the 100 doable changes listed in this book. Be specific. Don't

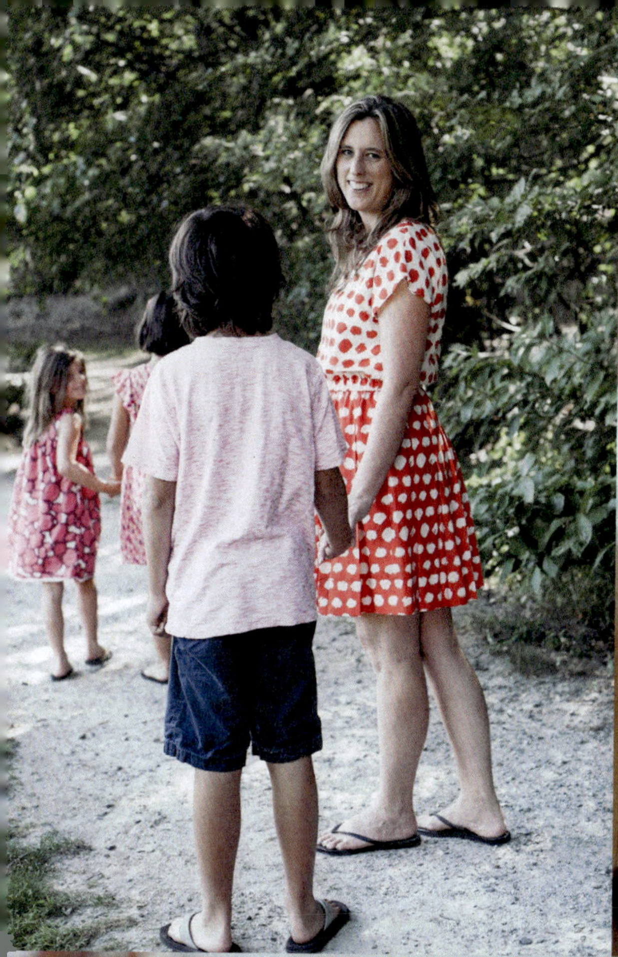

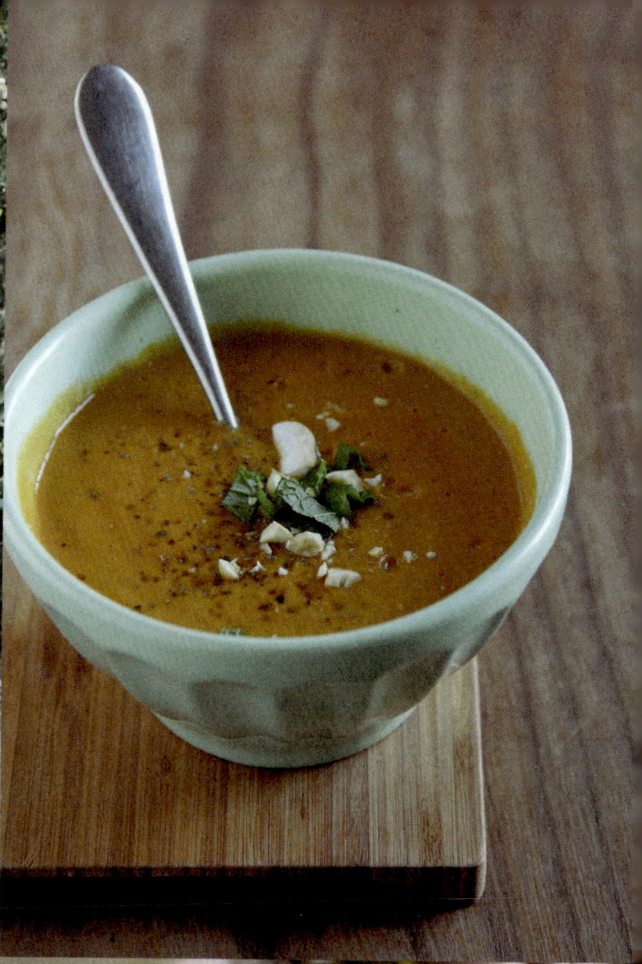

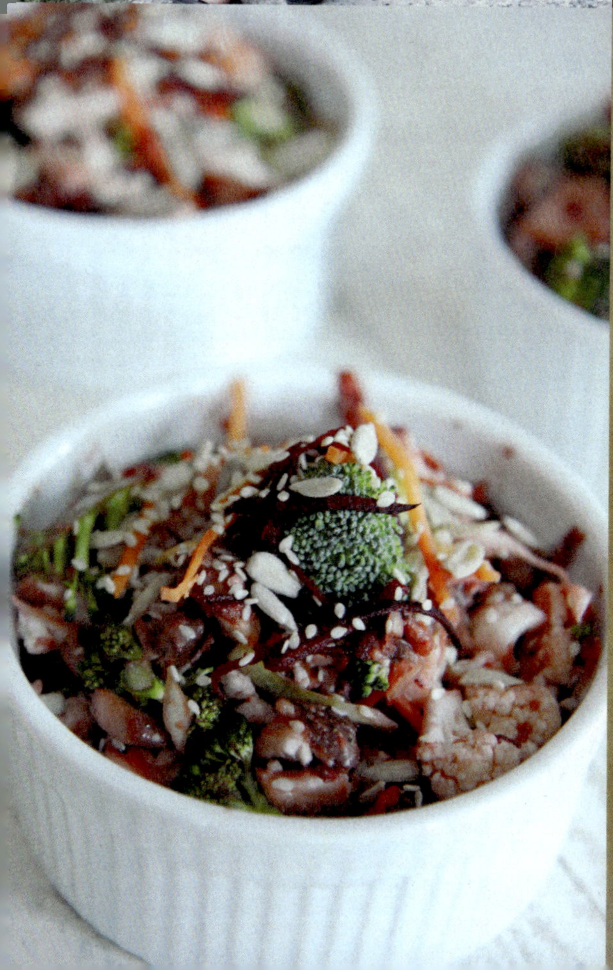

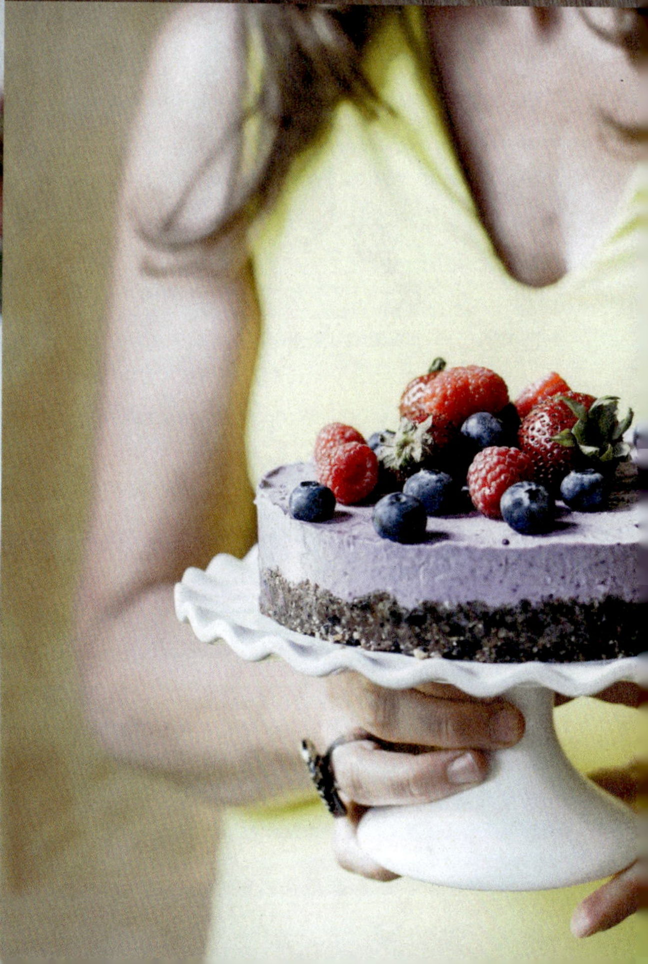

write, "I want to upgrade my breakfast." But instead, "I want to start each day with a smoothie." Don't say, "I want to have more family dinners." Say, "I want to have three family dinners each week." The goal here is not to be reasonable, but specific. Some other examples are: "Exercise every morning for 30 minutes" or "Drink 8 glasses of water a day" or "Sleep eight hours at night" or "Eat a big salad every day for lunch." See how you can actually work those things into your rhythm.

(You can download the choices worksheet at www.plansimplemealsbook.com/hub).

Take your list and see how you can create mini-routines that plan your tasks with rhythm. Don't forget that we are trying to focus on doable changes, so it may be that you pick one item, like green smoothies, from your right column, or you may decide it is doable to revamp your whole morning routine. It's up to you.

Next, try to build mini-routines around mealtimes. Consider the three meals as milestones in your day: breakfast, lunch and dinner. Think of all the things that you need to do to ramp up to that meal, and then all the things that ramp down afterwards. For example, every morning once you wake up, your rhythm builds until breakfast, and then winds down as you make your way out the door and on to your day. Consider all the details in order to make this happen. Write all the small things that you need to accomplish. You'll start to connect all your small tasks to create mini-routines. In mapping your small habits you can create and accomplish bigger goals in your family — goals that support your family brand you created in Step One.

The year brings us all kinds of different days. Weekend days, school days, work days, holidays, summer days, and winter days. While every day is unique, once you set mini-routines, they can become fluid rhythms because they can expand and contract. Like on a lazy Saturday morning, maybe breakfast means you sit down and enjoy tea, read a magazine, talk to your kids, or make a bigger breakfast. Whereas, school days take on their own rhythm with less leisure time and more emphasis on getting out the door.

Let's consider how all this plays into dinner. So many parents talk about 6–8pm as the most difficult hours of the day, but when carefully planned, I believe this time of day can have the biggest positive impact on our families. It's a time when all the busyness and hustle of work, school and play are coming to a close. We are all coming down from the good, the bad, and everything in between, and what better people to hold that space with than the ones we love most. After dinner is a time to start relaxing and winding down for bed. So in our model of ramping up to an event and then ramping down, see how beautifully dinner acts as the main attraction and the transition.

With this in mind, begin to consider the ways in which you can use the times before and after dinner to work to your advantage. As you're ramping up to dinner, you might consider doing all the busy things like taking out the trash, feeding the dog, and cleaning the kitchen—all things that require more energy. Do these when you're coming in from an energetic day because then it will feel better to relax afterward. It's difficult to accomplish laborious chores immediately after eating dinner, because your natural flow is to relax and unwind.

The time after dinner, as often as possible, should be aimed towards settling down and preparing for a good night's sleep. This might inform what food you choose to serve. It wouldn't make sense to eat some high-sugar dessert after dinner when you're trying to ramp down, right? I suggest instead veggies or food that's easy to digest. Trying eating early, so your body can digest and prepare for sleep. Then think closely about how your children's time is spent after dinner. Reflect on which activities wind kids up and which wind them down. Focus on quiet activities like practicing instruments, doing homework, and reading, which will help soothe children and lead them towards sleep.

LET'S RECAP PLANNING AND MINI ROUTINES.

Planning is simply writing down what you want to accomplish, so it does not get lost in your thoughts. You may choose to write on a calendar, but you can also write on pieces of paper or a kitchen chalkboard. I highly recommend keeping all things food related, like your week of meals and shopping list, in a notebook or binder, so you can repeat it another week, or even a different year.

Once you plan the big picture — which has components that you look at yearly, monthly, weekly and daily, then focus on creating mini-routines that will turn your dreams into a natural rhythm that will stick because it makes sense in your life.

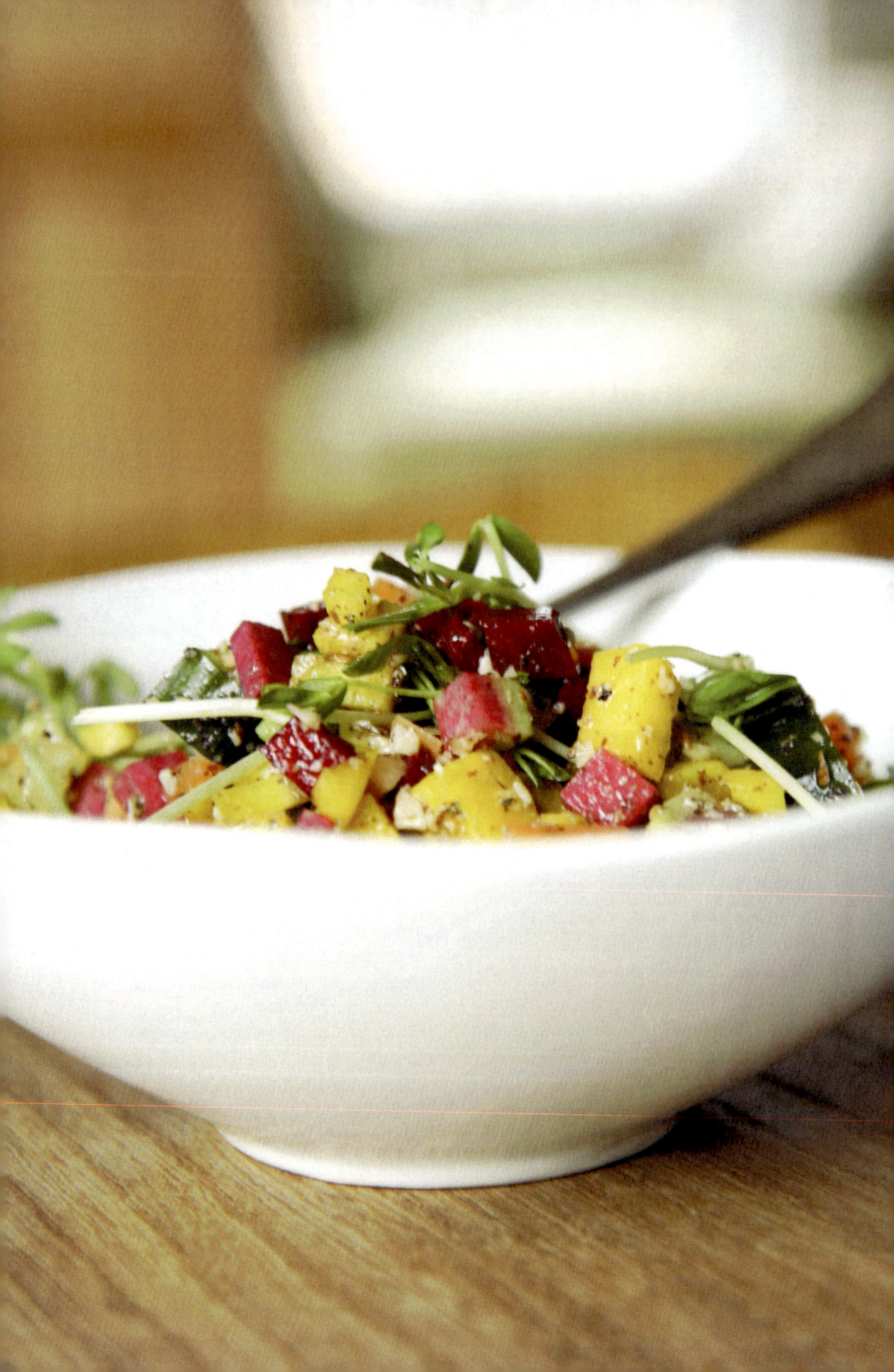

Food: Lunch

"The true secret of happiness lies in the taking a genuine interest in all the details of daily life."

– François de La Rochefoucauld

I see lunch as a big opportunity for parents to really up their health game and eat for their future. It is an opportunity for kids to eat healthy food independently and not necessarily in the most optimal situations, which strengthens their healthy muscles for later in life! On weekends, we use lunch as more of an opportunity to share a meal together — on weekends we follow the principles of dinner.

ADULT WEEKDAY LUNCH

I highly recommend that moms get in the habit of salads for lunch whenever possible. In the cooler months if you need something warm, just steam greens and veggies and pour a creamy dressing over that. You may have the same salad every day as you get into this habit, but as you start to experiment with different greens and veggies, you will discover that the possibilities are endless — if you want them to be. Personally, I feel much better eating the same healthy food every day rather than a variety of unhealthy options.

Five steps to rock salads at lunch — at home and work

1. Prep veggies every three days
2. Think bigger than just lettuce
3. Get great with dressing
4. Dress it when ready to eat. (Unless you are using the jar trick.)
5. Enjoy it in a big beautiful bowl.

A few new twists to salad that may serve you...

1. Eat any dip over a bed of green.
2. Use pasta toppings over raw zucchini.
3. Used to sandwiches for lunch? Sub bread for a bed of lettuce.
4. Miss the idea of bread? Get a brown rice tortilla and stuff it with salad. I mean stuff it! Think a whole head of romaine or a whole bunch of kale.

LUNCH IN A JAR

Get flexible on the go! I love packing my lunch in a jar then pouring it into a large bowl when I am ready to enjoy it.

WHAT A GREAT WAY TO KEEP GREENS CRISP!

Play around with what goes in a jar. The only real rule is to add the dressing and protein first, so leafy greens won't get soggy.

1/5 Colorful Veggies
Carrots
Beets
Cucumber
Avocado
Radish
Turnips
Squash
Tomato
Celery
Fennel
Artichoke Hearts

2/5 Dark Leafy Greens
Spinach
Kale
Parsley
Pea Shoots
Lettuce
Collards
Chard
Mache

1/5 Grains
Quinoa
Brown Rice
Millet
Amaranth

1/5 Protein
Raw Sprouted Seeds
Cooked Lentils
Tofu
Garbanzo Beans
Black Beans
Well-sourced
   Meat or Fish

Dressing

105   PLAN SIMPLE MEALS: GET MORE ENERGY, RAISE HEALTHY KIDS AND ENJOY FAMILY DINNER

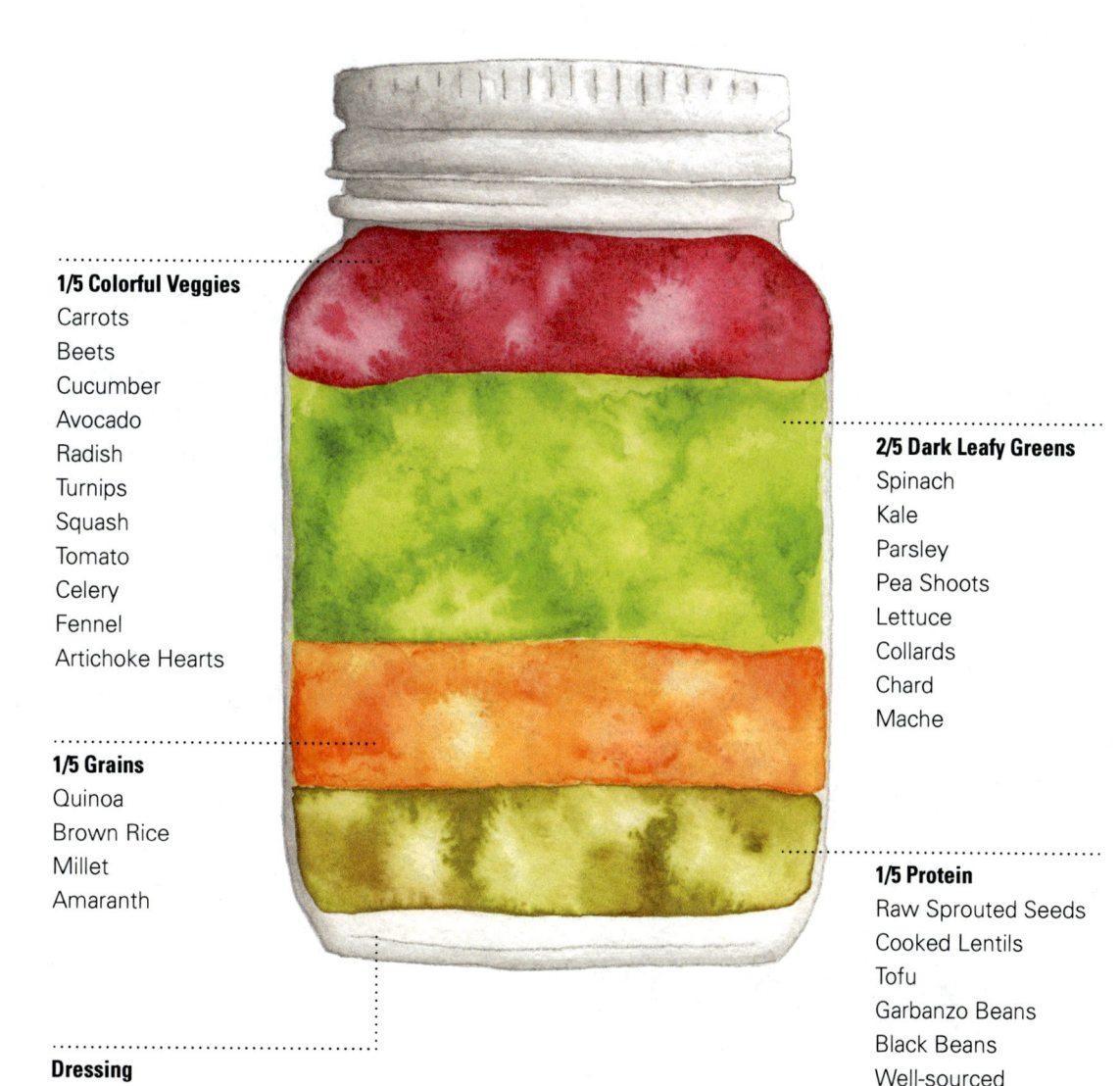

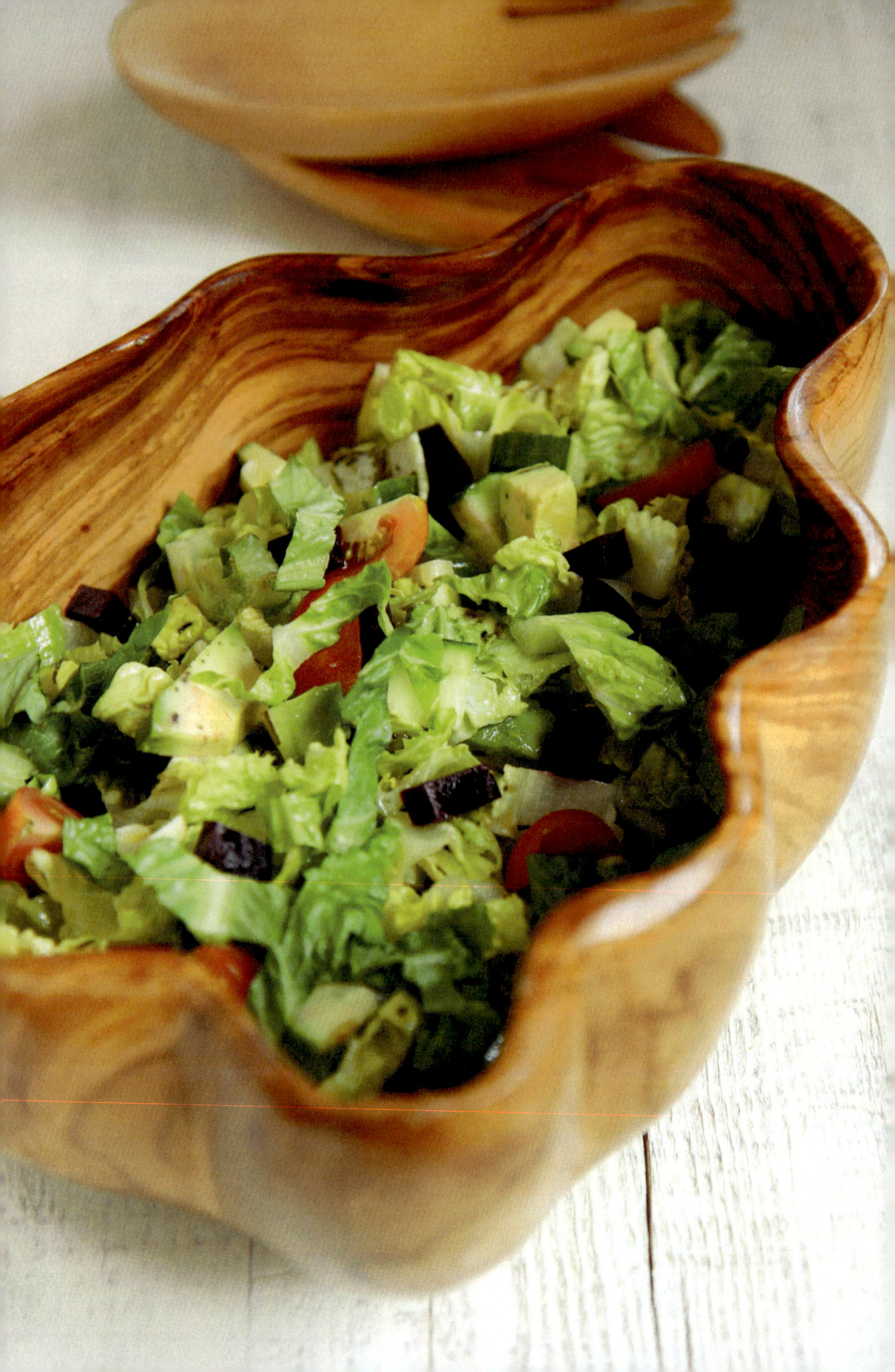

SALAD DRESSING IDEAS

SIMPLE DRESSING

INGREDIENTS

2 tablespoons Dijon mustard
½ cup apple cider vinegar
1 tablespoon maple syrup
1 tablespoon herbs de Provence
1 teaspoon cumin
1 teaspoon sea salt
¼ cup olive oil

DIRECTIONS

1. Put all ingredients into a lidded jar.
2. Shake until everything is mixed.

TIA T'S TOMATO DRESSING

INGREDIENTS

1 large tomato
3 or 4 fresh garlic cloves
1 full sprig of rosemary
1 tablespoon of red wine vinegar
1 teaspoon maple syrup
2 tablespoons olive oil
(extra virgin is a little too bitter)

DIRECTIONS

1. Blend everything but oil.
2. Slowly add oil, allowing to emulsify.

ASIAN ALMOND DRESSING

INGREDIENTS

5 tablespoons almond butter
1 tablespoon apple cider vinegar
1 tablespoon honey
1 tablespoon tamari
2 tablespoons sesame oil
1 tablespoon lime juice

DIRECTIONS

Blend in high-speed blender.

CREAMY CASHEW DRESSING

INGREDIENTS

1/2 cup raw cashews (soaked)
1/2 cup water
1/4 cup olive oil
2-4 tablespoons lemon
2 tablespoons any herb
1 tablespoon brown rice miso
    (sea salt or tamari can work too)

DIRECTIONS

Blend in high-speed blender.

GOOD PRODUCTS DO HELP KIDS EAT AT SCHOOL!

Kids Konserve nested stainless containers are awesome for snacks.

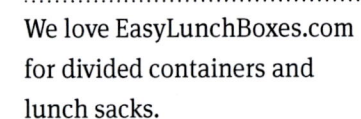

We love EasyLunchBoxes.com for divided containers and lunch sacks.

I love LunchBots thermos for warm meals because of its wide mouth. Remember to pour warm water into a thermos to heat before adding hot food.

KIDS' LUNCH

The goal for any kid's lunch is to keep it easy to eat and full of nutritious food that helps them be present and productive during school day. I find the simpler and more repetitive lunch is, the more successful my kids feel in general.

For children, lunch is a time to learn how to eat a meal away from parents. For smaller children, this starts with simple things like understanding the order in which to eat different foods, and how to open containers. For older children, this is about how to feel awesome about their homemade meal when others may be eating highly-processed foods.

Time is also a big factor at all ages. Lunch is an opportunity to be social and schools generally don't give it enough time, so navigating how to sit and get to eating and chewing is big! The more you can preview and talk through lunch at home, the more comfortable your kids will become.

And do remember it is a learning process. Don't punish uneaten lunches. Use them as an opportunity to understand what is going on and empower your child to do it differently next time, or for you to pack it differently. (Uneaten lunches do make a good snack.)

HOW YOU PACK LUNCH CAN MAKE A DIFFERENCE.

Food can change over the course of the three or four hours it sits in a lunch box! If you are in doubt, test on weekends, and try it yourself.

I love post-it notes for lunch box reminders and notes. You can write a love note or explain which container to eat from first.

For older children, 7+, add age-appropriate chores and get support with packing lunch.

REALLY UNDERSTAND WHAT IS BEING SERVED AT SCHOOL.

Remember, lunch is a time to really step into healthy eating, rather than to slip into what's easy or convenient.

Always feel OK replacing a planned lunch that is not made yet with good leftovers that the kids loved from the night before.

LunchBots also makes this great divided container that we use for snacks that need compartments — veggies, crackers and hummus or a few kinds of fruit.

I JUST WANT TO REITERATE THE IMPORTANCE OF TWO THINGS.

One, that not all food tastes good packed in lunch. There are many healthy foods that don't keep well when packed at 8 am, and by afternoon, they either look or taste awful. We're going to consider all that as we go through the formulas and hopefully you'll get a lot of strategies for different fruits and vegetables that stay fresh until lunch.

The second thing I want to reiterate is the importance of packing kids' lunches if they are away for school each day. Very often, I fear, parents work so hard on the other meals throughout the day that lunch is a time to "let ourselves off the hook." I don't want to make anyone feel guilty if that is what they choose because I empathize with busy parents. I know that we are all doing the best we can. However, I challenge you to scrutinize the lunch menu at your child's school and question if it's the best choice for a healthy life. Maybe ask yourself: Does every meal have gluten? Does every meal have dairy? Is every meal highly processed? Does every meal have high sugar? Which meals are a little bit better? If you're trying not to pack every lunch, are there certain days that make more sense than other days? If it's a school where there is a choice, how can you empower your kids to choose the best things for themselves? That's huge, as soon enough kids grow up, and move out of the house and become adults. They will have to live in the world independently and make their own decisions about food. How can you start influencing them now so that they will be prepared with valuable knowledge when that time comes?

For younger kids, take into consideration that lunchtime at school can sometimes be stressful. Beyond food, other factors make lunchtime unique, like sitting at tables, socializing with other children, and eating without adult supervision. Depending on what the school's set up is, lunchtime can be overwhelming, and occasionally opening up a lunchbox in front of friends can make a child feel vulnerable. Maybe their neighbors are eating differently or making different choices. It just opens up all sorts of things for kids. Empower your kids ahead of time so that lunch feels successful and they are confident around their peers, even at a young age. You can do that by explaining what's in the lunchbox, and by sticking to that idea of rhythm.

We love Klean Kanteen for water and smoothies. The insulated model keeps smoothies cool, and we try to always cultivate the habit of drinking water — my kids sleep with their bottles!

SCHOOL LUNCH FORMULA

Kids' lunches can be way more repetitive than other meals. If the goal is to get healthy food into your child so he or she can thrive in school, then the goal is to provide him or her with good food they will actually eat. If dips always disappear, pack dips three days a week. If soup is a big hit in cold months, then make two kinds of soup each week and alternate them. You can always get creative with the extras — different chopped fruits, different types of veggies, muffins, homemade cookies, or a granola bar.

LUNCH RHYTHM
PASTA DAY

Pasta Day came into existence because my kid's school had it first, only their version was often full of dairy and gluten. Because I still wanted them to feel like they were partaking in the special day, I'd send them with better alternative pasta options that kept them clear and focused for afternoon classes.

PASTA PESTO

INGREDIENTS

2 cups packed basil leaves
½ cup pumpkin seeds
   (Almonds and pine nuts are also yummy, but pumpkin seeds work in a nut-free school)
4 tablespoons olive oil
3 tablespoons nutritional yeast
2 cloves garlic
Pinch of sea salt to taste
Gluten-free pasta*

DIRECTIONS

1. Put all pesto ingredients in a high-speed blender and blend until smooth.
2. Add more olive oil and/or water to create desired consistency.
3. Cook pasta according to directions.
4. Toss pasta and pesto.

*Make sure to test your gluten-free pasta on a weekend to see what it does after a few hours. Extra sauce helps, and we find that pasta with quinoa or corn seems to hold up the best over time.

A COUPLE OF NOTES ON MAKING IT LAST IN A LUNCH BOX

This lunch is mostly a matter of putting together the pieces! The pesto can be made on Sunday evening or in the morning on Monday, but double it up if your week is particularly busy.

If you want the pasta warm, pack it in a stainless thermos that you have warmed by filling it with hot water and dumping the water out just before filling with food.

Make sure the pesto is on the watery side as the pasta will absorb water as it sits, especially the gluten-free variety...

WHAT ELSE CAN BE PACKED IN THIS LUNCH?

- Grape tomatoes, a pear, and trail mix
- Carrot sticks, strawberries and a sweet treat that you prepared over the weekend
- Cucumbers, an orange, and a jar of chia pudding
- Lightly steamed green beans, raisins, and a side of applesauce
- Celery and a super-foods fruit smoothie

HOW ELSE CAN YOU PREPARE PASTA?

- For pesto, play around with different nuts and seeds. Add spinach or kale for extra nutrients and a softer taste. Add avocado for creaminess.
- With tomato sauce
- Ramen style rice noodles with broccoli
- With salad dressing and chopped veggies (cool for warmer times)

LUNCH RHYTHM
SALAD DAY

Of course you don't want to slather fresh greens with dressing at 7 am because they will be soggy by lunchtime. The good thing about salads is they don't require any reheating, so they're better for travel. One of the things my daughter loves is either a brown rice or a quinoa salad with lots of chopped veggies. There are many sturdy veggies that don't even need grains too. You can toss them with a vinaigrette and they will still taste great by lunch. My kids also enjoy more traditional salads, so sometimes I'll pack them a very sturdy romaine lettuce along with a ranch-inspired vegan dressing.

On salad day, I will pack a protein — some beans, a hardboiled egg, or a protein-packed muffin or smoothie are well received.

RICE AND VEGGIE SALAD

INGREDIENTS

1 cup cooked brown rice
1/4 cup chopped cucumbers
1/4 cup chopped radishes
4 tablespoons apple cider vinegar*
1 tablespoon dijon mustard*
2 tablespoons olive oil*
A dash of salt*
maple syrup to taste*

DIRECTIONS

1. Mix the dressing ingredients (*).
2. Toss the dressing with the rice and veggies.

MAKE THIS YOUR OWN

Carrots and beets would be great if that is what is in your fridge. Add white beans or chickpeas for protein. Quinoa is a great alternative to brown rice.

This is for one serving assuming you are using leftover rice.

QUINOA TABOULI

INGREDIENTS

2 cups quinoa
2 tablespoons olive oil
4 tablespoons lemon juice
1 teaspoon sea salt
1 cucumber (diced)
1 tomato (diced)
1 cup flat parsley (chopped)
1/2 cup red onion (diced)

DIRECTIONS

1. Cook quinoa as directed.
2. Put quinoa in a bowl and mix with lemon juice, olive oil, and salt.
3. Toss in remaining ingredients and mix well.

THIS RECIPE MAY BE YOUR END GOAL.

Start with quinoa and less parsley, or serve the ingredients separately. Give your young eater the time to love all the parts of a salad like this, and then mix them when you know she is ready. This may be best done on a weekend.

SIMPLE BEAN SALAD

INGREDIENTS

3 cups black beans or chickpeas, cooked
5 tablespoons fresh lime juice, or to taste
1 teaspoon sea salt
1 teaspoon ground cumin, or to taste
5 tablespoons olive oil
¼ cup diced cilantro
A variety of fresh veggies

DIRECTIONS

Mix all ingredients together in a bowl.

Cooking a bunch of beans on a Sunday (or free day) is a great thing to have in the fridge to throw together in fresh salads all week.

This salad is super flexible! Any fresh herb would work — cilantro, mint or basil would be great. You can also vary the type of beans and use white beans, French lentils or garbanzo beans.

Also any sturdy vegetables would work, just make sure to use a variety of colors. One cucumber, yellow pepper, tomato, and avocado all diced with the beans makes an amazing salad.

Another way to eat this salad is to use it as a dip with corn chips. An easy method for school.

CINDY'S QUINOA SALAD

INGREDIENTS

½ cup broccoli
½ cup carrots
½ cup cooked chickpeas
1 cup cooked quinoa
1 tablespoon parsley
1 tablespoon olive oil
A pinch of sea salt
1 tablespoon lemon juice
1 teaspoon maple syrup
A pinch of cumin

DIRECTIONS

1. Mince broccoli and carrots (a food processor is good for this).
2. Put wet ingredients at the bottom of a bowl with minced parsley, cumin, and sea salt to taste.
3. Add in veggies, chickpeas and quinoa, and toss.
4. Put in lunch container.

CAESAR SALAD

DRESSING INGREDIENTS

¾ cup raw pine nuts

½ cup water

2 tablespoons lemon juice

1 teaspoon maple syrup

3 tablespoons nutritional yeast

2 cloves garlic

½ teaspoon ground black pepper

½ teaspoon sea salt

DRESSING DIRECTIONS

Blend everything in a high-speed blender.

SALAD INGREDIENTS

Romaine lettuce

Lightly streamed broccoli

Carrots

SALAD DIRECTIONS

To pack this in a school lunch, you can serve the dressing on the side, and either kids dip veggies or know how to pour dressing over the salad.

Nuts and seeds are a good addition for crunch.

If you want your child to have animal protein, you could serve grilled chicken as a side. Or you could also serve it with a muffin and fruit for a very satisfying meal.

A good sauce and salad container is a great thing to have. We like our divided Easy Lunchboxes for this coupled with their smaller dressing container.

LUNCH RHYTHM
DIP DAY

Dip is a great item to build lunch around.

Think bigger than hummus. If you love hummus, consider making it from scratch. Really any bean, and many seeds and nuts, make great dips when blended in a food processor. If you follow the formula on this page and mix those with herbs, citrus and a little bit of salt, you'll end up with a huge variety of dips made out of all types of different things. Then you can dip vegetables into them, or healthy crackers. You can even steam the vegetables a little bit and you have a healthy and easy lunch that travels well and stays fresh.

CUT A VARIETY OF COLORFUL VEGGIES INTO DIPPABLE FINGER FOOD SHAPES FOR KIDS.

Matchsticks or coins work great. Veggie ideas include cucumber, celery, broccoli, carrots, baby tomatoes, bell peppers, radishes, green beans, snap peas, or cauliflower.

If your kids have been doing carrots and cucumbers for a while, see if you can add a new veggie to the mix. If you are transitioning from lots of crackers and not many veggies, start with carrots and cucumbers, which are generally kid-approved.

You could also quickly steam broccoli, cauliflower or green beans, which makes them easier to chew.

PACK VEGGIES AND CRACKERS ALONG WITH DIP IN A BENTO-STYLE LUNCH CONTAINER.

We love Easy Lunchboxes as pictured. Pair with fruit and one of the sweet treats from Sunday – if there are any left!

Mary's Gone Crackers are one of our favorite crackers, and kids also love brown rice crackers, rice cakes, sweet potato chips, or gluten-free bread for dipping.

MAKE A KID-APPROVED DIP FROM THE FOLLOWING PAGES, OR BUY ONE FROM THE STORE.

Dip is really easy to make — it is almost like a smoothie and can be made on a Sunday for sure.

Read labels to make sure there are no weird extra ingredients if you go the store route.

QUICK GUACAMOLE

INGREDIENTS

Avocado
Lemon juice to taste
Sea salt to taste

DIRECTIONS

Mash avocado with a fork, mixing in lemon and salt.

TRADITIONAL HUMMUS

INGREDIENTS

5 cups cooked chickpeas
¼ cup fresh lemon juice (about 1 large lemon)
¼ cup tahini
1 clove garlic
2 tablespoons olive oil, plus extra for serving
Sea salt to taste
½ teaspoon ground cumin
2 to 3 tablespoons water

DIRECTIONS

1. In the bowl of a food processor, combine Tahini and lemon juice. Process until the mixture is creamy.

2. Scrape down sides. Add the olive oil, minced garlic, cumin and salt to the whipped tahini and lemon juice mixture.

3. Add half of the chickpeas to the food processor and process for one minute. Scrape sides and bottom of bowl, add remaining chickpeas and process for 1-2 minutes or until thick and quite smooth.

4. Alternatively, blend all ingredients in your Vitamix, using the plunger.

LENTIL HUMMUS

INGREDIENTS

2 cups water
1 cup dried yellow lentils
2 medium garlic cloves, finely chopped
3 tablespoons tahini
5 tablespoons olive oil
¼ cup lemon juice
2 teaspoons sea salt
¼ teaspoon freshly ground black pepper

DIRECTIONS

1. Heat water in a small saucepan over high heat until boiling. Add lentils and reduce heat to low.

2. Simmer until almost all of the liquid has been absorbed, about 15 minutes.

3. Drain through a fine mesh strainer and let cool to room temperature, about 20 minutes.

4. Place lentils, garlic, tahini, oil, lemon juice, salt, and pepper in a high-speed blender. You can also use a food processor, but high-speed blender will give a creamier texture.

EDAMAME HUMMUS

INGREDIENTS

3 cups organic, frozen edamame
4 cloves garlic
1½ teaspoons sea salt
½ cup tahini
8 tablespoons lemon juice (2-3 lemons)
2 tablespoons water

DIRECTIONS

Blend in a high-speed blender.

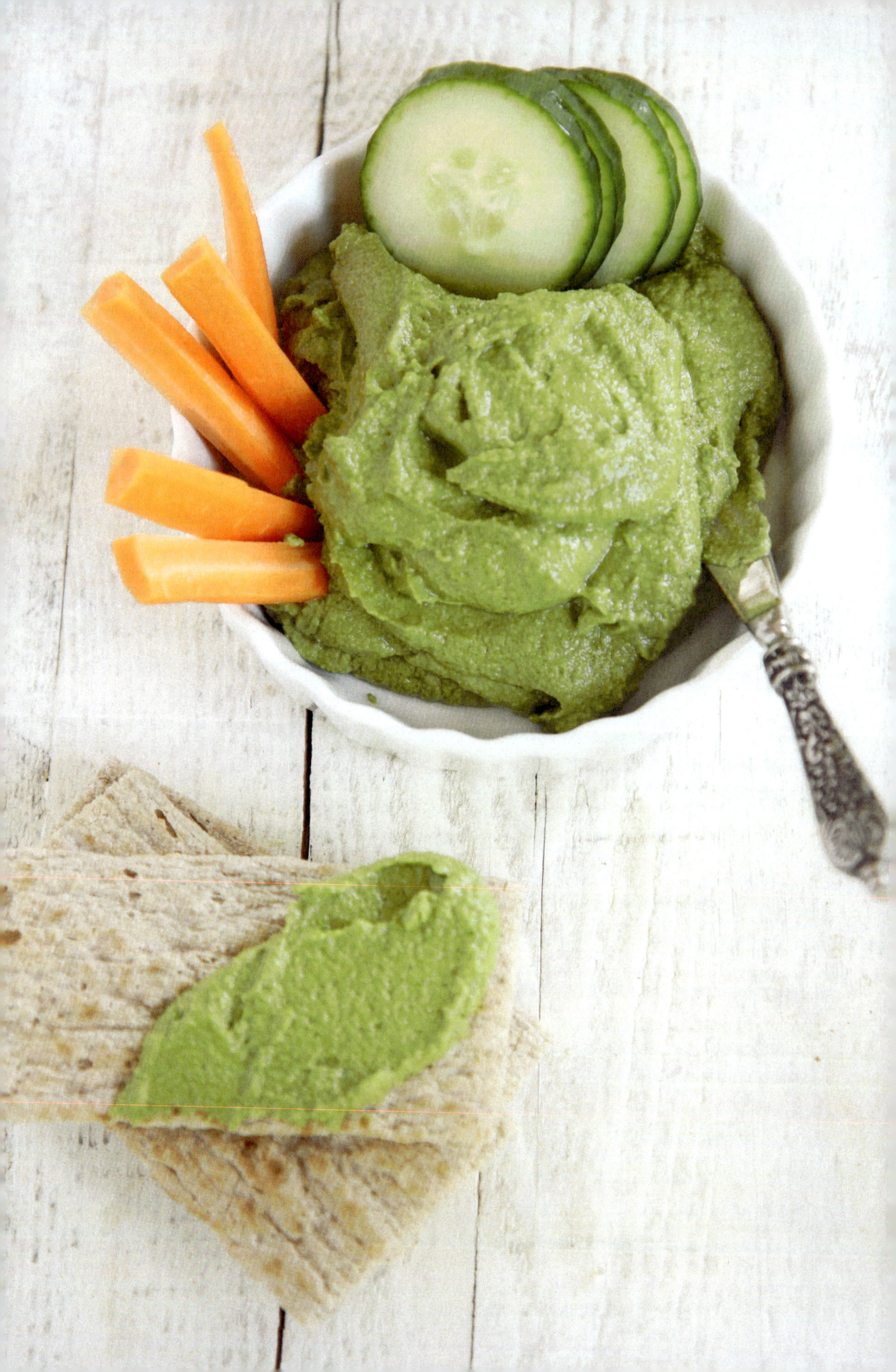

CILANTRO SUNFLOWER CAVIAR

INGREDIENTS

3 cups sprouted sunflower seeds
1 cup fresh squeezed lemon juice
¼ cup chopped scallions
¼ cup raw tahini
¼ cup tamari
1 large bunch of cilantro
1 clove garlic
1 teaspoon raw honey

DIRECTIONS

1. Place 3 cups of sunflower seeds in a bowl and cover with water. Soak for 8 hours.
2. Drain and rinse seeds and place in a strainer for about 2 hours. You will see the seeds get a very small "tail."
3. Place all ingredients in high-speed blender. I use my Vitamix with the plunger, as it is a very thick dip.

If you do not have a Vitamix, I would recommend a food processor for this recipe.

If you are someone who does not like cilantro, basil would be a nice alternative.

Soaking seeds and nuts is easy once it becomes habit!

LIBBY'S ONION DIP

INGREDIENTS

2 cups of cashews, soaked
1 onion
1 teaspoon olive oil
½ cup water
1 teaspoon salt
¼ cup diced chives

DIRECTIONS

1. Cut onion in large chunks.
2. Sauté onion in olive oil until it is caramelized.
3. Blend cashews, cooked onion, water and salt in a high-speed blender (such as Vitamix).
4. Stir in chives.

LUNCH RHYTHM
UNSANDWICH DAY

I have nothing against a sandwich (well except all the bread we eat!) but I feel like all too often we default to meat and bread or PB&J. On sandwich day we playfully make sandwiches more interesting and nutritious. Sautéed or grilled veggies in a sandwich or almond butter and honey with fruit — eliminating sandwich meat and sugar. Or move beyond bread, which I have found very freeing when trying to be gluten-free.

THINK BEYOND THE AVERAGE DELI SANDWICH

Sliced red pepper, avocado and Cheeze

Hummus, grilled zucchini

Cream Cheeze and cucumber

Avocado, raw veggies, and sea salt (or just avocado)

Pesto, tomato and lettuce

Almond butter, fruit and honey

THINK BEYOND BREAD

Sure you can find gluten-free sliced bread, but think of all the other options too.

Hummus and seasonal veggies wrapped in collard leaves

Bean or nut salads wrapped in lettuce leaves

Corn Tacos

Nori

Brown Rice Tortillas

WHAT TO SEND WITH A SANDWICH

Sliced Veggie Sticks — cucumber, celery, carrots, radishes.

Fresh fruit — pick two fruits that are different colors.

Nuts

A smoothie

NOTES ON SANDWICHES

It helps to toast bread in the morning if sandwich is being eaten 3 hours later. **Pay attention to what you put next to the bread.** Cucumber or tomato directly against bread leads to soggy bread, where avocado or a "cheeze" spread fares fine.

Children could put together the sandwich themselves at school if all your ingredients seem soggy! Just remember to show them how and make sure it is possible in the time allotted.

QUESADILLAS

Advice from Laura Fuentes at Momables — Save extra beans and make quesadillas for lunch the next day! Assemble the quesadillas at night, but wait until the morning to grill them. After you grill (or toast in a toaster oven), let sit for five minutes to cool, then cut and pack into lunchboxes.

TACOS

Envision this shell as a great vessel for any leftover beans. Guacamole, salsa, cashew sour cream, Daiya vegan cheese, and shredded lettuce would also make great toppings.

Depending on how long the lunch has to sit, you can pre-make the taco, or pack the shell and let the kids scoop up the toppings.

SUSHI

INGREDIENTS

Veggies for filling, such as cucumber, pea sprouts, avocado, and carrots
1 cup rice, cooked
Gomasio
Snack pack of nori

DIRECTIONS

1. Cut cucumber into matchsticks.
2. Mix one cup cooked brown rice with 2 tablespoons Gomasio.

PACKING

1. Pack a "snack pack" of roasted nori. They should have this in the international aisle of your supermarket, or even at Costco.
2. Pack rice, cucumbers, and avocado (or carrots) in a bento box. Your child can then make nori tacos for lunch, which you may want to show them briefly how to do at home!
3. You can add a small container of tamari for dipping.

SALAD WRAP

INGREDIENTS

Romaine lettuce
Shredded carrots
Sunflower or pea shoots
Avocado
Hummus
A pinch of sea salt
Brown rice tortillas

DIRECTIONS

1. Warm the tortilla to soften. You can soften it in a skillet over low heat with a small amount of oil or water if you are packing it for school lunch.
2. For school lunch, combine all of the ingredients and place in the middle of the tortilla and roll it up like a burrito. Wrap it in tin foil and instruct your child to open it from one side, so it stays together.
3. For the adult version, add double the romaine.

LUNCH RHYTHM
SOUP DAY

Soup is a great thing to make a large batch of and package the extra for lunch. Bean soup is great, as is a puréed squash soup in the fall. It could also serve as a cooling soup in the summer.

Check out the dinner section for lots of variations. The winners at school are puréed soups with toast sticks or crackers for dipping, and noodle soup.

NOODLE SOUP

INGREDIENTS

Miso

Kombu seaweed

Water

Gluten-free udon noodles or rice noodles

Choose 2 add-ins — tofu, broccoli, carrots, bok choy are good options

DIRECTIONS

1. Follow directions on miso container
2. Cook noodles according to package in a separate pot.
3. Add veggies to miso broth at end.
4. Mix two together in a thermos.

SQUASH SOUP

INGREDIENTS

Any type of squash
   (butternut is an easy favorite)

2 leeks

1 tablespoon olive oil

1 tablespoon ancho chili powder

1-2 tablespoons cumin

Salt to taste

DIRECTIONS

1. Peel and remove seeds from squash.
2. Bake squash at 350° for 45 minutes OR steam diced squash for 15 minutes.
3. Slice the leeks and while squash is cooking, sauté them in the olive oil until translucent.
4. Blend cooked leeks, squash, herbs, and water (1+ cups depending on desired consistency).

LUNCH RHYTHM
LEFTOVER DAY

You have to be careful choosing which leftovers to package because not all dishes taste awesome on the go. Pasta and fried rice taste great, as do beans and soup, and they all travel well. Figure out which items in your rhythm, more consistently than not, would taste good as leftovers. Then make the next day your Leftover Day and that way you'll be able to pack something that makes sense. One of my kids' favorite leftover food is soup. I'll also pack some toast, (gluten-free) for them to dip in or some crackers to go with the soup. Consider how you pack those leftovers and what containers they go into, so that it's the most successful by lunchtime.

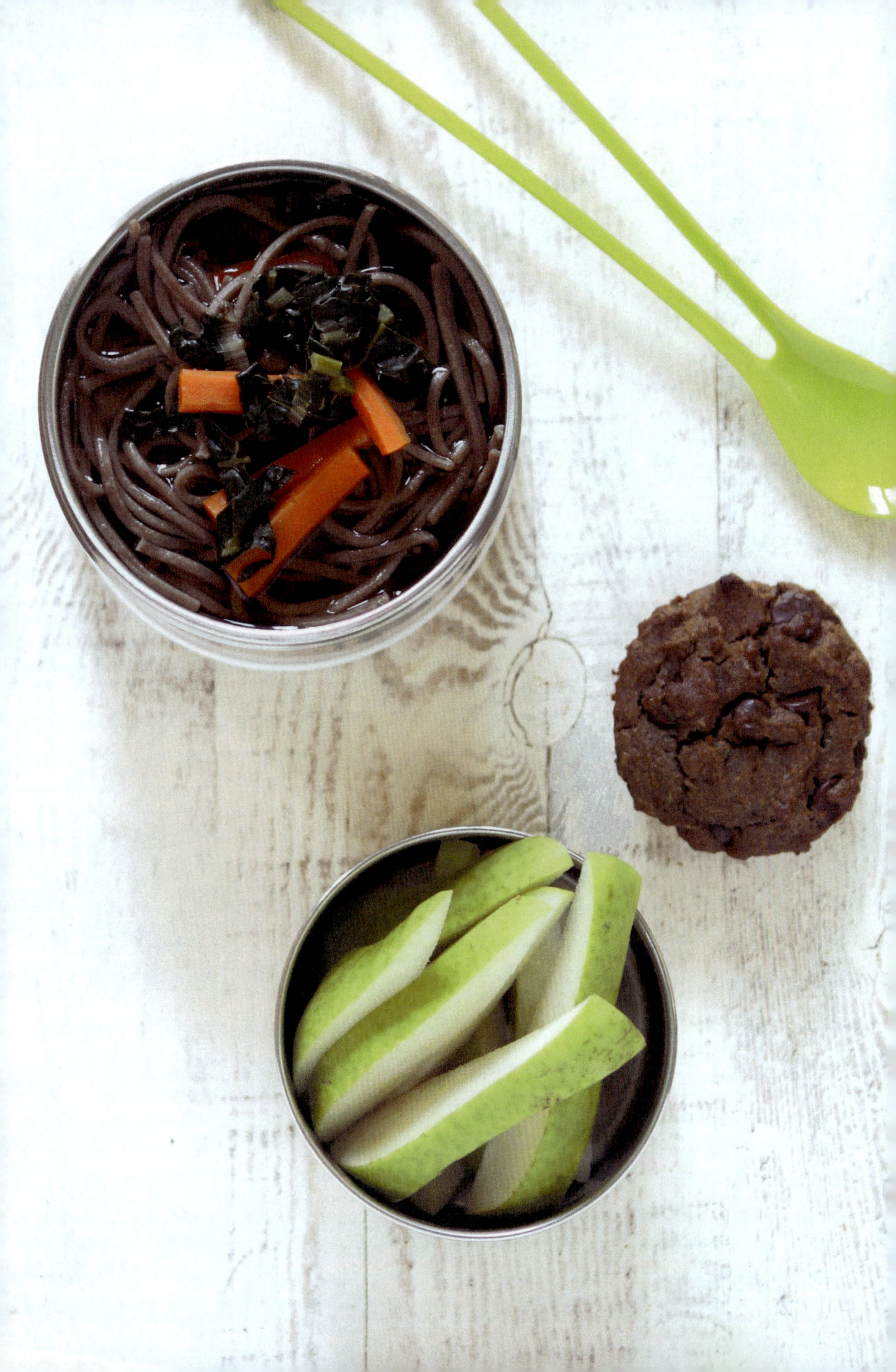

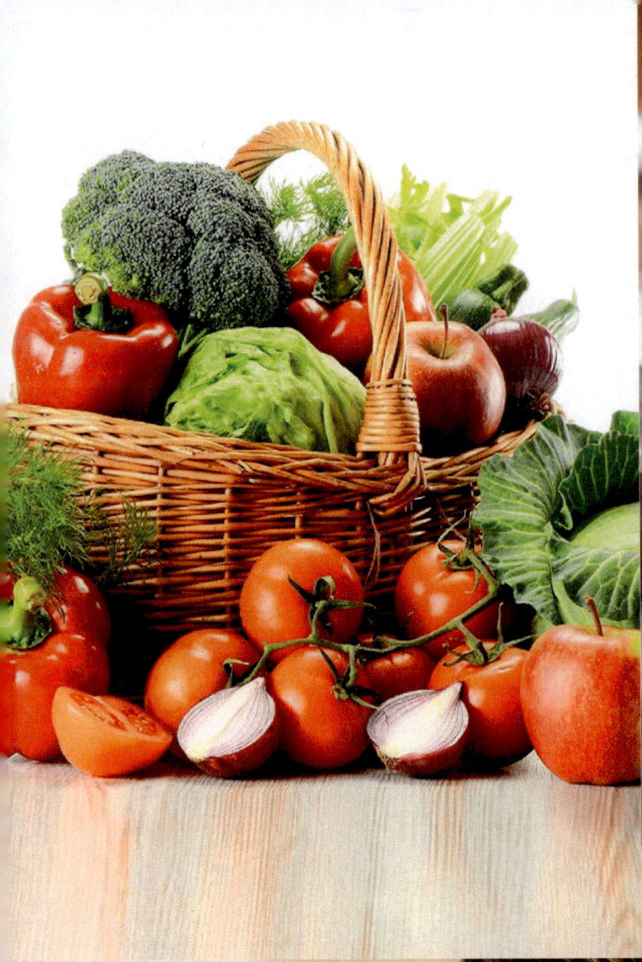
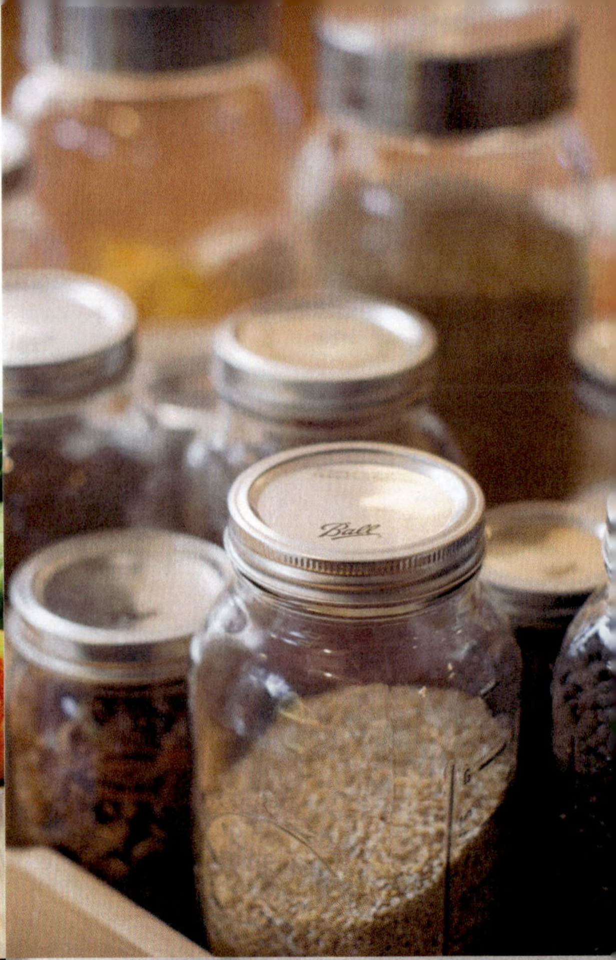
Ball
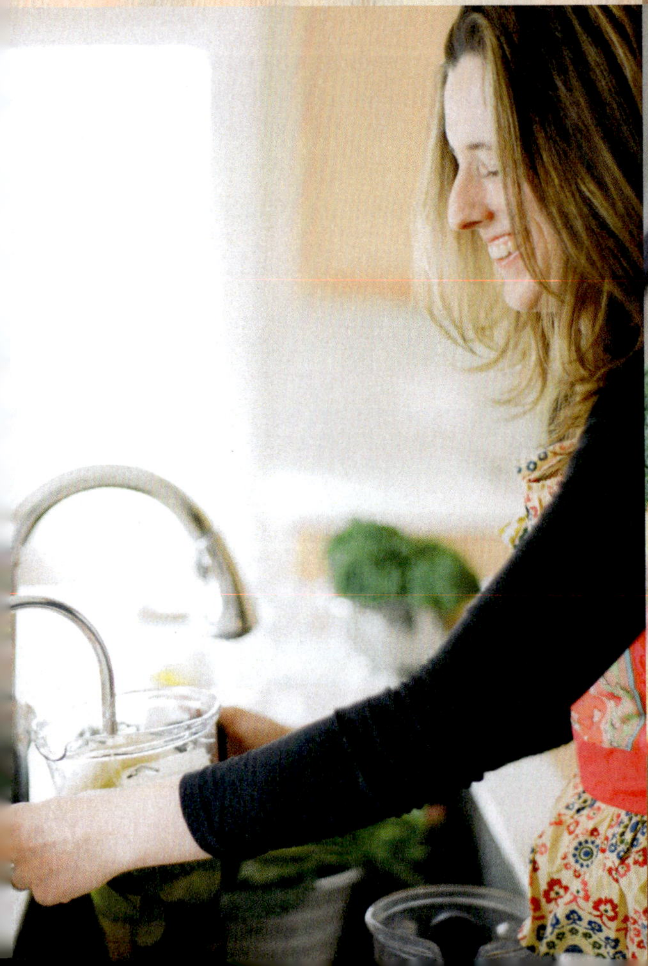
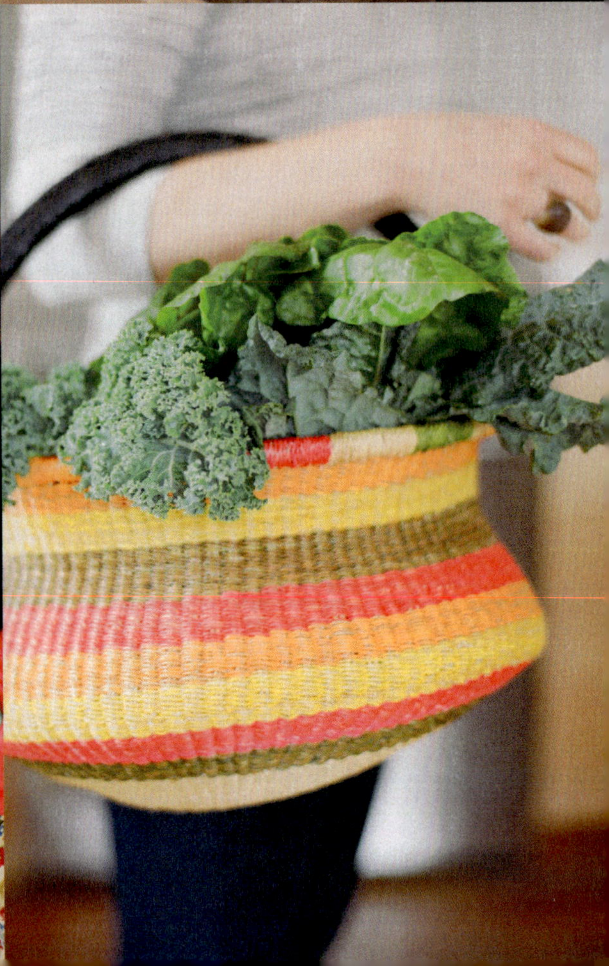

Doable Changes

Here are some doable changes inspired by this chapter.
Choose one, and commit to experimenting with it this week.

1. Let your child choose a new fruit or veggie to try next time you are all at the store.
2. Create a master list of the items you buy most often, and where you get them.
3. Make time every Friday to plan the following week of meals.
4. Write what's for dinner each morning on a Post-it.
5. Create a binder or electronic folder with your plans, so you can repeat them.
6. Make time to food shop every week. When you get home, wash and chop the food that you can.
7. Find a source of organic nuts and ship to your house.
8. Keep chopped veggies and fruit in the fridge.
9. Try fermented foods such as sauerkraut in your salad to help build the good flora in your gut.
10. Master the art of salads. Eat a salad every day for lunch.
11. Make a salad dressing twice a week, so salad is always easy.
12. Make your own hummus.
13. Pack lunch for your kids __ days a week
14. Always sit to eat.
15. Chop veggies once or twice a week, so a salad is easy.
16. Always add veggies
17. Try to make your own bread.
18. Be OK with doing things a bit differently than the "standard" American (or norm in your country).
19. Make time for yourself. Exercise, journal, or take a nap.
20. Move food forward throughout the day.
21. Try adding sea veggies to your repertoire — nori counts!
22. Find a good source for dried beans.
23. Order what you can online.
24. Browse a farmer's market.

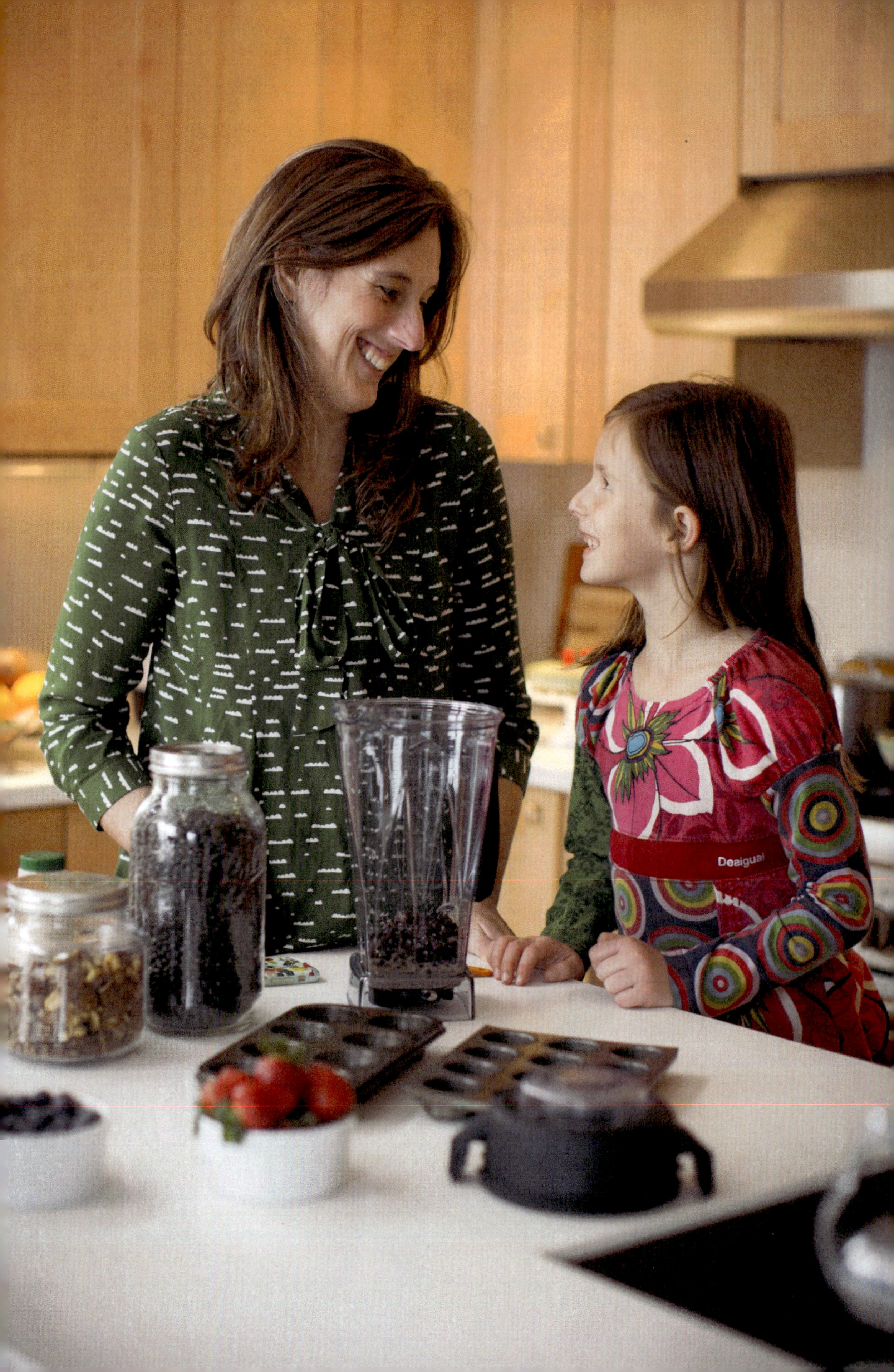
Desigual

STEP FIVE
Build your village

"Everyone thinks of changing the world, but no one thinks of changing himself."

—Leo Tolstoy

YOU: BE THE MODEL

Here's the thing: when I first changed the way I ate, it was a big transformation. Today people ask how my kitchen is so relaxing, and how I can just whip together dinners so calmly. I can promise you, it did not start this way. Remember that seven years ago, take-out was my friend, cooking an egg was stressful, and kale was not even part of my vocabulary. While I had experience with losing weight and dieting in previous years, I had never felt the connection between food and overall wellness that I feel so deeply today. I had never been aware that unhealthy food made me feel badly, even though now that's so obvious to me now.

Kids have different reasons for throwing tantrums and shoving vegetables off their plates. As parents, we often blame the food itself, but the food may not be the problem. As humans, we are instinctively drawn towards fruits and veggies, however that natural desire gets lost among the sparkly packages and sugary goodness that bombards our lives as modern consumers.

The dictionary definition of tribe is: "a social division in a traditional society consisting of families or communities linked by social, economic, religious, or blood ties, with a common culture and dialect, typically having a recognized leader."

The recognized leader is you.

In seeking my own wellness first, I found the foods and rhythms that worked best for me, and then those healthy patterns very naturally rippled out to my family. I realized I needed to lead by example before I could ever ask anything of my kids in a genuine

PARENTS

OUR KIDS

EXTENDED FAMILY

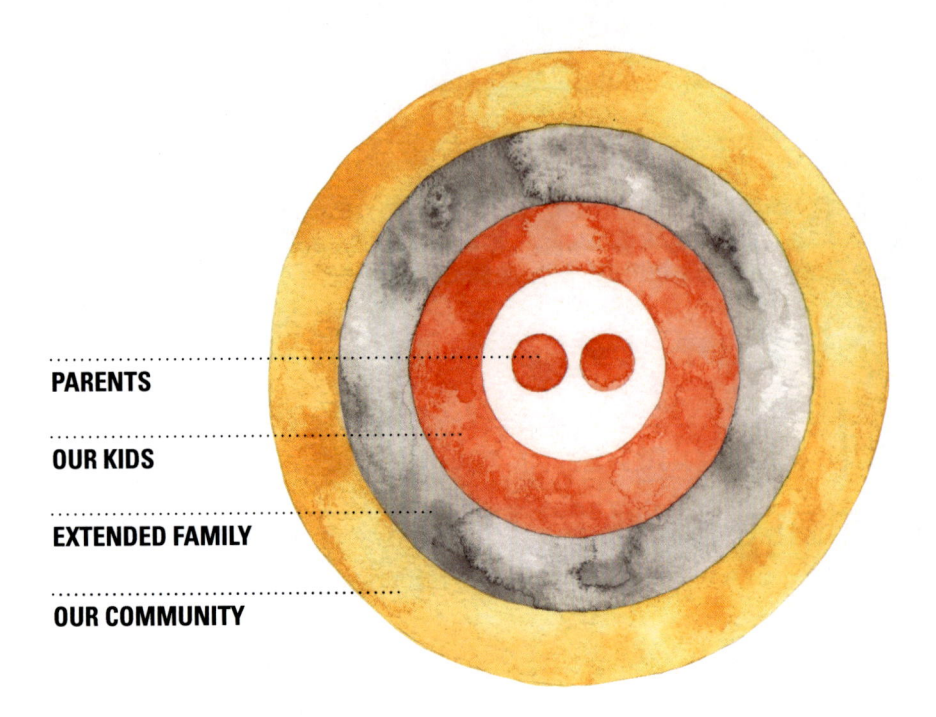

OUR COMMUNITY

way without just being a nagging parent. And nagging is what I believe causes the resistance, not the food itself.

Imagine yourselves as parents in the middle of a set of concentric circles. After we figure out ourselves, we start to influence our family. After we influence our family, we start to influence our extended family and our friends around too. The cool thing is, as we're influencing these people, they have their own audiences. They sit in the center of their own circle, and they start influencing their set of friends, and as you can imagine, the overall ripple effect is huge.

Creating a tribe is important both for ourselves to get support, but also to really make the world a healthier place. One of the things that you might experience as you start to make all these changes is that it's can be frustrating to feel resistance from others. Maybe your spouse isn't on board, or maybe one child's not on board, or maybe your mother-in-law's always sneaking your child food. Maybe you're constantly going to school events, or little league games, and all these processed foods that you don't want in your life are being offered to you and to your family. That can really be a test of your newly transformed lifestyle.

If you can start to pinpoint the people in your life who understand or at least appreciate your healthy choices, it makes a huge difference. That's exactly what I did. I actually had to pay for my allies at first: a health coach, a cooking class, the Waldorf School for my kids. Eventually, I found friends and family members who really appreciated eating well and learning about healthy food, and they started coming on this journey with me. Over time, the food options changed at my regular social gatherings and holiday events. As I began to spread the knowledge and awareness that had worked so beautifully in my own life, it just naturally weaved its way into the lives of my own friends and family.

136 PLAN SIMPLE MEALS: GET MORE ENERGY, RAISE HEALTHY KIDS AND ENJOY FAMILY DINNER

Now I say this in hindsight. I want to be clear that the health coach and the cooking instructor were my lifeline on many days when all odds seemed stacked against me. I also tried not to have too much of a tribe at the very beginning because I sensed that I needed to be alone to succeed. I could not go to a traditional Thanksgiving dinner one month in, so I opted out that year.

While it may seem overwhelming to change the minds of those around you, know that you always have control of your own choices, so start there. Make changes that you control, like bringing your own food everywhere. You can bring food to your kid's school, to events, to dinner parties. You can start off bringing it for yourself and build up to sharing, when everyone starts asking about your glow! When you share food, and people love it, because they will, share the recipes with them and make sure everybody knows how to make what you've made. Share desserts first. There is nothing more shocking than serving a delicious raw brownie or cheesecake made out of cashews and dates. They're amazing, but maybe new and different to those who've never tried them. Share things that you know will have a high likability to them and you'll start to build this tribe around you almost by default, but just remember that it all starts with you.

Start small, knowing that you can't change everyone's opinion. Push yourself a little to be healthy and take every day as a new and exciting challenge. Push gently on those around you to maybe grow and shift their perspective on food to make healthier choices. Of course pushing gently means never using guilt trips or making anyone feel shameful about food. Remember that everyone is on their own journey with food and in life. You can never force anyone to change, but you can lovingly share information with them if they are open to receiving it. But again, it all starts with you.

FAMILY: YOUR KEY TRIBE MEMBERS

Once I had shifted my own perspective on food, I then had acquired the necessary skills to bring my family along for the ride. While two of my children and my husband don't have food sensitivities necessarily, everybody can still benefit from eating better. I noticed positive changes immediately once I started offering my kids less sugar, and more fruit and vegetables. I watched things change little by little. I watched my son who did not love change get less frustrated on a daily basis. I watched my somewhat spacey daughter become more grounded. And when they were off sugar for a stretch, I could immediately see the crazies that happened after a sugary treat. We all started to learn these things together.

One of the most effective tools and strategies that made healthy eating work in our little tribe of five was family dinner. I really think that there's nothing more powerful than family meals — especially dinner.

I hear a lot of people say that they're just not all home at dinner time. If this is the case for you, gathering together on the weekends for breakfast or lunch — really anytime you can be together and bond as a family is beneficial. However, I also believe there's something magical at dinnertime. It is the pivot point from day to night. It's a beautiful time of day to connect with the people you love and share stories of your respective days.

For me, the practice of gathering at dinnertime really helped make my time in the kitchen feel worthwhile. I realized the powerful effect sitting for dinner had on our togetherness as a family unit. Our perspectives on life would shift just by the conversations we were having, the food we were sharing, and the ability to just slow down and sit down together at this time of day. It changed the way I saw cooking and providing for my family. I fully admit to the fact that I am a mom who worked after every child. I chose this not only because of need, but also for my own self-fulfillment. There was something about being in the kitchen that just made me feel like June Cleaver in 1950 and it was really out of sync with my personality. Like many females my age, I wanted to feel like a strong and independent woman, and not just a slave to domestic life.

Once I started reaping the benefits of sitting down together, which happened pretty fast once we made a commitment to it, the concept of making dinner, and washing dishes and cleaning up after dinner really shifted for me. Dinner and chores became my meditation.

Maybe it feels overwhelming to begin a practice like sitting down for dinner all of a sudden. If so, just take your next doable step. It might be that right now you sit down two times a week, so own those two days and work towards the next doable step for your family. Maybe that's dinner three times a week instead of two, or maybe it's five. Always focus on upgrading family dinner. Even if you're sitting down every night as a family you can still improve dinner in other ways. Try upgrading the conversation at the table so that it's not just everyone chatting over each other. Focus on not getting up and leaving the table so many times. Hopefully everybody can sit for a good amount of time, half an hour minimum. Learn listening skills, create a gratitude practice, and talk about the values that you created for your family's brand.

CONVERSATION STRATEGY FOR AGES 2 TO 99 — THE THORN AND THE ROSE

In this storytelling game, each person at the table takes their turn to share one good thing (a rose) and one concern (a thorn) that happened in their day. In our house, the Thorn and the Rose game has become "The Happy Sandwich," where an unhappy event that day, or an upcoming concern, is "sandwiched" between two happy experiences – one that has already happened, and one that is anticipated. To play, ask each child, "What went well today? Was there anything you wish had been better? Is there anything coming up that concerns you tomorrow? What are you looking forward to tomorrow?" Ending on a high note closes each family member's sharing with good energy and a sense of hopefulness. This is a wonderful game for all ages – so don't forget to share your Thorns and Roses too!

I find that the dinner is an amazing time and place to share stories, worries, accomplishments, and desires, as it offers a safe space for children to express their feelings. Through talking and sharing, we create our tribe. I could ask my kids every day in the car on the way home from school if everything is ok and not get more than a "yeah" or a "sorta." At dinner, when the day is finished and the mood is relaxed, that's when I really get to peel back the layers and listen to what's going on with my kids. To me, that's worth any amount of time spent in the kitchen.

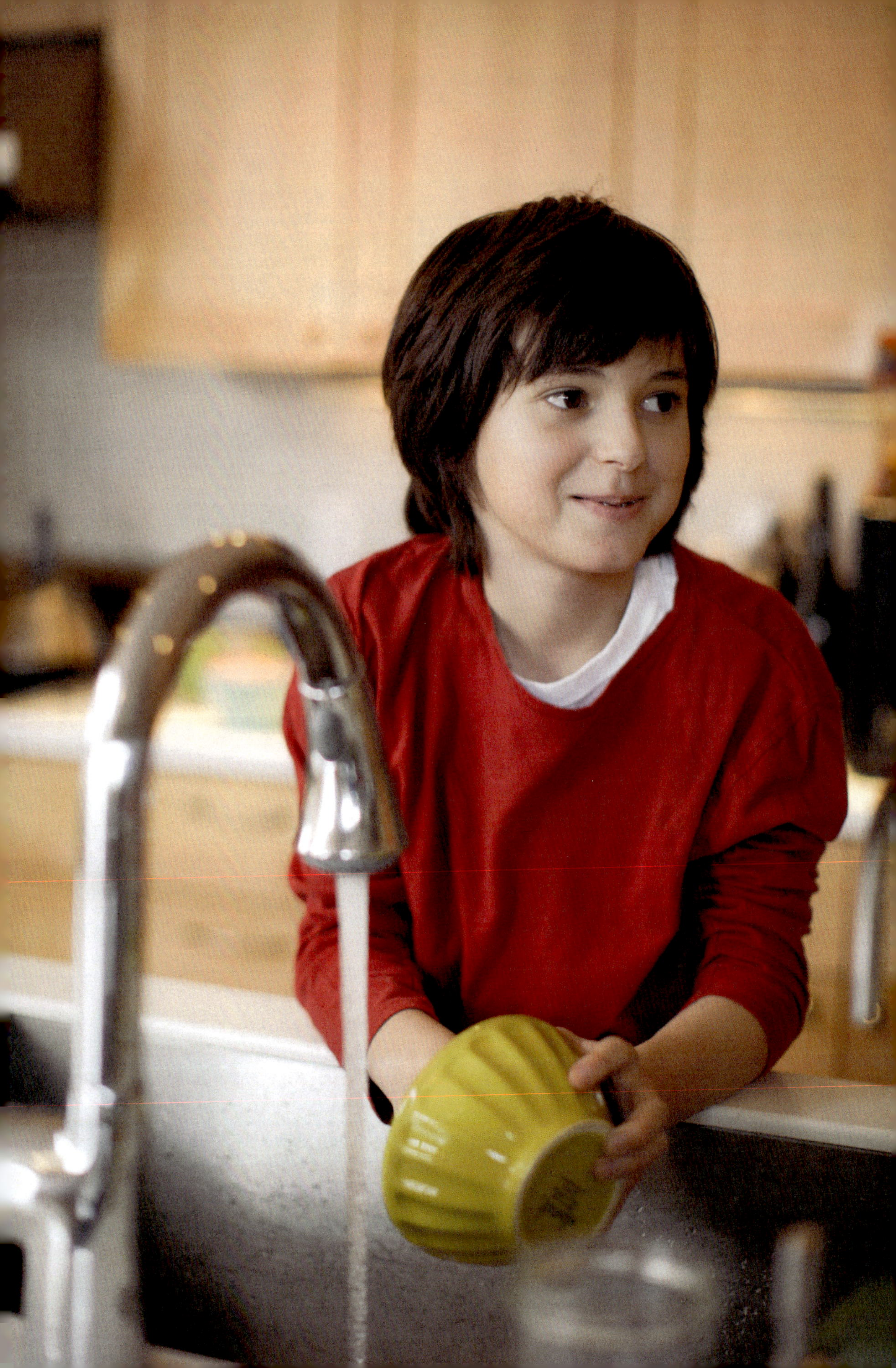

LET YOUR TRIBE HELP YOU WITH ALL THOSE ITEMS IN YOUR MINI-ROUTINES.

Remember in creating your core tribe, which is you and your kids and the family you live with, that you may be the leader but you don't have to do all the kitchen chores alone — even two-year-olds like little tasks. A two-year-old could carry something from one place to another. A two-year-old could stand by your side and help you wash dishes somehow if you give them a specific task. A seven-year-old could fully load a dishwasher or set a table. Sometimes as busy parents, we're just trying to get something done, and we forget we have a team at our fingertips. If you have any guilt, look at it this way. You are the only one who can teach your kids to do dishes after dinner, cook great food, and sit to enjoy it, and someday they will be alone and they will need these skills. If you don't do it for you, do it for them.

CHORES

Toddler (ages 2–3)
Unload silverware from the dishwasher
Fold dishtowels
Sweep the floor
Wipe cabinets or table
Wash vegetables
Help clean up spills and messes
Water the garden

Preschooler (ages 4–6)
Everything above +
Tear lettuce for salad
Measure and stir when baking
Help find items at the grocery store
Load the dishwasher
Pack snacks (with guidance)
Collect recycling
Help plant a garden
Set table
Clear table
Wash dishes (with supervision)
Carry groceries

Elementary (ages 7–10)
Everything above +
Wash, peel, and cut produce
Make a smoothie
Make simple dishes
Pack snacks and part of school lunch
Make salad dressing
Read recipes and help collect ingredients
Collect garbage and bring out to bin
Take out the compost
Harvest from the garden
Wash dishes
Load dishwasher
Empty dishwasher and stack items on the counter
Select produce and weigh it

Tween (ages 11-13)
Everything above +
Find a list of items at the store
Make homemade muffins and snacks
Cook simple meals
Pack entire school lunch
Take garbage/recycling to the curb
Weed the garden

Teen (ages 14+)
Everything above +
Make full meals
Plan meals
Walk (or if 17+, drive) to the store and buy items from your list
Clean out fridge/freezer/pantry

Chores can be a fun thing to do together! Cleanup after a meal has fun parts for every age, and it means the job gets done faster, and a family has more time to be together after dinner.

After you get your immediate family and those in your household really involved in the food, then you have the momentum to move out a little bit further to the next concentric circle. Just remember that sometimes people can be resistant to change. We all are. That's why you're learning to be the best leader you can, because it's hard to change things.

Grandparents, babysitters, and good friends, it might take them a while to catch on. Be patient. What you can start to do with these people is just share. Share whenever you can. If grandparents are over, be cooking and be explaining what you're doing. A great strategy I discovered was to figure out what I was anticipating from others, and "beat them to chase" so to speak. Like, if you're scared that the grandparents are just going to shower your kids with Oreo cookies, then make sure that when they're over, you're baking healthy cookies and explaining the difference. That way, you're not always fighting. You're more teaching, embracing, and letting in.

My parents were the first to embrace my healthy transition and wanted to learn more about it. Still, five years later, they continue to be curious because I'm making lots of healthy food every day. When I visit my parents, they often ask for recipes so they can replicate them on their own. Did my mom always buy the perfect gluten-free treat for my daughter along the way? No, but over the years she has come to understand and learn about labels, and now she discovers gluten and dairy-free goodies I don't even know about!

I've found that most people are interested and engaged when you approach them with openness and compassion. Just involving people and letting them into the process goes a long way. People really want to understand and learn too, and help you. Helping is a great way to learn. I'll explain in more detail how you can be an even greater advocate of healthy eating, but for now, let's focus on your next doable step: what food to serve for dinner.

Don't forget to listen. There may be people in your life who rock in the kitchen. You always appreciated their food, but you perhaps didn't acknowledge them. It is great to hang out with people who know more than you. They may even be part of your own family.

Once you are comfortable with family dinner, or maybe even before you feel ready, invite friends and extended family over on the weekends and just watch what happens at that table. It's quite amazing.

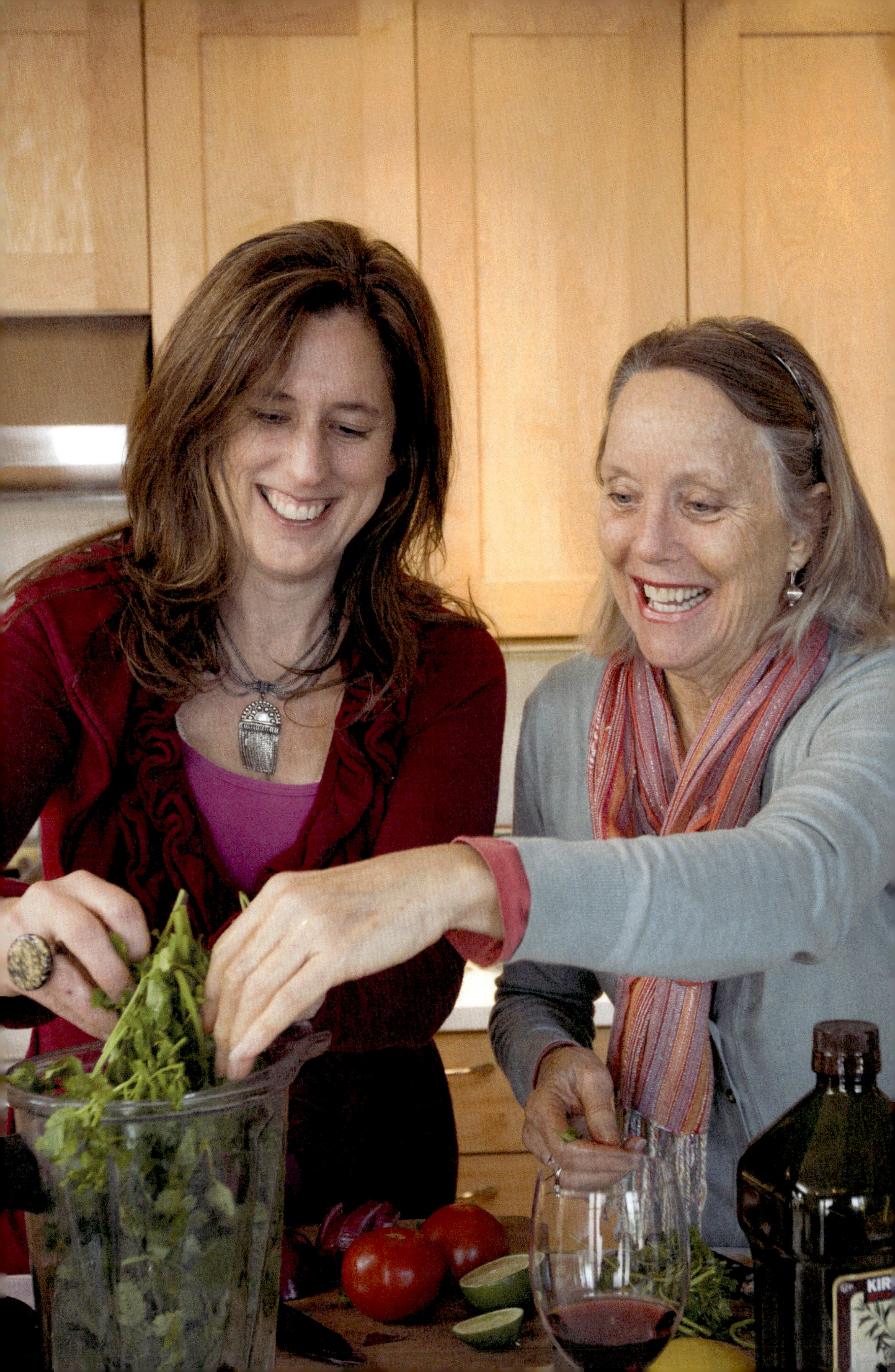

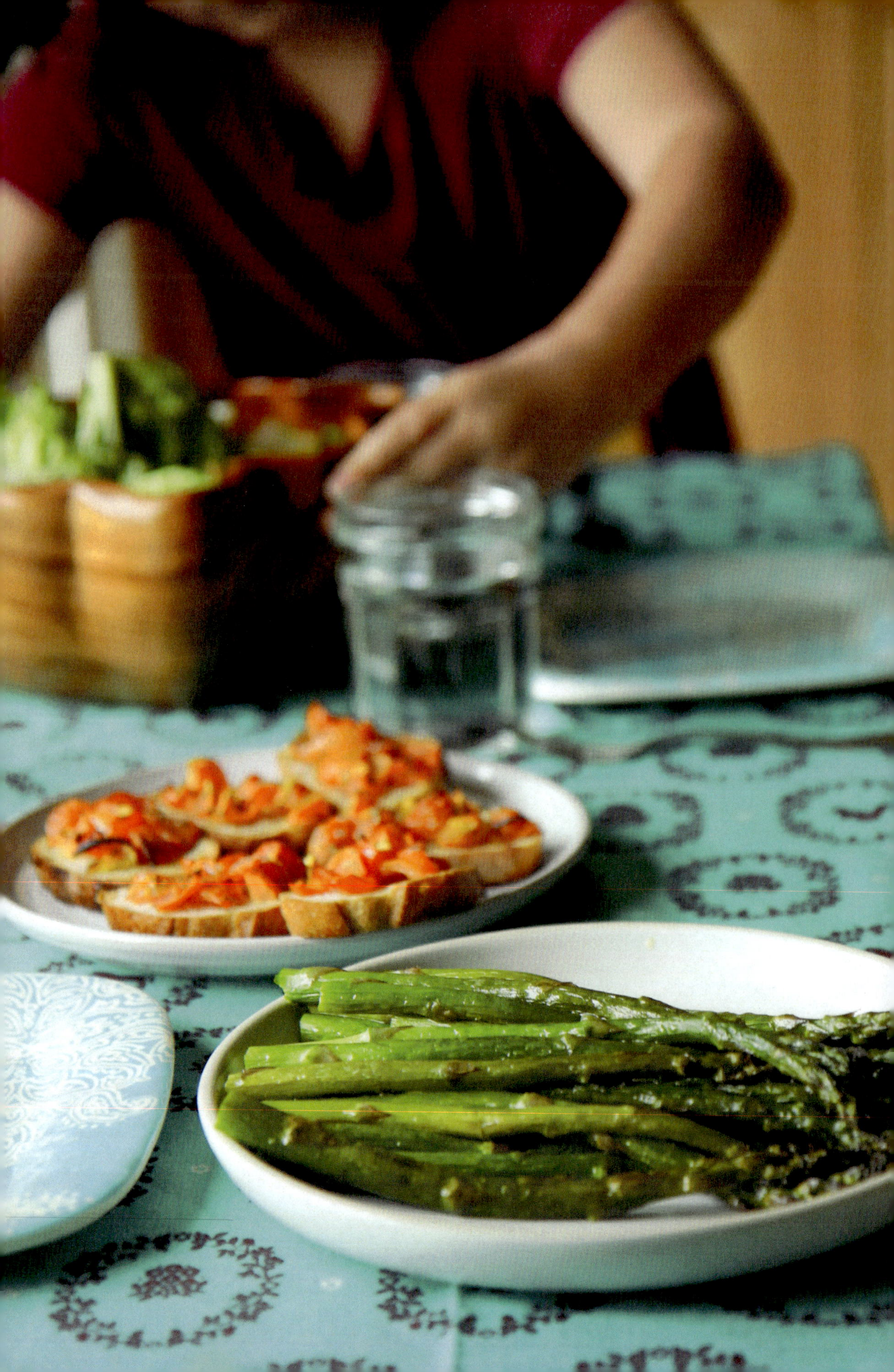

Food: Dinner

"The shared meal is no small thing. It is a foundation of family life, the place where our children learn the art of conversation and acquire the habits of civilization: sharing, listening, taking turns, navigating differences, arguing without offending."

— Michael Pollan, Cooked

First of all, let's go into the purpose of dinner. So far we've looked at breakfast, which is really about getting adults and kids off to a great start — towards green smoothies and away from cereal in a rhythm that flows effortlessly. Lunch becomes that opportunity where we can take care of our individual needs a little bit more — we teach ourselves and our family to listen to our bodies and nurture them when out in a world where this may still be a foreign concept. Dinner is different. At dinner we assemble at the table after our respective busy days. We come together to share food and company.

If there is a family "classroom," the dinner table is it. Dinner is the time where we can really teach our kids how to be good eaters. We can teach them about conversation. We can teach them about giving and receiving love. We can teach them listening skills.

And what's most remarkable is that all this happens naturally, effortlessly, just by the nature of sitting at the table together and sharing the same food.

Dinner is an opportunity that we should all embrace because it is the fastest path to a healthy family — in 45 minutes well spent, kids can be equipped for life. Consider all the tools I've introduced in the previous step about rhythm. By now I hope you have a sense of what you can do in your day to make dinner happen easier. Remember "moving food forward," working with your schedule, and being repetitive about what you eat are all things that can help create the space for family dinner.

Dinner is a great time to lovingly nudge our kids, which basically means lead by example, and challenge them in a safe environment to eat a variety of new foods.

VEGGIE-CENTERED MODEL

Let's start by reconsidering the plate. It is as easy as shifting around proportions and building meals around vegetables instead of around a protein or starch. The optimal proportions on your family plate should be 1/5 protein, 1/5 grain or starch, and 3/5 a vibrant rainbow of vegetables.

If this seems confusing, don't worry about it too much. Consider it your end goal rather than your starting place. Like the other meals, I've created seven formulas to help make dinner successful. These formulas will yield enough variety within a year and also be a way to make kids appreciate different foods and expand their pallets gradually.

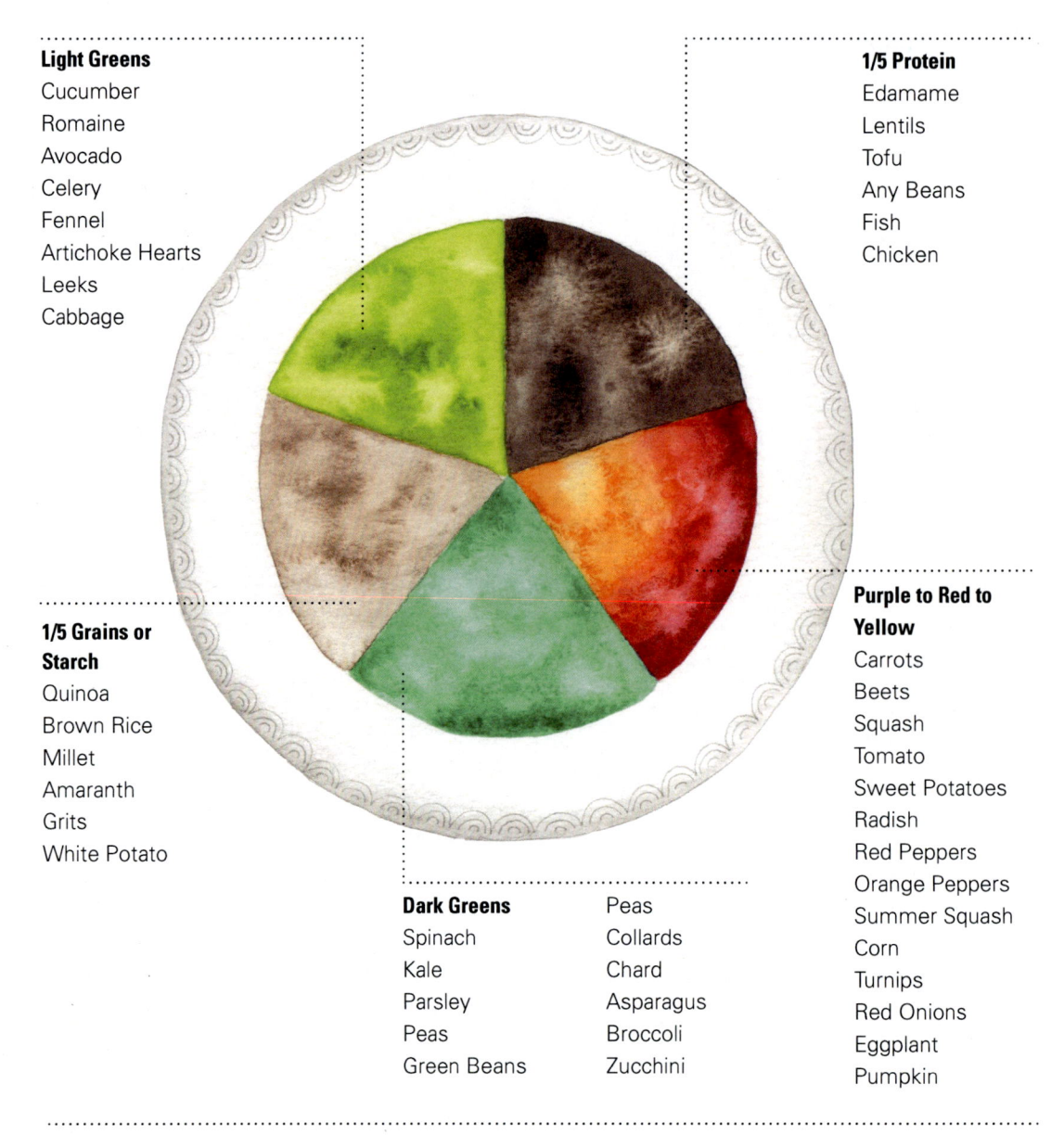

Light Greens
Cucumber
Romaine
Avocado
Celery
Fennel
Artichoke Hearts
Leeks
Cabbage

1/5 Protein
Edamame
Lentils
Tofu
Any Beans
Fish
Chicken

1/5 Grains or Starch
Quinoa
Brown Rice
Millet
Amaranth
Grits
White Potato

Dark Greens
Spinach
Kale
Parsley
Peas
Green Beans
Peas
Collards
Chard
Asparagus
Broccoli
Zucchini

Purple to Red to Yellow
Carrots
Beets
Squash
Tomato
Sweet Potatoes
Radish
Red Peppers
Orange Peppers
Summer Squash
Corn
Turnips
Red Onions
Eggplant
Pumpkin

FROM PICKY TO ADVENTUROUS

With dinner, we will consider different strategies for how to move a picky eater, or simply a child who has not yet been convinced about healthy food, forward.

(There is a worksheet over in the book hub, www.PlanSimpleMealsBook.com/hub)

❶ Know where you are.
Don't try to go from 0 to 100. Be OK with today and know that eating well is a process, much like learning to read, that your child will get with time and practice.

❷ Start with what your children like.
Build meals based on food they already like, at first. If your son likes carrots, make a new dish with carrots. If your daughter likes pasta or pizza, start playing with adding more veggies, and making the processed parts from scratch.

❸ Observe.
You want to commit to moving forward but not too fast. Sometimes "picky" does not have to do with the food but the situation. Other times it may be about texture and size of a vegetable. This may differ from child to child. Take time to notice without judgment.

❹ Have a plan.
Know that you may have to reintroduce one food 7 times. Charting your progress in writing is pretty helpful, so you know you are getting closer to 7 times. I find people who set out to try 7 times find success much faster.

❺ Have a partner.
Tell your spouse, your mom, or a friend about your experiments. Sometimes it is nice to do this with a group of moms. Make sure you have a tribe who has your back. Feel free to join our group at HealthyMomsMeetup.com if you want me and an amazing group of moms as your partners!

❻ Rinse and Repeat.
This process will feel different with each new food and at the various stages of each child. Get in the habit of doing this a few times in a row until making new things becomes second nature for you, and trying new things, becomes second nature for your child(ren).

❼ Celebrate.
Please don't praise your kids for eating. Do pat yourself on the back when meals go well, and simply say, "what a great meal!" As meals become more diverse, they will be celebrations in themselves!

DINNER RHYTHM
BEAN DAY

For us, Bean Day is on Monday, but it could be any day of the week for you. I grew up in New Orleans where it's tradition to have red beans and rice on Mondays, because it's also wash day. Beans take a long time to cook if they start dried, so it was something that could be stirred in between all the washing that needed to be done. Mondays were always the perfect days to do both these things together.

Beans can be simple, and every bean tastes different, so there are lots of ways to explore. I will challenge you to try to cook with dried beans. Though they may take longer than beans from a can, there's less chance of BPAs, and dried beans are available in many more varieties. They're usually fresher, easier to digest (especially if you sprout them before you cook them), and they're just delicious.

CHOOSE A TYPE

Black beans
Adzuki beans
Red beans
Soldier beans
Lentils
Chickpeas
Pinto beans
Calypso beans
Navy beans
Fava beans
Black-eyed peas

PREP BEANS.

Rinse beans and soak them overnight (except for lentils, black-eyed peas and adzuki beans).

For most beans, 2 cups dried beans equals 4 to 5 cups cooked beans.

CHOOSE A METHOD FOR COOKING.

Cooking Method 1

Cook plain and flavor after — especially if you want to use a portion for a cake or brownies!

Cooking Method 2

Sauté an onion in olive oil.

Add diced (or blended) tomato.

When it turns into an orange paste, add beans and water.

Salt to taste.

Cooking Method 3

Sauté an onion in olive oil.

Add finely diced celery and green pepper.

When it is fully cooked, add beans and water.

Salt to taste.

ADD EXTRA VEGGIES.

Do this step if your family loves beans and are ready to move onto the next variation.

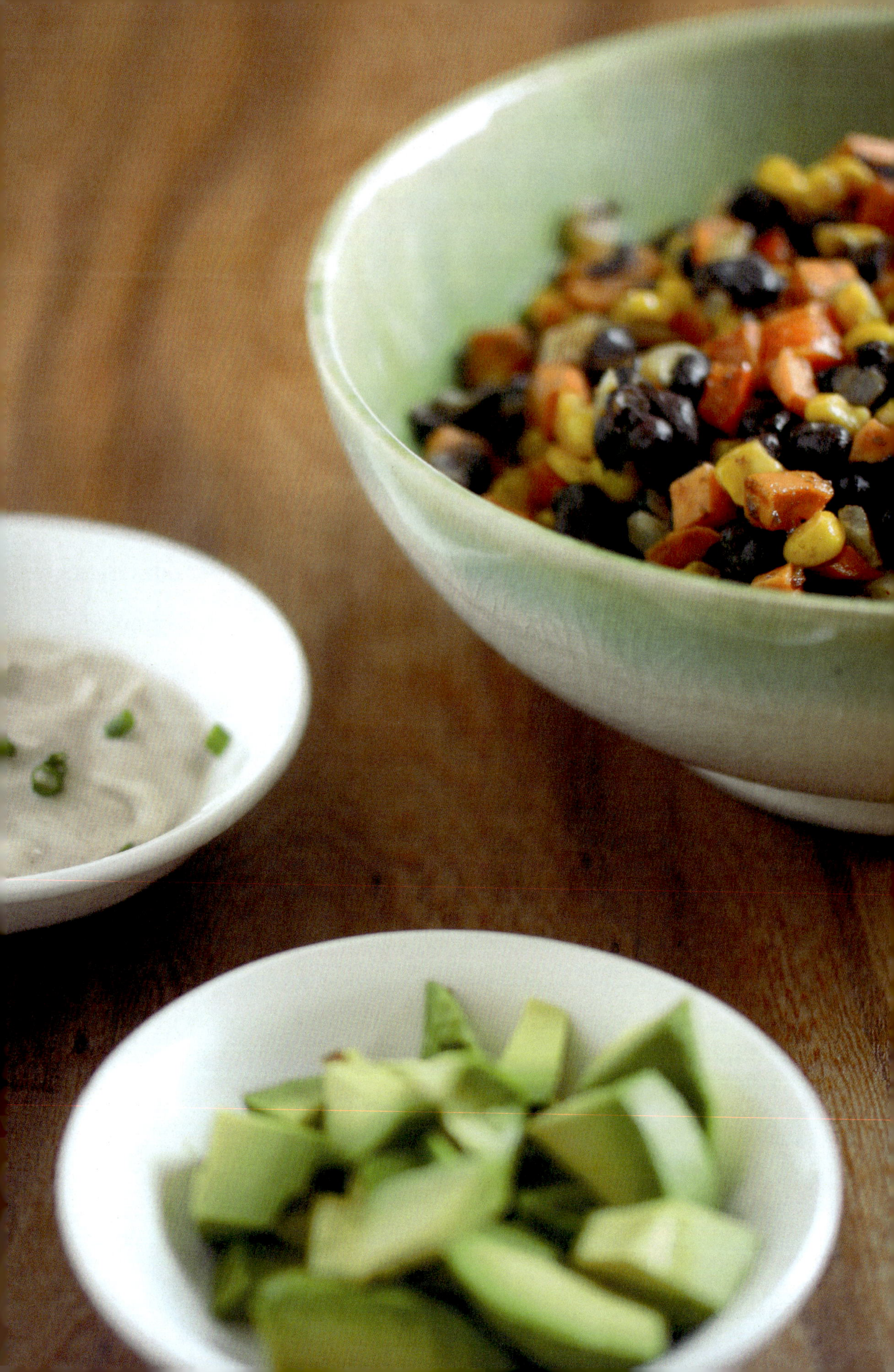

FALL ADD-INS

Carrot and thyme

Sweet potato and squash with cumin

Kale and extra tomato and basil

WINTER ADD-INS

Potato and spinach

Cauliflower, carrots and herbs de Provence

Brussels sprouts and garlic

SPRING ADD-INS

Swiss chard

Fennel and cabbage

Spring peas and onion

SUMMER ADD-INS

Eggplant, zucchini, and extra tomato

Cool with raw veggies, lemon, salt and fresh basil

Cool with fresh corn, beets and vinaigrette

A pressure cooker is a very helpful tool that's made such a difference in my house. With a pressure cooker, you can soak beans overnight, let them sprout for a few hours, cook them in enough liquid so the beans are covered for about 12 minutes, and they're done. Whereas normally if you put them in a big stock pot, they might take up to three hours.

BEAN FORMULA IN ACTION

NEW ORLEANS RED BEANS

INGREDIENTS

1 pound dry red kidney beans
2 tablespoons olive oil
5 cloves garlic
1 large onion
4 stalks celery
1 green bell pepper
2 bay leaves
2 teaspoons thyme
1 teaspoon oregano
1-2 teaspoons chipotle pepper
Sea salt to taste

DIRECTIONS

1. Soak beans overnight in a large bowl filled with enough filtered water to cover beans by 2".

2. Chop garlic, onion, celery and pepper very fine (the easiest way to do this is in a food processor if you have one), putting them in separate bowls.

3. Sauté the chopped veggies in the olive oil. Start with the garlic and onion, then add the celery and pepper after a few minutes.

4. When almost cooked through, add herbs, and stir into cooked veggies.

5. If using a pressure cooker, add beans and vegetable mix with just enough water to cover the beans and cook at 2 lines for 12 minutes.

6. If cooking on the stovetop, add beans and vegetable mix to a large pot with enough water to cover the beans by 1". Cook on medium-low heat, covered. After one hour, check on the beans; skim any foam off the top, then stir and add water to cover if needed. Continue checking each half-hour. Cooking time may be 1-2 hours depending on the freshness of the beans.

BLACK BEANS

INGREDIENTS

1 large onion
2 tomatoes
3 cloves garlic
1–2 tablespoons ancho chili powder
1 tablespoon cumin
Sea salt to taste
2 tablespoons olive oil
1 lb. bag dried black beans
Veggie broth or bouillon cube or powder
4 cups brown rice, cooked

DIRECTIONS

1. Rinse beans under cold water.
2. Soak dried beans in water to cover by at least 2 inches for six hours, or overnight.
3. Finely dice the onion.
4. Finely dice tomato, or throw it in the blender for pickier eaters or just for ease.
5. Sauté the onion in the olive oil until soft and translucent. Add the tomatoes and cook until you have a dark orange paste (about 10 minutes).
6. Add chili powder and cook for another minute.
7. Add the beans and cover with water.
8. Cook for 11 minutes in pressure cooker or up to 2 hours in a stock pot, adding water as necessary.
9. Serve over brown rice.

LENTILS

INGREDIENTS

1 lb. bag French lentils
1 onion
1 large tomato or 2 small ones
2 cups chopped cauliflower (half a head)
1 tablespoon olive oil
Sea salt to taste

DIRECTIONS

1. Finely dice onion, tomato and cauliflower separately.
2. Sauté the onion in olive oil until it starts to become translucent.
3. Add tomato and keep cooking until the mixture starts to turn orange.
4. Add lentils and cauliflower and quickly add enough water to cover.
5. Cook until lentils are tender, and cauliflower is falling apart, and salt to taste.
6. Serve over brown rice.

MOROCCAN CHICKPEAS

INGREDIENTS

2 eggplants, cut into quarter-inch cubes
1 onion, finely diced
8 cloves garlic, crushed
½ inch piece of fresh ginger, grated
2 teaspoons ground cumin
2 teaspoons ground coriander
2 cans organic crushed tomatoes
   (fire-roasted taste fantastic!)
2 cups water
1 lb. finely chopped kale strips
1 lb. bag dried chickpeas*

*If you are short on time, you can use three cans of chickpeas.

Fabulous served with quinoa.

DIRECTIONS

1. Rinse chickpeas under cold water.
2. Soak dried chickpeas peas in water to cover by one inch for six hours, or overnight.
3. Cook soaked chickpeas for 11 minutes in pressure cooker or 45 minutes in stockpot, adding water as necessary.
4. Drain cooked chickpeas and set aside.
5. Place eggplant cubes in a colander, sprinkle with salt and leave to drain for one hour, then rinse cubes and pat dry with paper towels.
6. Heat the oil in a large frying pan. Add the eggplant and cook until browned on the outside. Remove with slotted spoon and place on a paper towel.
7. Add the onion to the frying pan (which should still have some oil) and sauté; when soft and translucent, add garlic and ginger.
8. Stir in the cumin and coriander, then add eggplant, chickpeas, tomatoes and water and let simmer for 15-20 minutes.
9. Add the spinach or kale and more water if necessary, bring to a boil and cook for 1-2 minutes (a bit longer if using kale), until greens wilt.

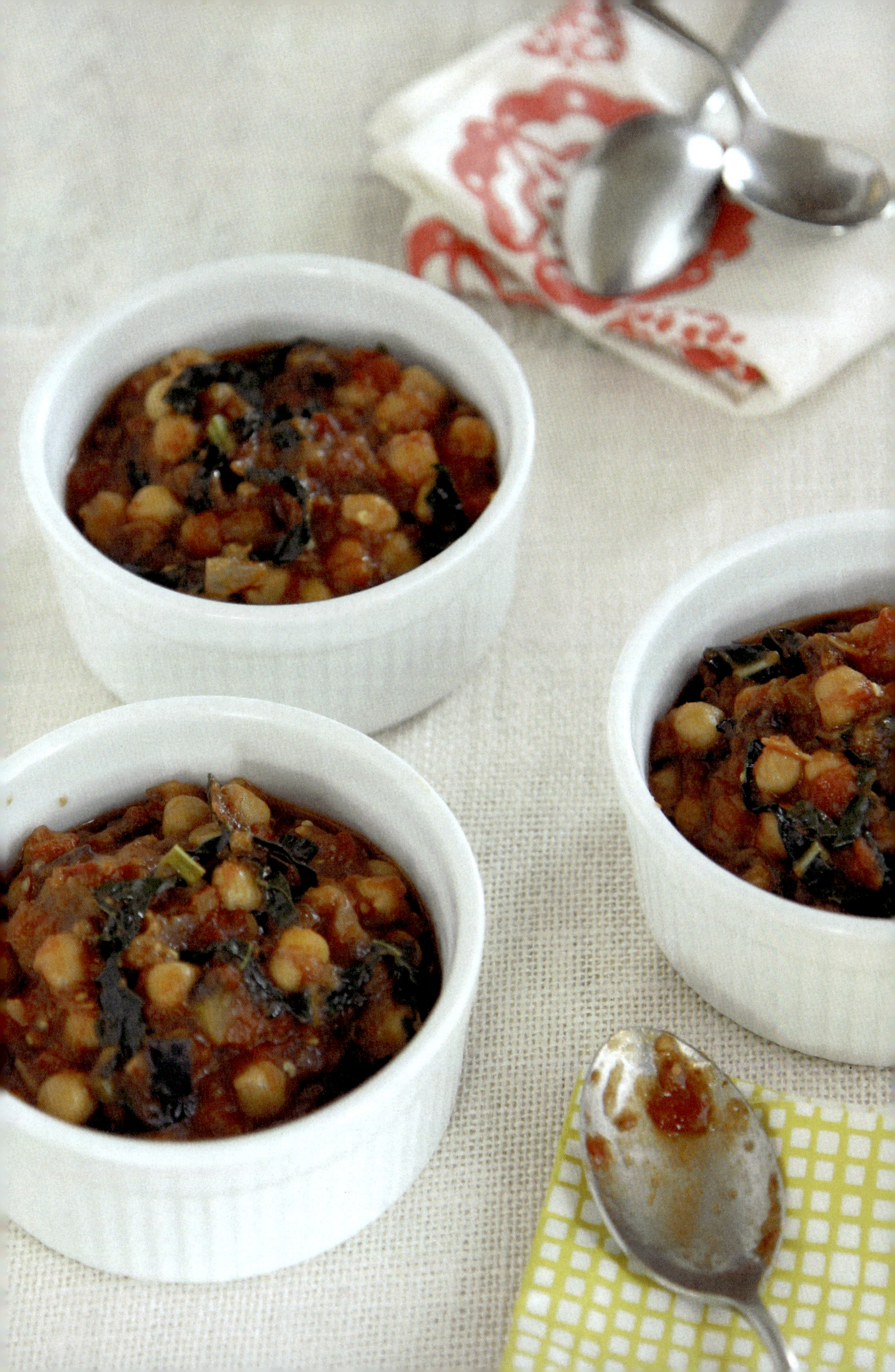

FAVORITE SIDES FOR BEAN NIGHT

Big green salad
Guacamole
Salsa
Green sauce
Sauerkraut
Cabbage salad
Radish salad
Sautéed greens (kale, chard, spinach)
Caramelized onion
Veggie sticks
Roasted carrots

PICKLED ONIONS

INGREDIENTS

Two red onions
Salt
Apple cider vinegar

DIRECTIONS

1. Cut onion into long, thin strips.
2. Put in a bowl with salt and lemon juice and massage the onions until they start to wilt.

SAUTÉED GREENS

INGREDIENTS

1 bunch of organic greens*
4 cloves garlic, minced
1 tablespoon olive oil
2 tablespoons mirin
1 tablespoon tamari

*Any greens work. I LOVE kale.
The kids LOVE spinach.

DIRECTIONS

1. Cut leaves in long, very thin slices — 1/8" if possible. (unless spinach or baby greens). The easiest way to do this is to roll them up lengthwise into tubes, then slice.
2. Warm a frying pan over low heat, then add oil.
3. Add greens to the oil. Toss them regularly and after 3 minutes, add mirin and garlic.
4. Keep sautéing for 5 more minutes or until greens start to wilt (spinach will wilt fast; collards take longer). Taste them and make sure they are tender and sweet. When you are satisfied with the texture, turn off the flame and add tamari.

NONA GIGI'S GREEN SAUCE

INGREDIENTS

1 jalapeño (de-seeded)*
1 bunch cilantro
Juice of 1 lemon
½ yellow onion
3 tablespoons olive oil
Sea salt to taste

DIRECTIONS

1. Blend everything in blender.

   *To de-seed the jalapeño, cut it in half the long way and take the seeds out under running water.

RADISH SALAD

INGREDIENTS

12 radishes, diced
3 tablespoons cider vinegar
1 tablespoon olive oil
A pinch of salt

DIRECTIONS

Mix everything in a bowl.

CABBAGE SALAD

INGREDIENTS

½ cup sesame seeds
2 tablespoons olive oil
2 tablespoons rice vinegar
1 tablespoon tamari
1 teaspoon maple syrup
1 pound napa cabbage, chopped
2 scallions, thinly sliced
¼ cup chopped cilantro

DIRECTIONS

1. In a bowl, mix the oil, vinegar, tamari and maple syrup.
2. Add the cabbage, scallions and cilantro and toss.
3. Add the sesame seeds and season with sea salt and pepper to taste.
4. Toss again and serve.

DINNER RHYTHM
TACO NIGHT

This night can be pretty flexible. It is a great way to repackage leftovers. It is also a great choice for when you have requests from your family. You may think of wrap night as an easy way to get "bready" products in that are gluten-free, but it is also a fabulous way to integrate greens in a fun way — lettuce, collards, and chard make delicious wraps!

THE WRAPPERS

A great thing is that corn tortillas don't have gluten, so you can start there if you're eliminating it. Some people do find it difficult to digest corn, so pay attention to your gut and your sleep after taco night. You can also find brown rice tortillas.

Thinking outside the box, many things can be used to replace the tortilla altogether. For an Asian style wrap, for example, you could use nori or romaine lettuce. You can find a bunch of suggestions for the filling on this page. Tacos are generally something that are much loved by kids. It is a great time for them to experiment because they love the idea of putting various contents into a shell and serving themselves.

PICKY TO ADVENTUROUS

1. Start with wrappers you know your kids will love, and then get more adventurous — corn tortillas and brown rice tortillas are pretty widely accepted then move into butter lettuce, nori, romaine, collards, chard once your kids love those.

2. Give healthy choices for fillings — encourage simple things and then play games to get more in. Start with black beans and guacamole. Serve tomato salsa and lettuce, and lead by example, then at some point have a game about the rainbow — maybe add shredded carrots.

FORMULA

1. Pick the main attraction

2. Add some extra veggies to the mix

3. Complement it with a sauce

PLAN SIMPLE MEALS: GET MORE ENERGY, RAISE HEALTHY KIDS AND ENJOY FAMILY DINNER

FALL FILLINGS

Chickpeas, squash and guacamole

Black bean, sweet potato, and carrot

Roasted root veggies

WINTER FILLINGS

Tofu and greens

Falafel and fennel

Sesame rice with avocado and cucumber (great in nori)

SPRING FILLINGS

White bean, spring peas and green sauce

Refried beans, chopped lettuce and salsa

Spring greens, carrot sticks, red peppers, and cucumber (works as a spring roll)

SUMMER FILLINGS

Quinoa cakes or veggie burger lettuce wraps

Grilled veggies

Shaved veggie rolls

WHAT IF SOMEONE WANTS MEAT?

This is a great night to add some animal protein if you have a divided house. I am 100% vegan, but I do buy very well-sourced animal protein from a farm and serve it to the kids every once in a while. They ask, and I want them to listen to their bodies so they can make great decisions when they are on their own.

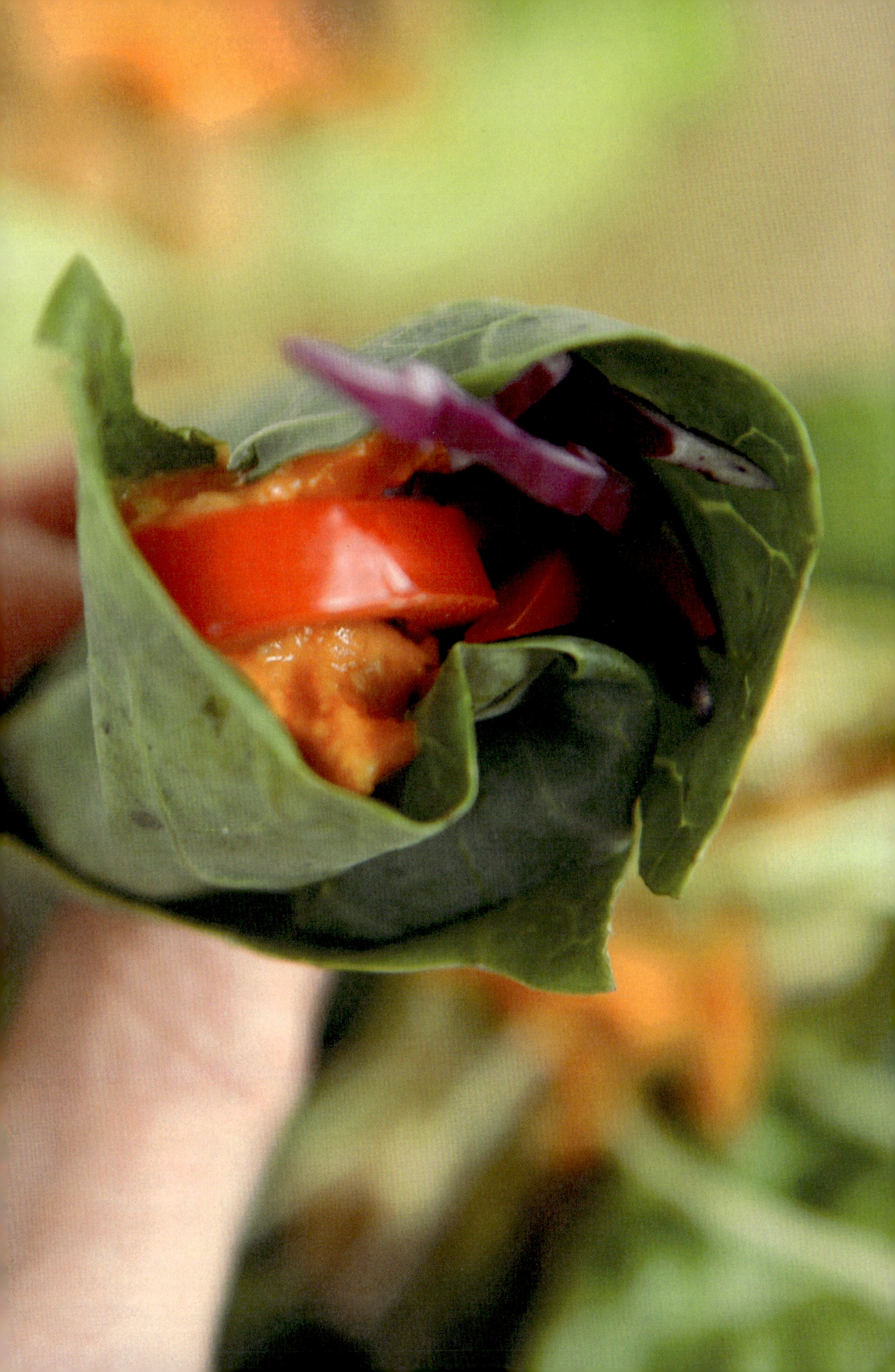

TACO FORMULA IN ACTION

THE "WYNN"ING FALAFEL FILLING

INGREDIENTS

3 cups cooked chickpeas
3 cloves garlic
1 small onion, roughly chopped
¼ cup parsley, roughly chopped
1 sweet potato, cooked
2 teaspoons sea salt
2 teaspoons ground cumin
1 teaspoon ground coriander
1 teaspoon olive oil

DIRECTIONS

1. Drain the chickpeas and place in a food processor.
2. Add in all the remaining ingredients. Process until everything is well blended. Turn off food processor and scrape down the sides a few times to incorporate all the ingredients. Transfer the mixture to a bowl.
3. Roll into balls or flat mini patties and place on a cookie sheet lined with parchment paper. Bake at 350° for 30 minutes, flipping halfway.

TOFU FILLING

INGREDIENTS

2 containers firm tofu
1 yellow onion
1 green bell pepper
1+ tablespoons cumin
1 teaspoon chipotle pepper
Sea salt
2 tablespoon olive oil

DIRECTIONS

1. Dice onion and pepper very fine, so pieces are approximately the size of lentils (the easiest way to do this is in a food processor if you have one).
2. Sauté the onion and pepper in olive oil.
3. Add the spices and salt, and stir.
4. Crumble the tofu into the mixture.

SWEET POTATOES, PARSNIPS AND BEETS*

INGREDIENTS

2 sweet potatoes

3 parsnips

2 beets

2 tablespoons of herbs de Provence

1 teaspoon sea salt

2 tablespoons olive oil

DIRECTIONS

1. Peel and dice veggies.

2. Toss in olive oil, salt, and herbs de Provence.

3. Roast at 350° for 40 minutes, stirring a few times.

*Many firm veggies work here, fennel, carrots, onion, squash. Dice them small and add some cooked beans (no liquid).

SHAVED VEGGIE FILLING

1. Shave or grate any veggie you can get in season: Carrots, beets, cabbage, fennel, kale, cucumber, zucchini, turnips, snap peas, red peppers.

2. Mix a combo of three with salt, sesame oil and sesame seeds.

ROASTED STEINER TOMATOES

INGREDIENTS

grape tomatoes

olive oil

sea salt

DIRECTIONS

Toss tomatoes in a olive oil and salt. Roast at 400° to desired tenderness.

VEGGIE BURGERS

INGREDIENTS

½ onion

½ cup zucchini

½ cup red bell pepper

½ cup carrots

1 cup lentils*, cooked

1½ cups quinoa or brown rice, cooked

Pinch sea salt

*Other leftover beans work here too.

DIRECTIONS

1. Place onion, zucchini, bell pepper, and carrots in a food processor and pulse. Add lentils and quinoa and process until everything is well integrated.

2. Make dough into small patties and place on a cookie sheet lined with parchment.

3. Bake at 350° for 30 minutes or until browned. Flip midway.

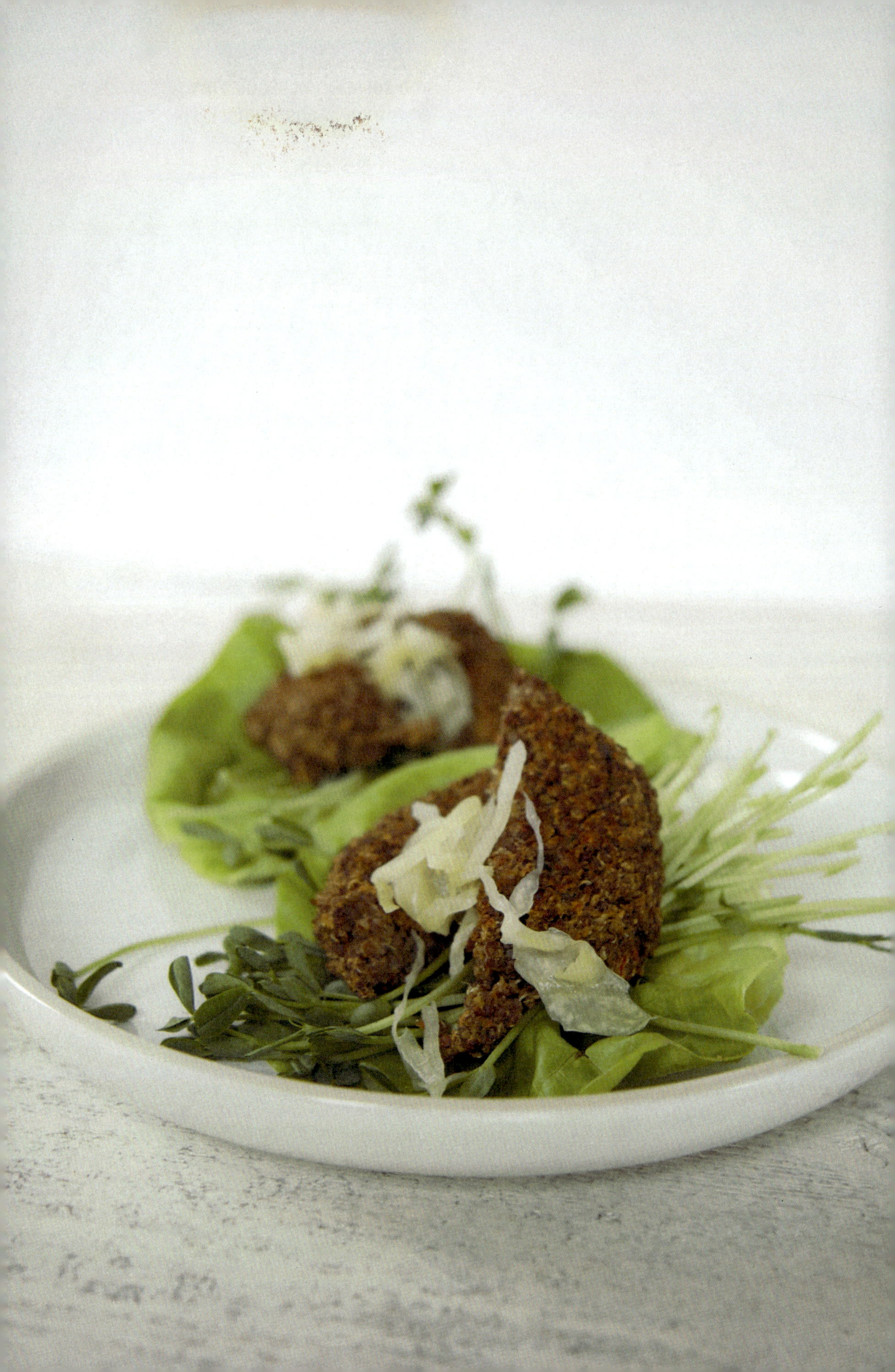

ADD SOME EXTRA VEGGIES (AS SIDE DISHES OR TOP THE TACOS YOURSELF FOR THE FAMILY)

Shredded lettuce
Shredded carrots
Shaved cabbage (napa, green or red)
Diced radishes
Sautéed greens (see bean sides)
Shaved fennel
Sliced avocado
Sliced bell pepper
Sautéed mushrooms
    (could also be the main event)
Diced sweet potato (if not part of filling)
Parsley
Sautéed or grilled zucchini
Pickled onions (page 156)
Sauerkraut
Sliced tomatoes

ADD A SAUCE (OR TWO)

SOUR CREAM

INGREDIENTS

1 cup cashews (soaked and rinsed)
1/2 cup water
1/4 cup lemon juice
2 tablespoons diced onion
1/2 teaspoon sea salt

DIRECTIONS

Blend everything in blender.

SALSA

INGREDIENTS

6 cups diced tomatoes
1 jalapeño chili, seeds and ribs removed (you could start with half for kids)
½ yellow onion, quartered
1 clove garlic
½ bunch cilantro
1 tablespoon fresh lemon juice
Sea salt to taste

DIRECTIONS

Blend in a regular blender or a food processor until mixed but still chunky. If using a high-speed blender (such as Vitamix), don't over-blend.

TAHINI WHITE SAUCE

INGREDIENTS

½ cup tahini
3 cloves garlic
½ teaspoon sea salt
2 tablespoons olive oil
Juice of 1 lemon
1 teaspoon parsley, chopped fine

DIRECTIONS

Blend everything in a high-speed blender or your food processor.

EASY GUACAMOLE

INGREDIENTS

Green Sauce (pg. 157)
3 avocados

DIRECTIONS

Mash avocados with a desired amount of green sauce.

ASIAN DIPPING SAUCE

INGREDIENTS

½ cup sun butter (almond butter works too)
¼ cup rice vinegar
3 tablespoons tamari
2-3 tablespoons maple syrup

DIRECTIONS

Mix all ingredients in a high-speed blender.

DINNER RHYTHM

KIDS COOK NIGHT

When kids cook food they will generally try it, so this is a really good tool to get little ones to expand their palates! Also, cooking with kids is a wonderful way to bond with them, and it is a valuable life skill that they can't get anywhere else but home. It's also delightful to think that one day they will be able to cook for you, and you have provided them a tool that will serve them into their college years and beyond!

Be sure to schedule Kids Cook Night when everyone gets home a bit early or on a weekend, as it may take a little extra time and patience. It's good to let kids know that good cooking does take time and food is not meant to be instantaneous. Obviously if you can get yourself into a relaxed state while they're cooking, they'll have a better experience of food altogether. Planning ahead and creating a rhythm will help. Maybe every Thursday you already know that you can get home a little bit early, and perhaps there's an extra hour and a half that the kids can help cook. On this day, a fun thing to do is to have a recipe book that older kids can read and younger kids can enjoy through pictures.

What to cook? I love the idea of something like fried rice, baked potatoes or pizza, and a salad with every kid-cooked meal — all of which are outlined on the following pages with a new veggie-centered perspective. The kids can learn a variety of tasks, like chopping, peeling and baking.

Ways for parents to feel centered before cooking with kids:

Make sure the kitchen is clean before you start. If it's not, make that a fun thing you do with your kids first.

Make sure some self-care happened earlier in the day; a walk, a yoga class, a phone call with a friend, a chapter in a book, lots of water, and lots of deep breaths.

We all have our days, but if feeling stressed at dinner is an always or usual occurrence, you have to figure out a way to take better care of yourself during the day. If this doesn't feel doable, get there by including your kids in your self-care. Think of exercises you can do with them, go to sleep when they do, or drink more water as a family — make it a game.

Approach Kids Cook Night with intention. Know that if you are centered first, it will be an enjoyable and valuable moment of bonding and teaching.

169 PLAN SIMPLE MEALS: GET MORE ENERGY, RAISE HEALTHY KIDS AND ENJOY FAMILY DINNER

KIDS COOK DAY IS A GREAT WAY TO MAKE A PICKY CHILD FEEL MORE ADVENTUROUS.

STAGE 1. LET THEM CHOOSE.

If they pick mac and cheese, find an alternative recipe so your child can learn how to make it from scratch and in a way that is gluten-free and vegan.

STAGE 2. GIVE THEM SMALL JOBS TO COMPLEMENT COOKING THE MAIN DISH.

For example, making a side salad to accompany the pasta. Since they are still the chef, likely they will stay engaged and try the side dishes too. Let them cook from a recipe book.

STAGE 3. ASSIGN A MEAL TO YOUR KIDS THAT YOU'VE SELECTED EITHER WITH THEM OR BEFOREHAND.

Pick something that pushes their food comfort zone. Have them shop for it as well.

GETTING KIDS STARTED IN THE KITCHEN

Learning to cook serves your children for a lifetime! Here are five easy ways to get your kids cooking:

1. Discuss the food. Don't lecture, just talk — notice the colors and textures, how much the veggies weigh, where the food came from, why you love it, a memory you have of it, etc.

2. Engage your kids. Not every child will come running to help you. Encourage them, empower them, and don't let them get away with never helping out.

3. Start a garden. We have a garden outside from June to October and are in love with the Tower Garden System that allows for growing indoors in colder weather and on patios in warmer weather. (See the resource section to learn more about it.)

4. All ages welcome! Start them early. Even a two-year-old can rip apart lettuce.

5. Let them own it. Cutting may seem scary, so teach them and stay close, but let them learn. They may not do things exactly as you would —have patience and accept mistakes.

HERE ARE SOME OF OUR FAVORITE KIDS COOK DAY THEMES

PIZZA

A great way to expand your idea of traditional pizza is to keep experimenting with new veggies and toppings that are healthy and fresh.

STUFFED POTATOES

A.K.A. baked potatoes. You may start with white, but also expose them to the wide variety of sweet potatoes. Experiment with what you put in them — butter and cheese (with or without dairy) is an OK starting place, but the point is to expand. Add broccoli, sautéed onions, black beans, and spinach.

SALAD MANIA

Salads don't involve the stove, just washing, cutting and some color theory. Challenge kids to use five different veggies. Teach them how to make dressing from scratch.

FRIED RICE

Fried rice is a simple and quick dinner, even with kids helping. It is great to incorporate foods from other cultures and make them healthier at home. It is also a useful way to clean out the fridge or use frozen veggies. Also, fried rice leftovers make a convenient lunch.

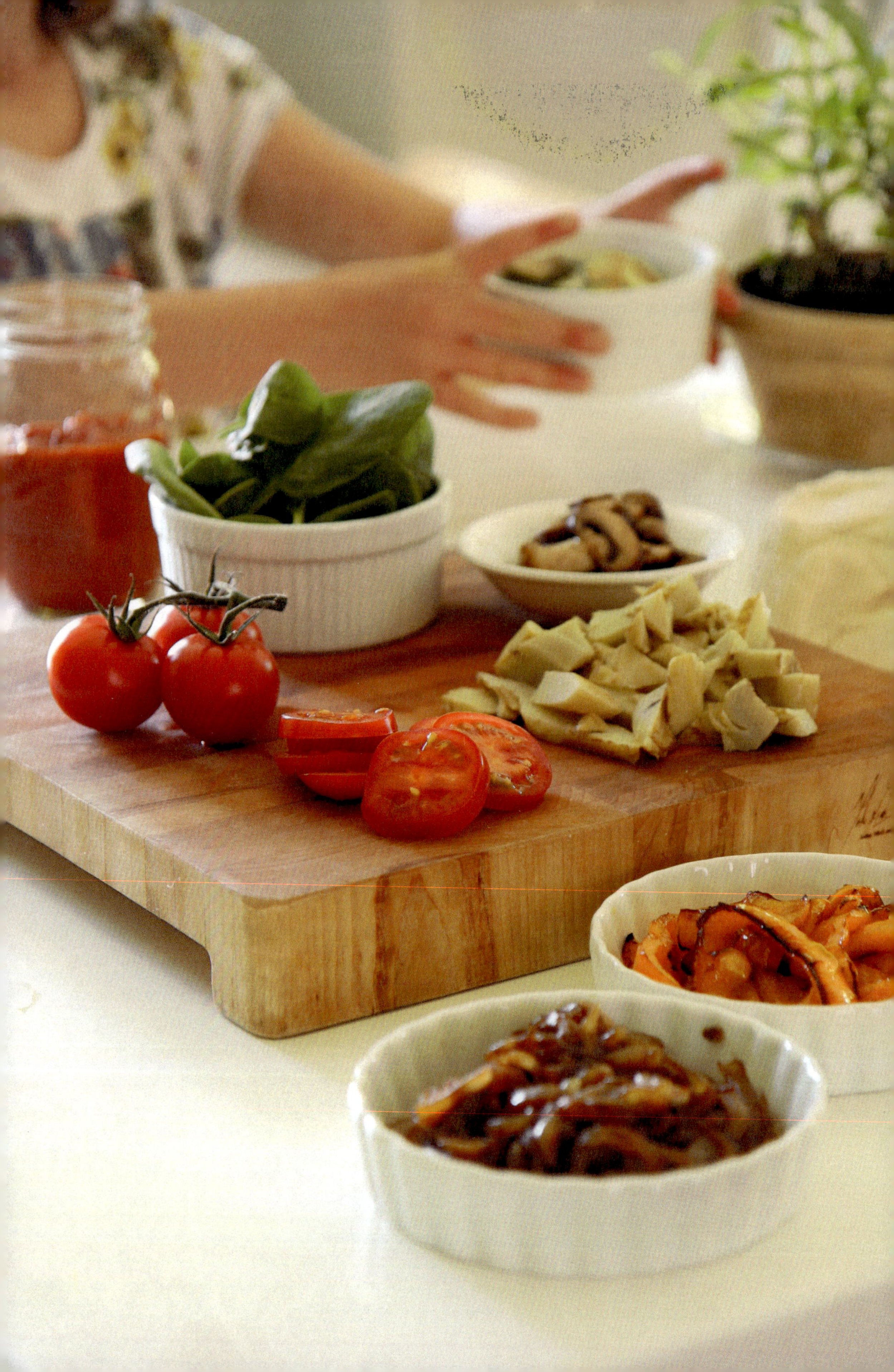

KIDS COOK IN ACTION

VEGGIE PIZZA

INGREDIENTS

2 brown rice tortillas per person (or pizza dough)
Tomato sauce
Squash, thinly sliced
Olive oil
Sea salt
Spinach
Onion

DIRECTIONS

1. Roast squash by tossing it in olive oil and a pinch of salt, and roasting it at 350° on a cookie sheet for 15 minutes.

2. Caramelize onions by cutting them very thin and sautéing in salt and olive oil for 10 minutes on medium heat, tossing regularly.

3. Place plain tortillas in the oven for a few minutes so they get crunchy.

4. To make a pizza, stack 2 tortillas, and dress the top one. (This will prevent them from becoming soggy).

5. Spread on tomato sauce that you made and froze. Don't have any? See the recipe on page 181.

6. Add veggies on top.

So many veggies work here — corn, arugula, mushrooms, zucchini, peppers. Chicken would also be a topping if you like adding animal protein and you have leftovers.

Pesto would also work in addition to or instead of tomato sauce.

Letting your kids put on the veggies will encourage them to get eaten.

Read dairy-free cheese labels. Find the ones that are as simple as possible. We tend just to skip the cheese altogether and love it just as much!

BAKED SWEET POTATOES

INGREDIENTS

5 sweet potatoes (or number of eaters +1)
A bunch of broccoli
3 cups of cooked black beans
Romaine lettuce
1 cucumber
1 avocado
Cumin
Sea salt

Let the kids set the table with serving bowls.

If there is anyone not participating, let the children who are preparing the meal call the others to the table. When you discuss your meal together, talk about the efforts of the children who helped prepare it, too!

A little pride goes a long way: Studies show that children who help choose ingredients and prepare meals actually enjoy the food more, even if they're usually picky eaters.

DIRECTIONS

1. Make sure you start the potatoes at least an hour before dinner, as they may take that long to cook.

2. Delegate a child to wash the sweet potatoes, broccoli and lettuce.

3. Show a child (age eight or older) how to turn on the oven to 400°.

4. Rub potatoes with a bit of olive oil. (Easy job for kids!)

5. Place the potatoes on a cookie sheet and place on middle rack in the oven. Check them at 45 minutes. You should be able to poke them easily with a knife, and see some orange on the knife when you remove it.

6. Cut the broccoli. Tip: Get more for your money by peeling and dicing the stalk – deliciously tender! (This is a job for a teen or parent.)

7. Kids can break up lettuce, cut cucumber, cut avocado (Mom may want to cut in half and take out pit), cut pepper, and toss all of the ingredients in a salad bowl.

8. Sauté the plain black beans that we left on Sunday with some salt and cumin.

9. Lastly, steam the broccoli for 2-3 minutes, so it is cooked but still a little crunchy.

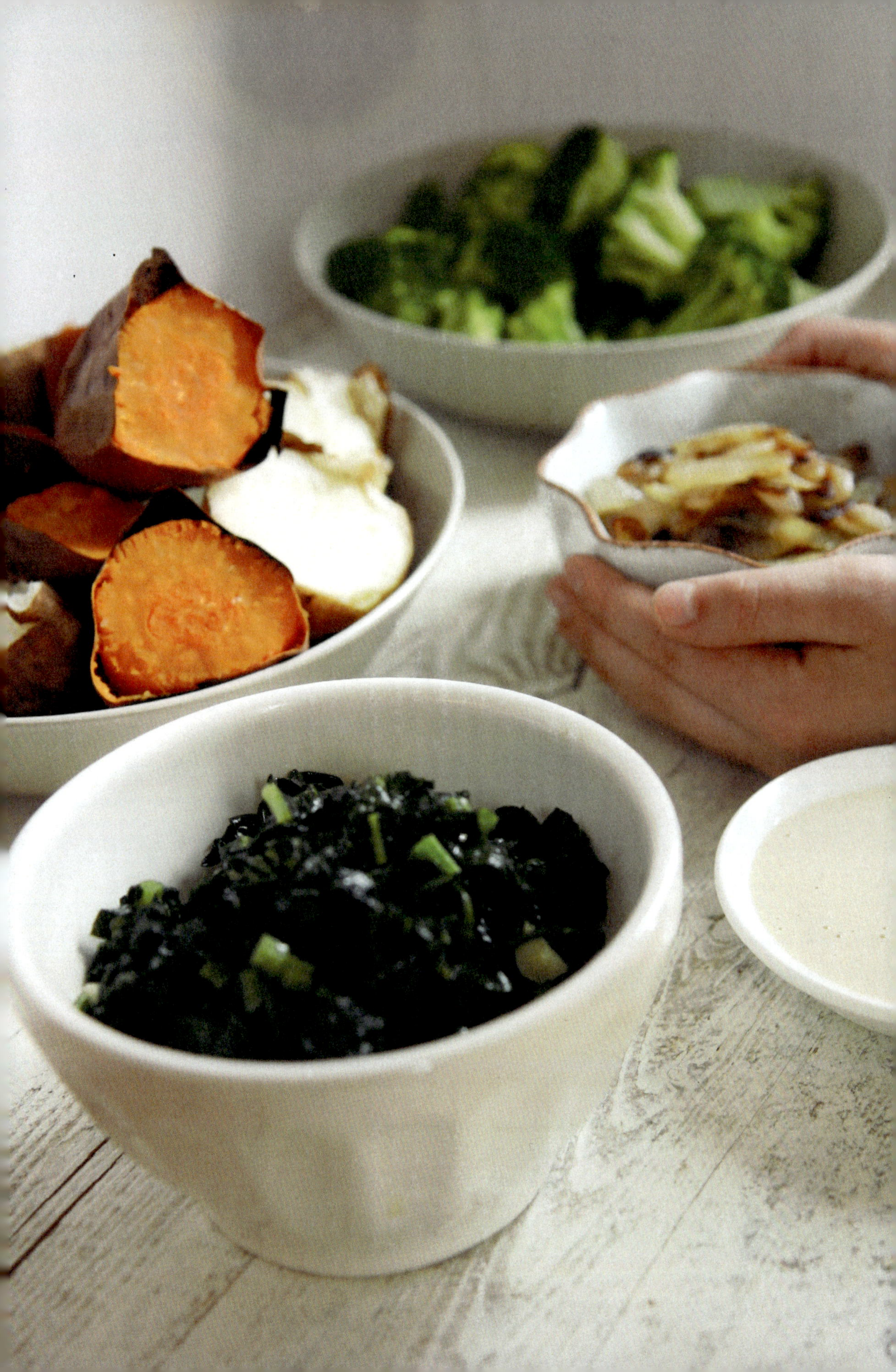

THE DAY'S VEGGIE FRIED RICE

INGREDIENTS

2 cups rice
6 cups veggies
2 tablespoons sesame seeds
2 tablespoons grapeseed oil
1 tablespoon sesame oil
1 tablespoon mirin
2 tablespoons tamari

DIRECTIONS

1. Cook 2 cups brown, white or wild rice according to directions on package.

2. Use a mandolin to thinly slice veggies or dice them with a knife into very small cubes.

3. Using a wok or large skillet, sauté veggies that are most firm in grapeseed oil first. As they start to cook, add shorter cooking veggies, mirin, and sesame seeds.

4. Add cooked rice and mix everything together, adding tamari and sesame oil at the very end. (If at any time the veggies need more cooking, add a splash of water.)

VEGGIE COMBO IDEAS – USE 2 CUPS OF EACH

Broccoli, carrot, peas
Daikon radish, bok choy, carrot
Corn, carrot, peas
Sweet potato, kale, green beans
Broccoli, mung beans, carrots
Asian greens, zucchini, onion
Napa cabbage, red pepper, asparagus
Edamame, corn, carrots

PLAY WITH TYPES OF RICE...

Sushi rice
Brown rice
Wild rice
Black rice

KIDS CAN...

Wash veggies
Measure
Help toss food in wok
Crack eggs

You can easily add tofu if you want a plant-based protein.

You can also add a small amount of animal protein. Fried rice traditionally has an egg. Cook 4 eggs omelet style and serve on the side if your family prefers animal protein. You can also add leftover chicken or fish.

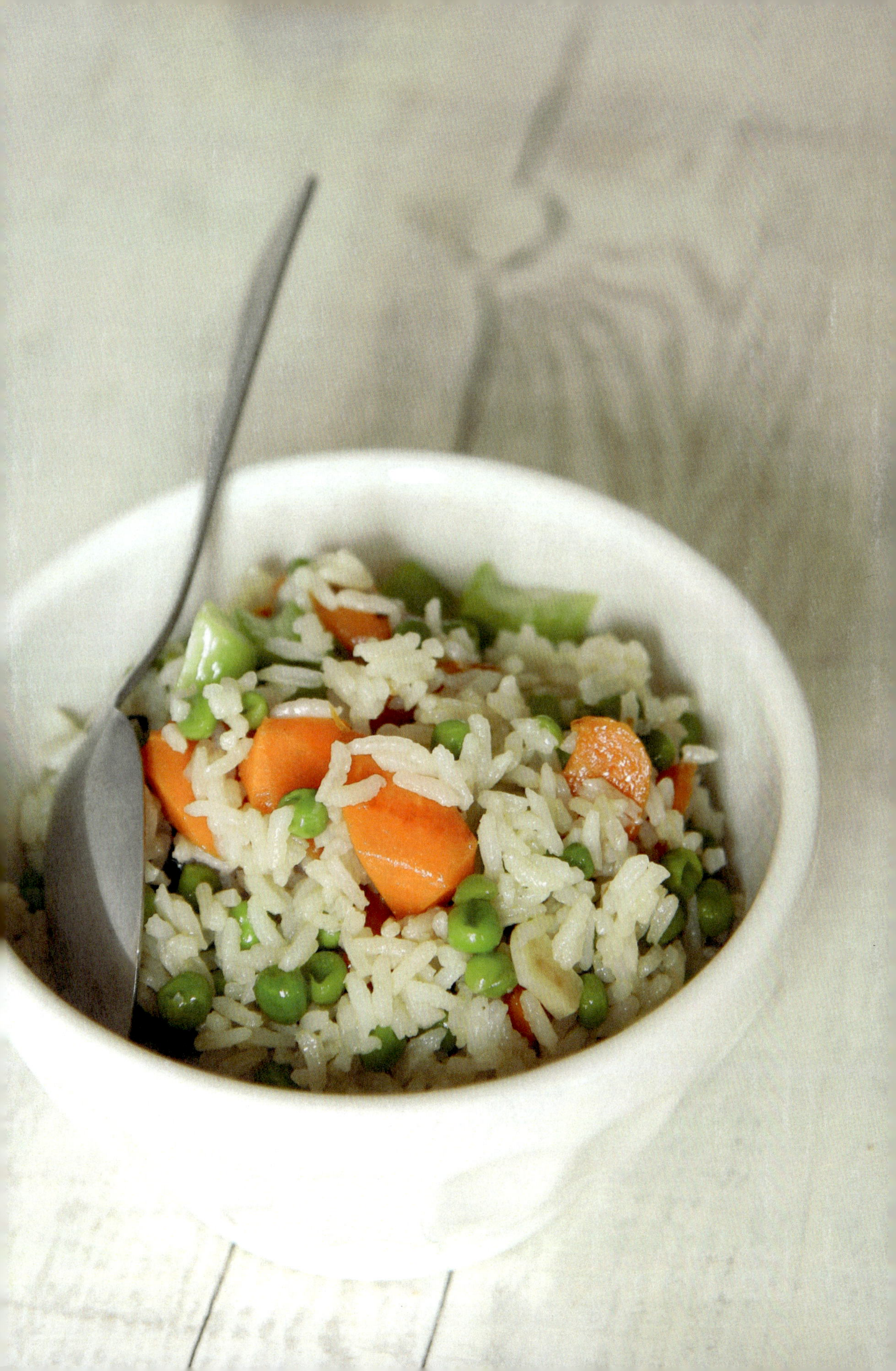

DINNER RHYTHM
PASTA NIGHT

We must recover from the Macaroni and Cheese epidemic. Pasta was meant to be a base for sauce, not something we eat plain, so as parents we need to help our kids move away from macaroni and cheese or pasta with butter and toward nutrient-rich foods with some pasta. This can and should be seen as a process. Maybe even look at it as a game to go from incorporating one veggie into pasta to six!

PASTA AS A TEACHING TOOL

This is perhaps one of my favorite days for encouraging kids to be adventurous. Personally, Pasta Day has had a huge impact on our family. One day, I made a big pot of pasta with tons of veggies sautéed in garlic and olive oil. It was amazing — but the kids would not eat it.

Of course I was crushed, but I decided to use their negative feedback constructively. I knew that they love pasta. I put garlic in everything. They had enjoyed many of the veggies over the years, but not all together and not with pasta. I had changed their favorite food too quickly, so I set out to use rhythm and pasta to get my kids to eat a wide variety of veggies.

PICKY TO ADVENTUROUS

The progression went something like this: Start with a puréed sauce. If you have a plain pasta eater, add sauce gradually over the course of a few weeks.

Once that works, sauté garlic, olive oil and one vegetable to add to the pasta. Pick a vegetable your kids love, like peas or carrots. Dice them really small, so they are barely noticeable in the pasta. Maybe the first time you ever serve this it's mostly pasta with some peas or some carrots, and the garlic, and the olive oil and the salt.

Then over time you keep adding more veggies and new vegetables. Maybe the first time it's just peas and the second time its peas and carrots and you're applying it over the course of the month. All of a sudden it's whatever is fresh from the farmer's market like zucchini, peppers or tomatoes.

PASTA THROUGH THE SEASONS…

FALL

Marinara

Sweet potato and Swiss chard

Squash, green beans, broccoli

WINTER

Kale pesto

Mushrooms and spinach

Cabbage and carrots

SPRING

Peas, asparagus, broccoli

Peapod, carrot, ginger

Basil pesto

SUMMER

Zucchini, summer squash, tomato

Corn, green beans, carrots

Fresh tomato and garlic

GET ADVENTUROUS WITH DIFFERENT TYPES OF NOODLES!

Brown rice

Quinoa

Corn

Udon noodles

Asian rice noodles

Bean noodles

Zucchini

PLAN SIMPLE MEALS: GET MORE ENERGY, RAISE HEALTHY KIDS AND ENJOY FAMILY DINNER

TOMATO SAUCE

INGREDIENTS

12 tomatoes

½ to 1 head garlic

A bunch of finely chopped basil

Olive oil

Sea salt

DIRECTIONS

1. Wash tomatoes and peel garlic.

2. Put tomatoes & garlic in a high-speed blender.

3. Pour the mixture into a large skillet.

4. Add basil and olive oil.

5. Simmer on low for 30-40 minutes, stirring frequently.

"UN-MEATBALLS"

INGREDIENTS

1 chopped onion

3 cloves garlic

½ cup fresh basil (2 tablespoons dried)

1 cup sunflower seeds

2 cups black beans, cooked

3 cups quinoa, cooked

½ teaspoon dried oregano

Sea salt

DIRECTIONS

1. Place onion, garlic, basil and sunflower seeds in food processor. Add black beans.

2. Transfer the mixture to a bowl with the quinoa, oregano and sea salt.

3. Mix everything together.

4. Roll dough into small balls and place on a cookie sheet lined with parchment.

5. Bake at 350° for 30 minutes or until brown.

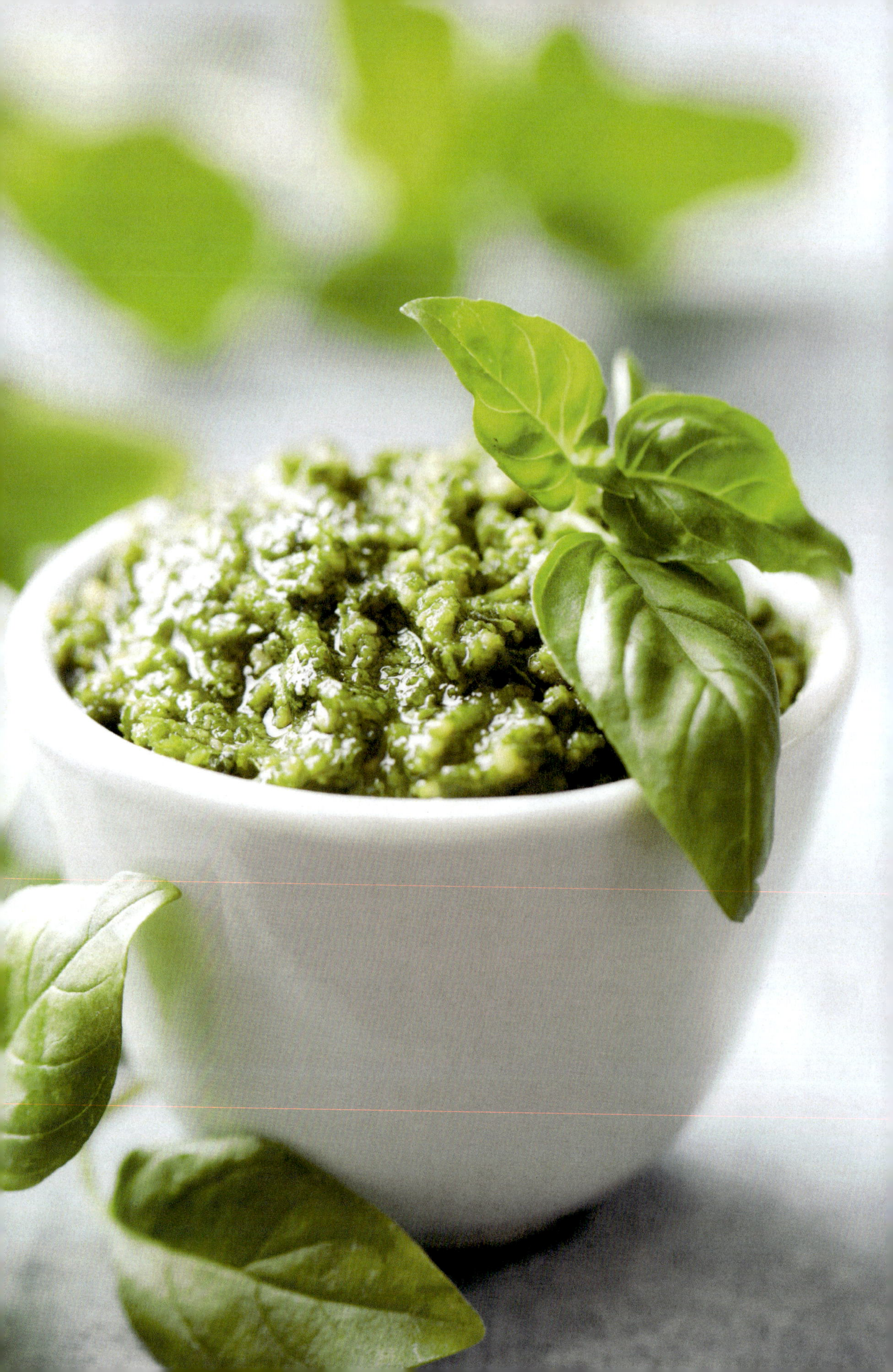

PASTA WITH PESTO

INGREDIENTS

Gluten-free spaghetti
2 cloves garlic
2 cups spinach
2 cups basil
1 cup pistachios
¼ cup olive oil
Sea salt to taste

DIRECTIONS

1. Cook pasta according to the package.
2. Blend pesto ingredients in a food processor or your Vitamix.
3. Mix in a small amount of water to pesto before tossing it with the pasta. You can do this in the blender, or if you have made a double batch, put pesto and water in a pot when you drain the water from the pasta, then add the pasta back to the pot to integrate.

USING PESTO

Since pesto is loved by all in our house, it's fun to experiment with different herbs, nuts, and greens!

Pesto can serve a wide variety of purposes, so it is a good topping to have on hand.

A dollop tastes fabulous in veggie soup.

It's a great dip for cut veggies.

It makes quick lunch when spread on a rice tortilla with greens.

It's perfect over zucchini.

Pesto and half of a grape tomato on a cracker makes fabulous and quick hors d'oeuvre for guests.

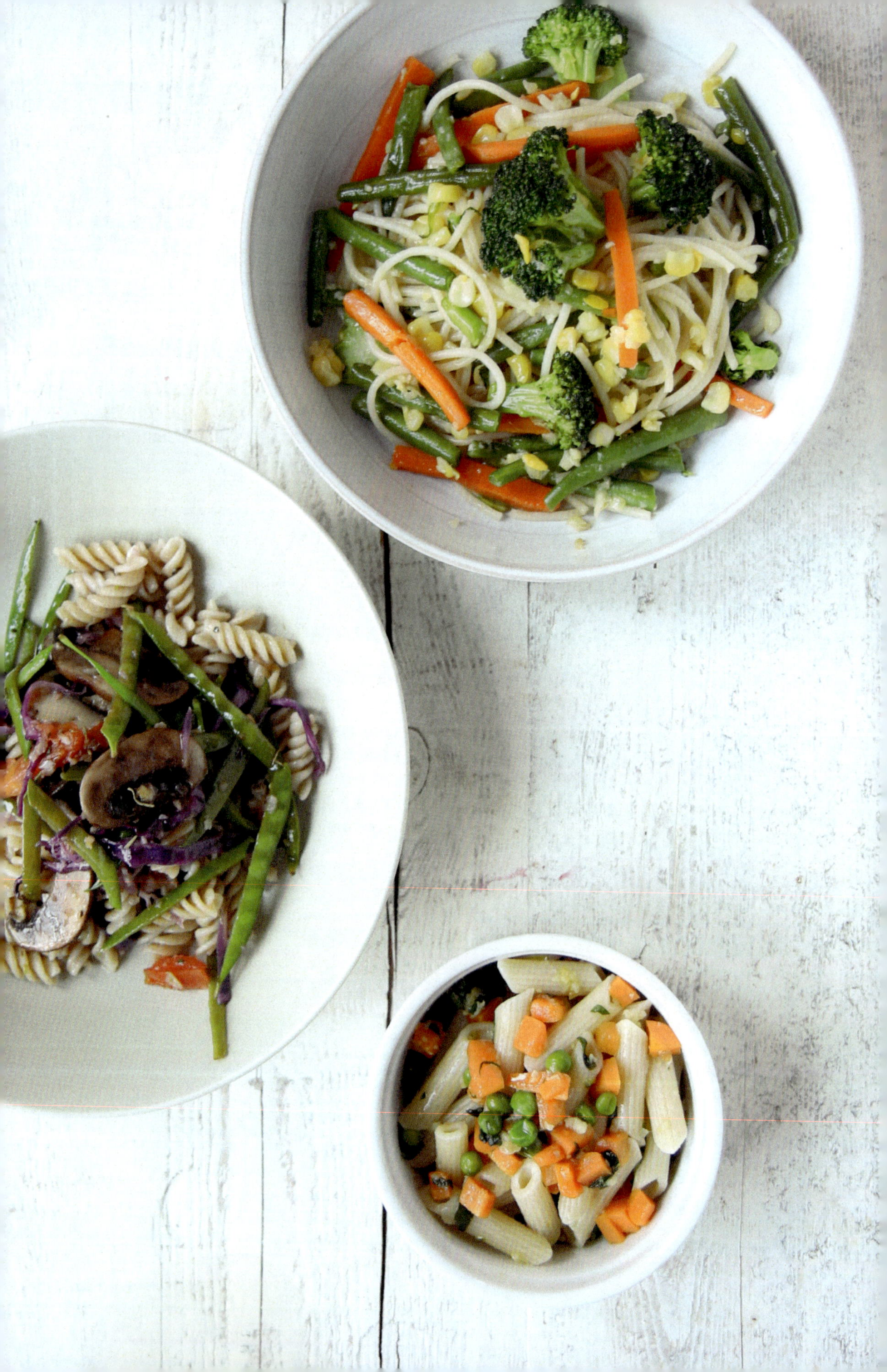

GARLIC PASTA

INGREDIENTS

3 kinds of in-season vegetables, enough to measure about 8 cups chopped

8-12 cloves of garlic, peeled and minced (or use garlic crusher)

1/3 cup olive oil

DIRECTIONS

1. Chop the vegetables to complement the shape of the gluten-free pasta that you will use: for example, with penne, chop into thin rectangles; for shells, dice the veggies.

    Note: If you are using a vegetable that will not cook through in 4 minutes in olive oil, cook first in salted boiling water until just tender.

2. Cook pasta according to directions on the bag. Add the veggies and continue cooking until they are cooked through.

3. Pour olive oil into a large skillet. Add the minced garlic and cook on medium heat for a few minutes.

4. Add the pasta and toss with the garlic sauce.

This is a very easy recipe to make with a wide variety of vegetables.

If you have picky eaters, you can take them to the farmer's market to pick out the vegetables. If that is not possible, the repetition of pasta with veggies will encourage them to try it over time.

DINNER RHYTHM
RICE BOWL NIGHT

Rice Bowl Day is my personal favorite of the week — it is the meal I could imagine changing up and having daily! It is a way to really drive home the veggie-centered model.

HERE ARE A FEW OTHER REASONS I ADORE THIS DAY:

- You can put lots of small dishes on the table for a make-your-own style meal. Kids are generally more adventurous when they serve themselves.

- I talked earlier about the importance of staying seated. Rice bowls are a dish that cater to serving a variety of veggies at the table. So you and your family are not constantly popping up from the table.

- The serving bowls reinforce the veggie-centered meal proportions. On Rice Bowl Night you might have five bowls: one with rice, one with some sort of beans, or tofu, or whatever you've decided for your protein, then three (or four) bowls of vegetables.

PICKY TO ADVENTUROUS

With smaller serving bowls, you allow children to choose for themselves, and you can observe the choices they make. Watch as they develop in their choices over time. At first, my son wanted a plate instead of the bowl and kept all the ingredients separate. My daughter didn't mind the bowl, but at the beginning she only wanted beans and rice and resisted the other vegetables. Over time, I watched as she progressed in her choices. She slowly plopped the avocado, then the tomato, then eventually all the veggies. It's amazing what happens after six months of Rice Bowl Days. You can see the kids' palates changing and them becoming more adventurous.

1. Start with the rice plus two other ingredients. Some kids may start with a plate and keep foods separate, but gently work toward the bowl model.

2. Change up the grain.

3. Add different veggies weekly.

THROUGH THE SEASONS

FALL

Delicate squash, chickpeas, green beans, spinach

Sweet potato, black beans, kale, green sauce

Broccoli, sweet potato, baked tofu, bok choy

Chickpeas, root veggies, kale

WINTER

Sprouted legumes, broccoli, kale, avocado

Brussel sprouts, sweet potato, carrots

Leeks, cauliflower, chickpeas

SPRING

Corn, beets, carrots, chard

Lentils, fennel, pea sprouts

Edamame, carrots, bok choy

Peas, green beans, white beans, basil

SUMMER

Zucchini, fava beans, tomatoes

Corn, cucumbers, beets, radishes

Romaine lettuce, red onion, cucumber, tomato

BOK CHOY

DELICATA SQUASH. Cut in half. Scoop out seeds. Cut super thin slices with skin on. Toss in salt and olive oil. Spread on cookie sheet. Roast at 350º until done.

188 **PLAN SIMPLE MEALS:** GET MORE ENERGY, RAISE HEALTHY KIDS AND ENJOY FAMILY DINNER

THE ESSENCE OF RICE BOWLS IS VEGGIES AND LEGUMES SERVED OVER A GRAIN WITH A REALLY YUMMY SAUCE. IF YOU ROCK THIS MODEL, YOU COULD NEARLY LIVE OFF OF RICE BOWLS!

THIS IS A GREAT WAY TO TEACH HOW TO EAT THE RAINBOW AND TRAIN YOURSELF TO FIND IT IN EVERY SEASON.

SOME EASY COMBOS...

❶

Black beans
Corn
Avocado
Tomato
Brown Rice
Green Sauce

❷

Tofu
Bok choy
Spinach
Carrots
Sushi Rice
Flaxy Sauce

❸

Lentils
Broccoli
Avocado
Shredded carrots
Kale
Quinoa
Lemon Sauce

❹

Chickpeas
Green beans
Sweet potatoes
Mushrooms
Millet
Onion Dip

189 PLAN SIMPLE MEALS: GET MORE ENERGY, RAISE HEALTHY KIDS AND ENJOY FAMILY DINNER

RICE BOWLS IN ACTION

The veggies in a rice bowl can be steamed, roasted, sautéed or raw — or a combo.

Many of the recipes in this book work in rice bowls. You can use the sautéed green recipe for any type of green — kale, bok choy, napa cabbage, spinach, chard.

Pay attention to how you cut the veggies. Grating and dicing look good to grown people and are easier for young eaters to accept.

Kids may start eating this all plain, but sauces really are what make the dish — like dressing on a salad. I love to top everything with hot sauce!

If you feel short on parts, avocados, diced cucumber, or sprouts taste great with most combos.

SPROUTED LENTILS AND GREENS

INGREDIENTS

2 cups broccoli,
2 cups kale cut into thin strips
1 cup sprouted lentils
1 avocado

DIRECTIONS

1. Steam kale, broccoli, and sprouted lentils for a few minutes.
2. Serve over brown rice.
3. Add sauce and avocado to finish the dish.

BAKED CHICKPEAS

INGREDIENTS

4 cups chickpeas, cooked
2 tablespoons olive oil
1 teaspoon cumin
1 teaspoon sea salt

DIRECTIONS

1. Preheat oven to 350°. Blot chickpeas with a paper towel to dry them.
2. In a bowl, toss chickpeas with olive oil, cumin and salt.
3. Spread them on a baking sheet, and bake for 30 to 40 minutes, until browned and crunchy.

ROASTED ROOT VEGGIES

INGREDIENTS

4 carrots
2 red beets
2 golden beets
1 sweet potato
2 parsnips
2 tablespoons olive oil
1 teaspoon sea salt
1 tablespoon herbs de Provence

DIRECTIONS

Dice veggies. Toss in olive oil, herbs and salt. Bake for 35 minutes or until tender.

ROASTED KALE

INGREDIENTS

1 bunch kale
1 tablespoon olive oil
Pinch of sea salt

DIRECTIONS

1. Toss kale in salt and olive oil. Spread on a cookie sheet.
2. Put in oven and watch carefully. Remove after 5-10 minutes.

LEMON SAUCE

INGREDIENTS

1 cup fresh basil
Juice from 1 lemon
Handful sunflower seeds
2 tablespoons tamari
1 teaspoon maple syrup
2 tablespoons olive oil
¼ cup water
2 cloves garlic

DIRECTIONS

1. Blend everything in a high-speed blender.
2. Transfer to a small pitcher that your family can use to dress their rice bowls.

FLAXY SAUCE

INGREDIENTS

3 cloves garlic
2 tablespoon shredded ginger*
2 tablespoons tamari
3 tablespoons lemon
1 tablespoon maple syrup
¼ cup tablespoons hemp seeds
¼ cup tablespoons flax meal
3 tablespoons – 1/3 cup water

DIRECTIONS

Blend everything in a high-speed blender.

* I used to be scared of ginger and then I discovered the micro plane. Now I freeze ginger and micro plane the amount I want, when I need it. No peeling necessary.

DINNER RHYTHM
SOUP NIGHT

While not all kids may love soup, it's easy to prepare, extremely healthy, and a perfect meal to begin to build a rhythm around. Depending on your child, you may begin serving purées and moving toward chunkier soups with vegetables. Not to say you'll never have purée again, but if you're worried about a picky eater, that's a good way to progress.

I've found that rhythm can be useful with Soup Day, like with veggies in the kindergarten classroom. For example, Soup Day is actually my son's favorite day of the week, but it's my daughter's least favorite. I serve it every week, and my son jumps for joy and my daughter sometimes grimaces, but she is learning to eat it, and sometimes she gets out of her way enough to actually enjoy it.

Soup night can have fun things to dip: garlic bread, quesadillas, and plain toast sticks. Sometimes that is a way to draw in skeptics. That said, in our house you have to also be willing to eat your soup with a spoon!

PICKY TO ADVENTUROUS

1. Start with simple purées — possibly orange colored.
2. Add more herbs and vary the color of the purées.
3. Make soups where the veggies are diced super fine, start simple, and always have a component your kid loves.
4. Add more veggies and create chunkier soups.

SAVE FORWARD

Soup is a great thing to double up on. You can freeze it for a rainy day, or put it in the fridge for lunches or a second dinner on a busy week.

THROUGH THE SEASONS

FALL

Squash soup

Ratatouille

Broccoli soup

Fall veggie soup

WINTER

Root veggie lentil soup

Carrot soup

Chili

Miso soup

SPRING

Zucchini purée

Tomato roasted pepper purée

Noodle soup

Spring veggie soup

SUMMER

Gazpacho

Cool cucumber soup

Bean Soup

Summer veggie soup

A basic veggie soup can vary greatly depending on the ingredients and time of year. This is a great thing to master in the fall and winter with an abundance of hearty veggies.

Soups are more forgiving than baking, but sometimes a recipe helps. There are a few here, and I encourage you to experiment! I have listed some "play" strategies at the end of each recipe.

TOMATO CARROT SOUP

INGREDIENTS

6 cloves garlic
10 large carrots
16 oz. can fire-roasted tomatoes
8 oz. water (half of tomato can)
½ cup cashews or almonds
    (chopped and soaked for an hour)
Sea salt to taste

DIRECTIONS

1. Place garlic, carrots, tomatoes and water in a soup pot and cook until carrots are tender.
2. Blend veggies with cashews in a blender (you can do this in batches) and return to the pot.
3. Add sea salt and pepper to taste.
4. Sprinkle with cashew or almond pieces.

PLAY: Use the cashews to make any purée creamy.

GREEN MACHINE

INGREDIENTS

2 baking potatoes
1 tablespoon olive oil
Sea salt
5 zucchini
1 large white onion
2 cloves garlic
1 handful parsley
1 tablespoon cumin

DIRECTIONS

1. Add 3 inches of water to a large soup pot fitted with a steamer. Add zucchini (washed and cut in thirds), 2 baking potatoes (washed and cut in quarters), onion (quartered), garlic, and 1 tablespoon of sea salt.
2. Steam veggies until tender. Put cooked vegetables, water from steaming, parsley, and cumin into a blender (you may have to do this in batches).
3. Return purée to pot, and season with cumin and more salt as needed.

PLAY: Try other green veggies or a combo of a few — broccoli and asparagus both taste great.

"ITALIANISH" BEAN SOUP

INGREDIENTS

3 cups tomatoes, diced
4 cups cannellini beans cooked
   (or 2 cans rinsed)
3 tablespoons olive oil
1 leek, halved lengthwise and sliced
¼ cup garlic, thinly sliced
1 cup carrots, diced
1 cup celery, diced
1 cup zucchini, diced
¼ teaspoon sea salt
1 bunch Swiss chard, cut into 1-inch slices
¼ head Napa cabbage, cut into 1-inch cubes
2 cups russet potatoes, diced
3 cups vegetable broth
2+ cups water
1 teaspoon dried thyme
1 bay leaf

DIRECTIONS

1. Using a fork, mash half the beans into a paste.
2. Heat 2 tablespoons oil in a soup pot over medium heat. Add leek and garlic; cook, stirring, until translucent and tender, 2 to 3 minutes. Do not brown.
3. Stir in carrots, celery, zucchini and the remaining 1 tablespoon oil until nearly tender, 3 to 5 minutes. Season with salt and pepper.
4. When the carrots and celery are nearly tender, stir in chard and cabbage. Cover and cook, stirring occasionally, until wilted, 4 to 6 minutes.
5. Add potatoes, broth, water, diced tomatoes, bean purée and whole beans, thyme and bay leaf. Bring to a simmer over medium heat.
6. Cover and cook, stirring occasionally and reducing the heat and cooking until all the vegetables are tender —15 to 20 minutes
7. Salt to taste.

PLAY: Add 1 cup of tiny gluten-free pasta instead of potato. Use string beans or corn instead of zucchini. Top with pesto if you have some in the fridge.

LENTIL SOUP

INGREDIENTS

1 tablespoon olive oil
1 onion, finely diced
1 teaspoon curry powder
1 teaspoon paprika
1 teaspoon sea salt (or more to taste)
3 cloves garlic
6 tomatoes
1 lb. red lentils
1 large baking potato, diced small
6 carrots, diced small

DIRECTIONS

1. In a large stock pot, sauté onion in olive oil, adding spices and salt.
2. Blend garlic and tomato in a high-speed blender, and add to onion mixture.
3. Let cook for 5 minutes, stirring frequently.
4. Add lentils, potato and carrot and coat with mixture.
5. Cover with water and let cook for 20 minutes (you will likely have to add water throughout the 20 minutes).

PLAY: Serve soup over spinach and top with green beans. Try all the different kinds of lentils.

SQUASH SOUP

INGREDIENTS

1 butternut squash
2 leeks
2 tablespoons olive oil
1 tablespoon cumin
1 tablespoon pumpkin spice
Sea salt to taste
Water

DIRECTIONS

1. Cook squash: The easiest way to do this is to cut squash in half lengthwise and scoop out seeds. Place the squash face-down on a cookie sheet and bake at 350º for 45 minutes until cooked. A faster way is to peel off the skin, cut into chunks (while deseeding) and steam for 10 minutes.
2. Wash and cut leeks: You can usually use the bottom half of a leek, but stop when it gets too tough to cut. Sauté the leeks in the olive oil for 5-10 minutes, stirring frequently so they don't burn.
3. Put the squash, leeks, and spices in a blender with 3 cups of water to start. Keep adding water until desired consistency is reached. You may have to do this in batches. Add sea salt to taste.

PLAY: Think of this as "anything orange goes" soup — try a variety of types of squash, carrots, and sweet potato.

VEGETABLE SOUP

INGREDIENTS

6 carrots
2 stalks celery
1 large potato
2 cups frozen corn
1 small squash
2 leeks, finely diced
1 onion, finely diced
8 cloves garlic
5 tablespoons miso
Salt to taste
2 tablespoons herbs de Provence

DIRECTIONS

1. Dice veggies into similar-sized pieces.
2. Put everything except miso in pot and cover with water.
3. Dissolve miso in ½ cup warm water and add to soup.
4. Cook until carrots are tender, about 25 minutes.
5. Add sea salt and pepper to taste.

PLAY: This soup is very flexible and can be made with any firm veggies in any season — beets, green beans, parsnips, broccoli stalks (make sure to peel), zucchini. Switch the herbs de Provence for cumin and paprika for a different taste.

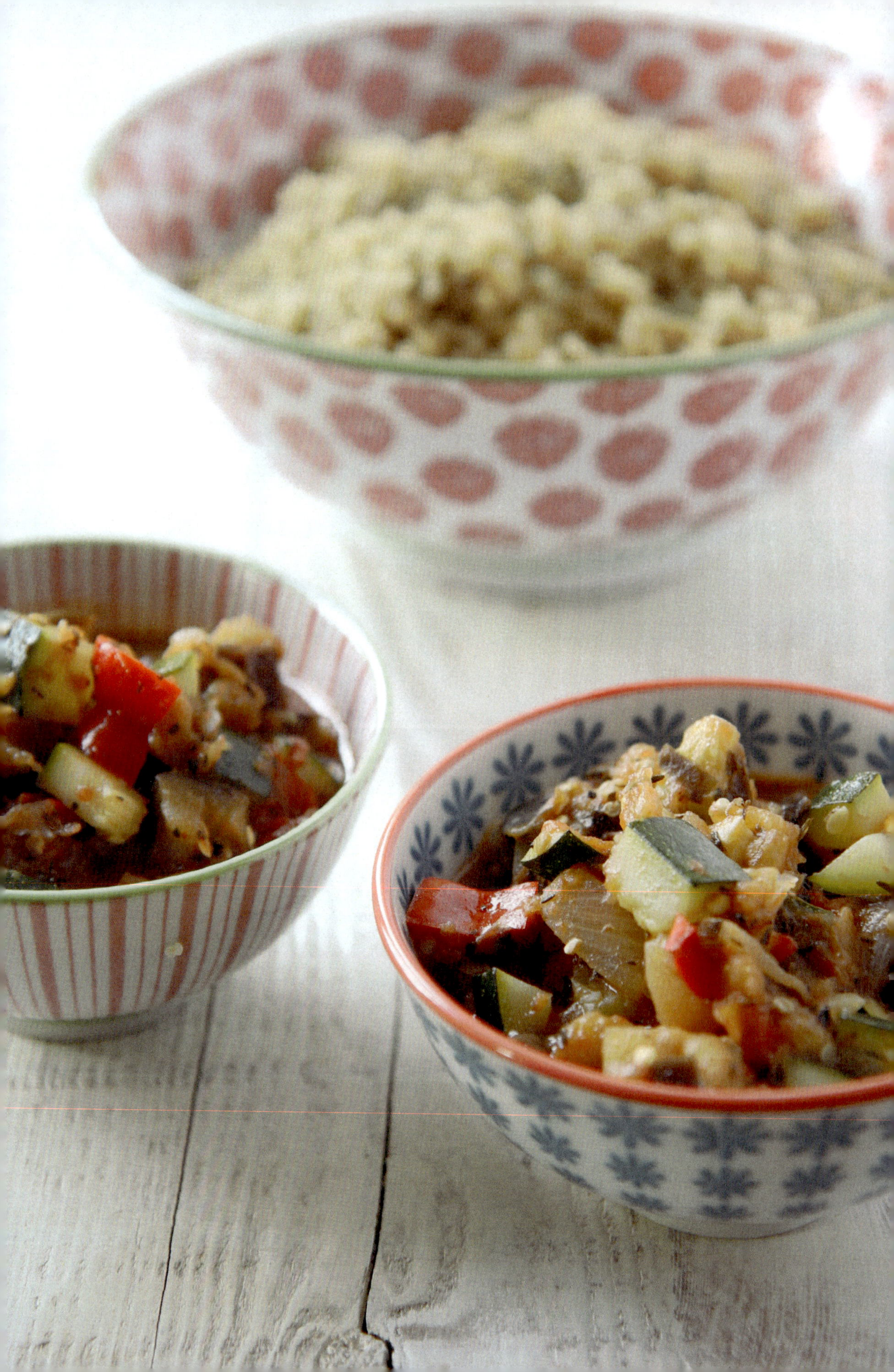

RATATOUILLE

INGREDIENTS

1 large eggplant or 2 small eggplants
5 zucchini
1 onion
1 red pepper

6 tomatoes
4 tablespoons olive oil
4 tablespoons herbs de Provence
Sea salt
2 cups cooked quinoa

DIRECTIONS

1. Dice all the vegetables in the smallest possible cubes, keeping them in separate bowls. Blend the tomato.

2. Place eggplants in a colander in the sink or on a plate. Toss in a tablespoon of sea salt. Let them sit and sweat for at least 30 minutes. Rinse them quickly under cold water and pat dry.

3. When you are ready to cook, sauté the onion in the olive oil. After about five minutes add the eggplant and cook until browned on each side.

4. Add red pepper, zucchini, blended tomato, and herbs. Let cook for 10-15 minutes. Salt to taste.

5 Ladle ratatouille over quinoa and serve with a big salad.

PLAY: Add chickpeas for added protein. Take away any of the veggies for a different feel. Add more tomato purée to make this into more of a liquid soup and serve in a bowl.

POTATO LEEK SOUP

INGREDIENTS

1 tablespoon olive oil
1 medium onion, roughly chopped
3 leeks, well-rinsed and chopped
4 russet potatoes, washed and cut into cubes (rough if blending)
4 cups vegetable broth
Salt to taste

DIRECTIONS

1. Sauté onion in olive oil.
2. Add leeks, potatoes, and broth to pot. Bring to boil. Cover, reduce heat and simmer until potatoes are tender, about 20 minutes. Remove from heat and let mixture cool slightly.

PLAY: This is a great one for kids to help make. Enjoy chunky or blend soup in batches to make it smooth. Add a touch of almond milk for a creamier texture.

GAZPACHO

INGREDIENTS

3 tomatoes cored
1 cucumber, roughly cut
1/2 of a red pepper
1 handful fresh basil, chopped
1 tablespoon olive oil
1 tablespoon apple cider vinegar
1 teaspoon of hot sauce
Sea salt to taste

DIRECTIONS

1. Mix all ingredients in the blender.
2. You can reserve a little of the cucumber or tomato to chop and sprinkle on top as garnish.

PLAY: Use yellow and green tomatoes, celery or green pepper instead of the red pepper for a green soup!

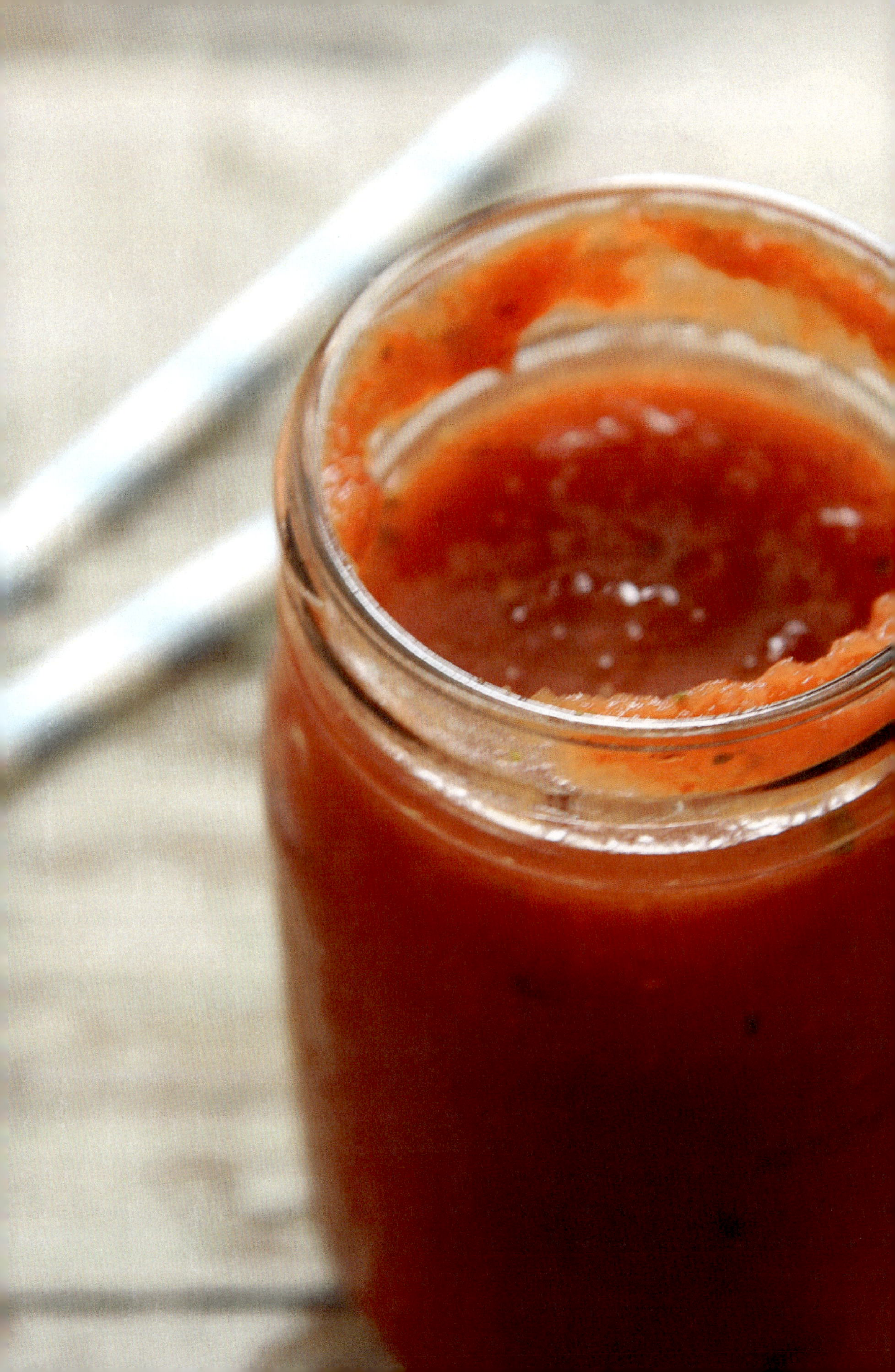

FOR DIPPING

CORN BREAD

INGREDIENTS

1½ cups cornmeal
½ cup brown rice flour
½ teaspoon baking powder
½ teaspoon baking soda
1 teaspoon sea salt
1 cup unsweetened almond milk
1 tablespoon apple cider vinegar
2 tablespoons maple syrup
¼ cup apple sauce
¼ cup coconut oil

DIRECTIONS

1. Preheat oven to 350°.
2. Add vinegar to almond milk and set aside.
3. Mix dry ingredients together.
4. Whisk wet ingredients together, adding milk and vinegar mixture last.
5. Add wet ingredients to dry ingredients, and stir with a rubber spatula. Pour into silicone muffin cups.
6. Place in oven for 14-18 minutes or until toothpick comes out clean.

POTATO CIRCLES

INGREDIENTS

2 potatoes (white or sweet)
1 teaspoon olive oil
Dash of sea salt

DIRECTIONS

1. Cut potatoes in 1/8" rounds.
2. Toss in oil and sprinkle with sea salt.
3. Spread on a cookie sheet. Bake at 350° until slightly brown.

"CHEEZE BREAD"

INGREDIENTS

10 corn tortillas
   (or 2 per person with an extra or two)
Cheese (vegan or organic dairy)
1 tablespoon olive oil

DIRECTIONS

1. Put a small amount of oil in the largest skillet you have. Heat up the skillet for two minutes over medium heat.
2. Add as many corn tortillas to the skillet as you can, without overlapping. Sprinkle each tortilla with cheese and cover with another tortilla. Flip when the bottom is browned.
3. When you are done with all of them, cut them into halves or quarters for dipping in the soup.

ON CHEESE

In our family, the vegan (dairy-free) brand we like is Daiya Cheddar, and more recently Kite Hill. Try to avoid soy cheeses when you can, and look for nut-based. This market is steadily improving, but is not perfect.

If you use dairy cheese, try an organic cheddar. Also, try to grate cheese yourself whenever you can. There are lots of extra (not so natural) ingredients added to pre-grated cheese to prevent it from sticking. No matter what you choose long term, try to avoid dairy when fighting a cold or with irritated sinuses from allergies.

SOME OTHER VERY SIMPLE OPTIONS FOR DIPPING IN SOUP...

Toast cut into sticks

Toasted corn or brown rice tortillas

Your favorite gluten-free cracker

DINNER RHYTHM
FARM TO TABLE NIGHT

It's a really good practice to order weekly produce, via a farm share, a farmer's market, or some other farm-to-table service in your area. It's especially beneficial for kids to experience what it's like to take vegetables directly from a farm and make a meal out of them. For some this formula may feel less structured than other days, but I encourage you to embrace the challenge. Many farm share options or weekly farm deliveries offer solely vegetables, so it's a good way to really challenge yourself with new ingredients — even if you start by just roasting them all separately, making soups, or figuring out a salad!

Some farms offer meat and eggs, and if your family eats those you might find they are way more expensive — I encourage you to stretch your budget slightly for the good of your family and the planet. Telling the stories of where your food comes from is really important, and will get your kids asking good questions when it's time for them to buy food.

WHAT TO MAKE

Make anything that is in this book or on your mind, but stretch yourself to make it from all that local food you have. That might mean that instead on 4 zucchini, you use 2 zucchini and 2 summer squash, and you push yourself to find a recipe that uses peppers because you have 14. See what you've got. Do 10 minutes of research on Google. Make a choice and start creating.

ON BUYING MEAT

"Essentially what you want to do when you're getting your protein from animal products is to find people who are raising the animals in ways that are natural to the animal. I saw a bumper sticker the other day: 'Eat cheap food and die.' That's essentially true – if you buy cheap beef, chicken or fish, you're getting a lot more than you pay for: you're getting a horrible dose of stuff that's very unhealthy. Again, know who and where and what, and ask the difficult questions. And if they can't answer your questions, don't buy it. Buy something else." From an interview with Greg Georgaklis, founder of Farmers to You.

(Full article available for download at www.plansimplemeals.com/hub)

DINNER RHYTHM
COOKBOOK NIGHT

Do you have lots of cookbooks that just collect dust? Cookbook Night is a great way to just push yourself to create new meals. On busy days, I highly recommend repeating what you already know and creating variety by adding different veggies or spices. When you have a little extra time, challenge yourself to make something totally new. This is how you will grow as a chef and gain confidence in the kitchen. By making Cookbook Day a regular practice, you will finally use those cookbooks and even add more great ones over time.

SOME OF OUR FAVORITES

It's All Good
by Gweneth Paltrow

We love her salads, every one! We also love her sweet potato muffins and her dumpling filling.

Chloe's Vegan Italian Kitchen
by Chloe Coscarelli

We love her Pesto Mac 'n' Cheese, Pumpkin Risotto, and Strawberry Basil Milkshake.

Deliciously Ella
by Ella Woodward

We love her Chickpea Flour Wraps, Coconut Thai Curry with Chickpeas, and her Acai Bowl.

The Blender Girl
by Tess Masters

We love her Chock-full Chocolate Surprise, Fresh Spring Rolls, and Pad Thai.

YumUniverse
by Heather Crosby

We love her salad dressings, "sammiches," and her super-veggie pot pie!

Oh She Glows
by Angela Liddon

We love her Caesar Salad, Broccoli & Cashew Cheese Burrito, and her Peanut Butter Cookie Dough Bites.

Soupelina's Soup Cleanse
by Elina Fuhrman

I love her Veggie Broth, Lentil Stew, and Cauliflower Me Maybe.

Crazy Sexy Kitchen
by Kris Carr

I love her Beetroot Ravioli, Black Bean Burger, and Curried Nada-Egg Wraps.

The Kind Diet
by Alicia Silverstone

I love her Radicchio, Radish and Fennel Pressed Salad, her Candied Pears, and Crispy Peanut Butter Treats.

Beauty Detox Foods
by Kimberly Snyder, C.N.

We love her Black Bean Burritos, Lentil-Mushroom Tarts, and Raw Gorilla Wraps.

DINNER RHYTHM
CLEAN OUT THE FRIDGE NIGHT

Before I started planning what we eat, my biggest problem was wasting food. Tossing food in the garbage is just throwing away money. In our modern times, learning to be resourceful and economical with food is such a valuable lesson for adults and kids. I know it has made a huge impact on me!

This day will look different depending on what you have left, and what time of year it is, but here are some suggestions:

- leftover veggie soup
- leftover veggie salad
- leftover buffet (little bits from lots of meals). Serve with a big salad.
- leftover burritos, or wraps

Cooking from what you've got is a skill that you will get as you get more and more comfortable in the kitchen. Look around you for people in your life who do this really well and watch what they do. Ask them questions. And then practice cooking with what you have on a regular basis, and it will click. I am getting better and better at this, but I admit it is not my favorite day. My husband is best cooking to use what's left, so sometime I step up to the challenge and sometimes I delegate!

A FEW OTHER THEMES TO WEAVE IN THROUGHOUT THE YEAR:

- **Grill Day** is a fun option during to gather outdoors during the summer. It is also a good way to delegate if you have a spouse or a neighbor who loves to grill.

- **Around the World Day** is a great way to come up with meals if you are a bi-cultural family, live in a diverse neighborhood, or you simply want to learn what other ethnicities eat for dinner. It's a great way bring variety into your kids' lives and educate them simultaneously. You could "visit China" one night for dinner, Japan, or India. Observe how the conversations at the table might change based on the food that's served. You can use YouTube and Google for some great visuals to spark conversation!

- **Old Family Favorites Day** is a great time to make food that you grew up with. If it does not fit into your new healthy lifestyle, see if there is a way that you can change it to make it work. Pass down stories and memories of your childhood to your kids as you share a beloved recipe with them.

DINNER RHYTHM
MAKE A SALAD WITH EVERY MEAL

Tip: Order salads at restaurants and pay close attention to the combos. Study the art of great salad.

1. MAKE A DRESSING.

Choose a dressing that you can enjoy for a few days and make enough to fill a small ball jar.

Making your own dressing is important. There is a lot of unnecessary additives in the store bought varieties.

2. CHOOSE 3 VEGGIES.

Chop into similar size pieces and place them at the bottom of the salad bowl.

Cucumber
Sliced carrots
Sliced avocados
Sliced radishes
Sliced celery
Sliced apples
Parsley
Cabbage
Fennel
Beets
Cooked corn
Snap peas
Raw broccoli
Mushrooms
Artichoke hearts
Kelp noodles
Daikon radish

3. CHOOSE LEAVES.

Chopped romaine
Mixed greens
Arugula
Mache
Pea shoots
Sunflower sprouts
Spinach
Boston bibb
Baby kale
Micro greens

4. SPRINKLE WITH CRUNCH.

Sunflower seeds
Quinoa
Hemp seeds
Flax
Walnuts
Pecans
Almond slivers
Arame (sea veggie found in Asian section of the grocery)
Dulse (sea veggie found in Asian section of the grocery)

SALAD IN ACTION

FALL INSPIRED SALAD

INGREDIENTS

2 cups arugula
1 cup spinach
A handful of walnuts
A handful raisins
½ cup apples, diced
½ cup quinoa, cooked
¼ cup cucumber, diced
2 radishes, diced

DRESSING INGREDIENTS

½ cup apple cider vinegar
¼ cup olive oil
5 tablespoons tamari
2 tablespoons maple syrup
1 clove crushed garlic

DIRECTIONS

1. Put dressing ingredients in a ball jar, cover, and shake.
2. Put your salad in a bowl or take away container (if you leave with it in the morning) that you love, and dress it when you are ready to enjoy.

KALE SALAD

INGREDIENTS

1 bunch of kale sliced into very thin strips
1 tablespoon cider vinegar
½ teaspoon sea salt
1 tablespoon cumin
2 tablespoons nutritional yeast
5 tablespoons hemp seeds
Juice from 1 lemon
2 cloves of garlic minced
2 scallions minced
2 tablespoons olive oil

DIRECTIONS

1. Massage kale with vinegar, salt and lemon for a few minutes.
2. Add all other ingredients except the olive oil, and mix well.
3. Add olive oil when ready to serve.

SALAD WITH ARAME

SALAD INGREDIENTS

Big bowl of mixed baby greens
Cucumber
2 tablespoons arame (sea veggie found in Asian section of market)
Shredded carrots

DRESSING INGREDIENTS

2 tablespoons brown rice vinegar
2 tablespoon tamari
1 tablespoon grapeseed oil
1 teaspoon maple syrup

DIRECTIONS

Dress when ready to serve.

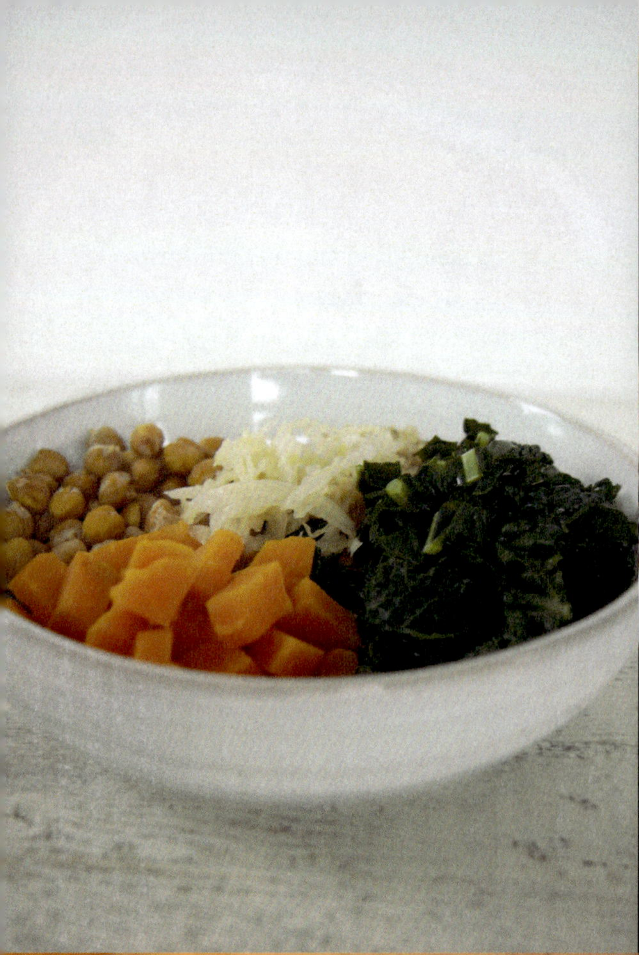
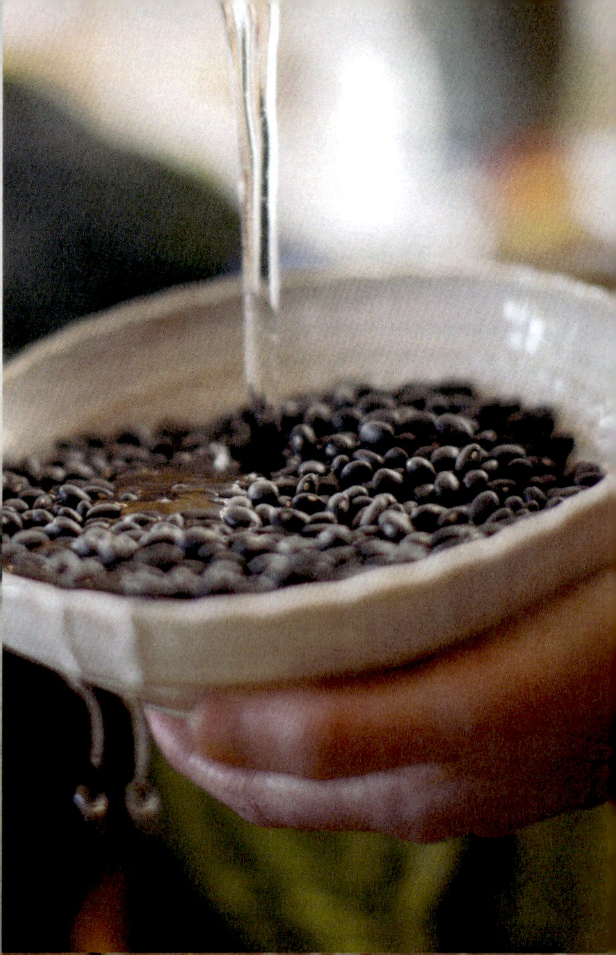
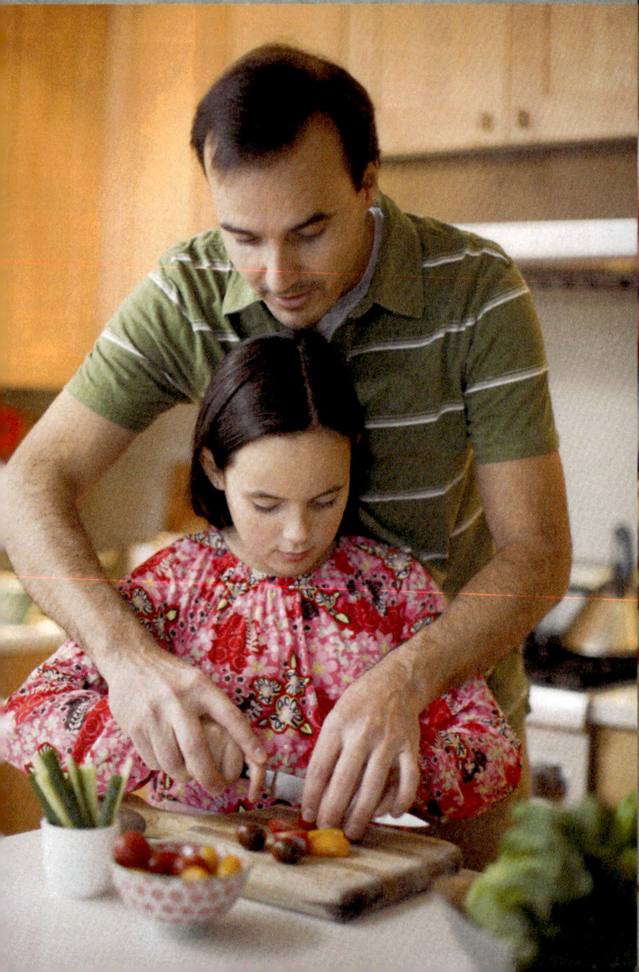
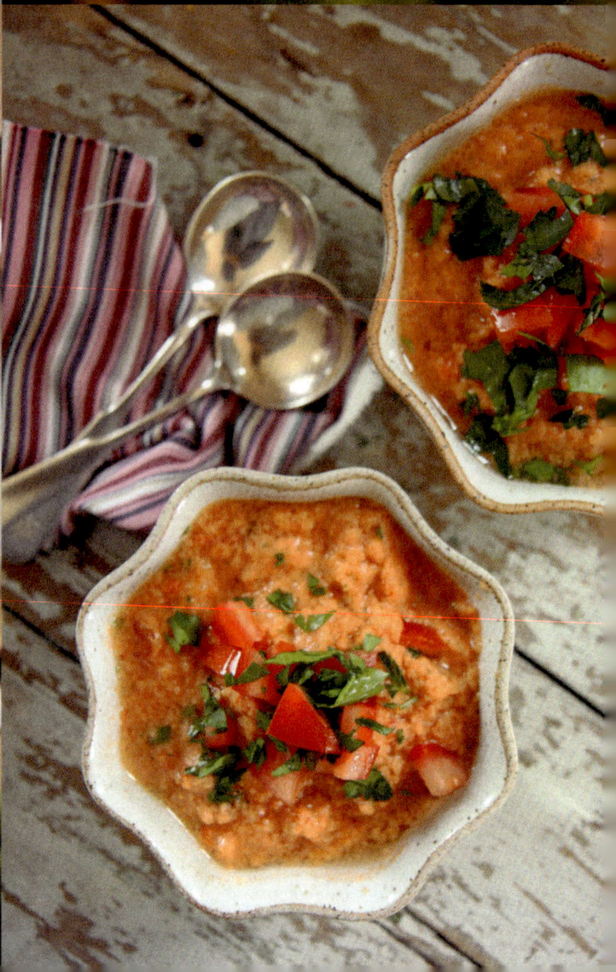

Doable Changes

Here are some doable changes inspired by this chapter. Choose one, and commit to experimenting with it this week.

1. Turn off your cell phone every evening and use the time to REALLY connect with your kids.
2. Redefine your plate, so it is 1/5 protein (beans, tofu, or animal protein if that suits you), 1/5 gluten-free grains, 3/5 of colorful veggies.
3. Choose a cookbook that can teach you new recipes that are gluten-free and vegan
4. Soak and cook dried beans vs. using the canned variety.
5. Plan to cook dinner with your kids at least once a week.
6. Choose one veggie you would love your child to eat and commit to including it in dinner seven times.
7. Clean up the kitchen after every meal.
8. Get yourself a health mentor.
9. Share food with friends and family regularly, so they know your tricks.
10. Empower people in your house to help you chop.
11. Look up a new country with your kids, discover their culture, and try to make their food.
12. Tell your favorite family stories at the dinner table.
13. Clean out the fridge every Sunday.
14. Switch up the cook a few meals a week.
15. Teach your kids to make a whole meal.
16. Start each meal with a moment of silence.
17. Learn to make tomato sauce from scratch.
18. Present your meals each night in a way that is appealing and shows off the natural rainbow.
19. Find a veggie soup you love to make and make a big batch.
20. Sleep a full eight hours.
21. Make a list of five ways you can get exercise at home.
22. Make a list of ten ways you can get exercise as a family.
23. Pick one food that you always eat at a restaurant and figure out how to make it from scratch at home.

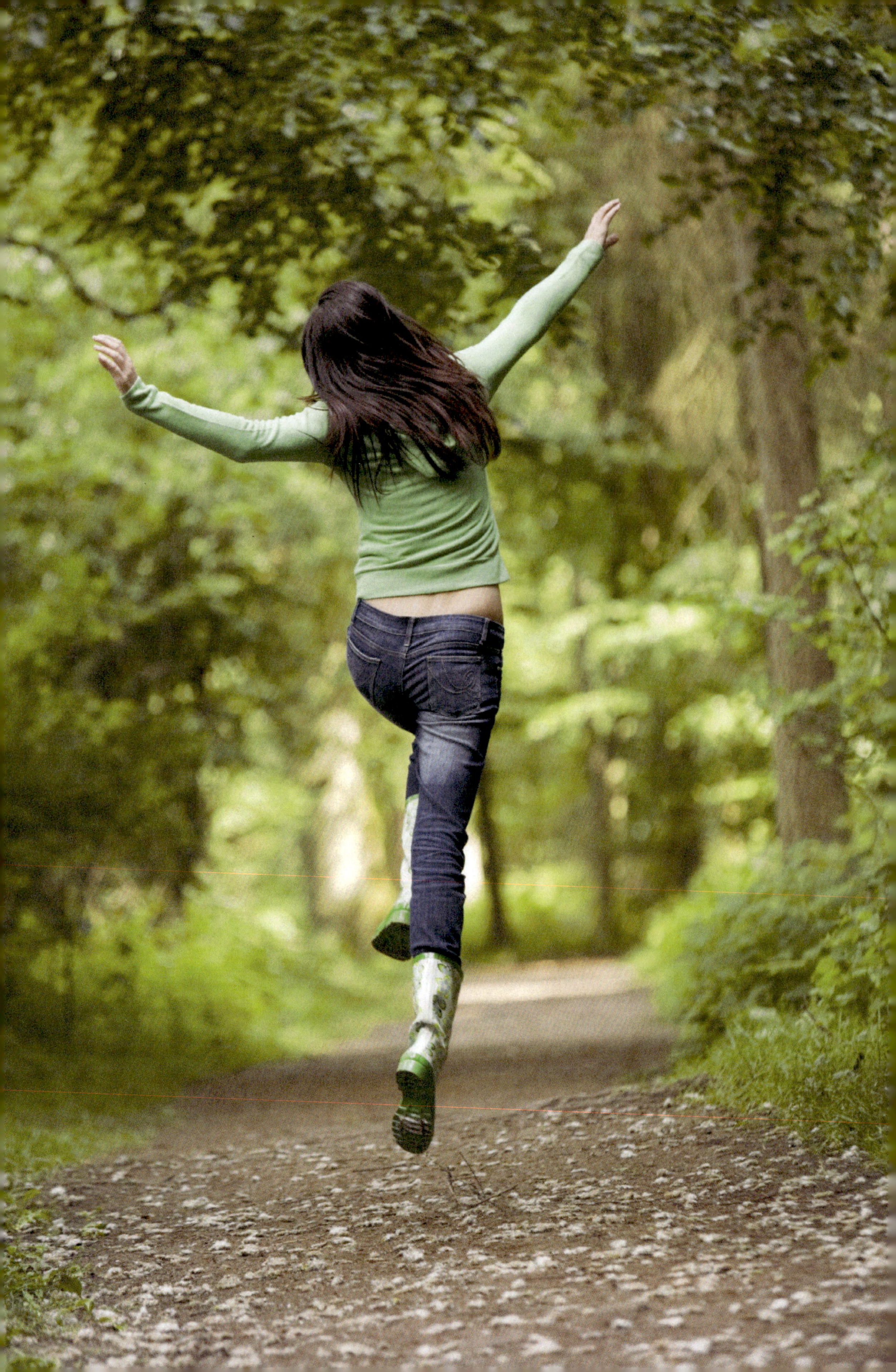

STEP SIX
Celebrate

"The more you praise and celebrate your life, the more there is in life to celebrate."

— Oprah Winfrey

When I took the step to move beyond my shortlist of healthy foods, it was April. Springtime made it pretty easy for me to stay focused on my health with warm weather and fresh vegetables. By September, my daughter had been dairy-free awhile but got sent home from school three times for vomiting. I knew something was still upsetting her digestion, so I took gluten out of her diet as well. Shortly after these bold and positive changes lurked the holiday season, starting with the biggest culprit of mindless over-indulgence: Thanksgiving.

Because the new food I was discovering made me feel so good, I had no problem eating differently among my peers or coworkers. However, I feared my children might feel negatively about being different or celebrating holidays in a nontraditional way. It was during this time I decided to dig deep and find a way to fully embrace the season of celebrating while also staying healthy and mindful for my family and me.

CELEBRATING YOU

Never forget to celebrate.

At its core, celebrating is just about cultivating gratitude along the whole journey we call life. There is no end destination. There may be goals, like weight loss and disease-free kids. There will certainly be lots of small doable steps to make those goals happen. But in its essence, a healthy lifestyle is a choice we make each day, including special days.

DOCUMENT YOUR JOURNEY

Daily, write down what you are grateful for, and the new lessons you learn through food. This conditions you to be in an appreciative mindset throughout the day and in your life in general. It causes you to live more fully and in each present moment as you unwrap the gifts in your everyday. As you make this a practice, include food. Notice how you feel based on the choices you make every day.

Maybe you are grateful for your morning smoothie, or a trip to the store, or a new farm you found on a weekend adventure. Maybe you gave up gluten for a week, and then had a piece of bread and got foggy. Don't sweat the bread, as it gave you a clue to your body and its ideal food. Same goes for a piece of cake or a piece of chocolate. Maybe you felt fine after a piece of chocolate, so you learned that lesson. But maybe the second time you indulged, it was late and you couldn't fall asleep. These are important lessons. Think of yourself as a detective looking for the clues to your optimal health. Have gratitude for the ability to even notice. Make sure you document at least three things each day.

{Download journal pages at www.plansimplemeals.com/hub}

Watch as this practice begins to shift your ability to be a great mom, wife, friend, worker, and wellness warrior each day.

CREATE HEALTHY RITUALS

Another way to celebrate is to create healthy rituals for yourself. Maybe it's that you sit down each day to have lunch and you say thank you for the food before you dig in. Maybe you create a ritual around your morning green smoothie. Maybe you always have a secret stash of trail mix in a cool reusable bag in your purse. Whatever are the healthy habits that serve you, honor them. Make them part of your routine in a way that feels effortless. Essentially, your new healthy habits become celebrations.

DATE NIGHT

Once you find ways to celebrate yourself, include your spouse with a weekly date night. A girls' night out is fine too, but if you have a spouse and you are raising kids together, date night is essential.

When we step into this new role of caring for our family and really feeding them well, sometimes our marriages can fall by the wayside. Or, once you get so good at preparing healthy food night after night, staying in becomes preferable to going out. But, with a little research, you can find delicious, healthy options in your area to share with your loved one.

I would look for a few things when deciding on the perfect location for date night. Some ethnic restaurants are great for veggie and gluten-free options. And, as vegan and paleo diets are getting more popular, those types of restaurants are popping up in cities all over. I especially look forward to the vegan café in our town that makes beautiful quinoa bowls. Or the raw food restaurant that is super inventive and delicious. I also like Indian, Thai and Japanese restaurants, because they offer lean proteins and many vegetable dishes. Often these places can be pretty reasonably priced too, if you're not looking to spend too much.

If you are having a splurge night out, then look for a restaurant that has its own chef. Ask the chef to prepare something for your needs, whether it's gluten-free, dairy free, or paleo. Just ask them to surprise you and see what happens. I've found mostly that the chef will end up celebrating with you. Restaurant staff tends to get annoyed by too many substitution requests. So instead, give the chef an opportunity to be creative and he'll be happy to accommodate you.

FAMILY: CELEBRATING EVERYTHING YOUR WAY

HOLIDAYS ON PURPOSE

As I mentioned, after about nine months of healthy eating and one month with a gluten-free six-year-old, it was Thanksgiving. Now, there are a few things that always bothered me about this holiday. One is that I never felt like I lived up to the images I used to see in home and garden magazines. You know, the ones with beautiful tables, effortlessly casual and chic, with blurred children running in the background and happy people lively with conversation? They looked so wonderful, so free and so happy. Yet I always felt either overwhelmed or kind of lonely at Thanksgiving time. Not that I didn't have lots of friends and family, but just that I couldn't shake the pressure to do Thanksgiving better. It never occurred to me to do it my way.

This particular Thanksgiving, I had absolutely no desire to make the traditional spread and I had even less desire to navigate someone else's table. By this time my daughter was gluten-free and dairy-free, I was vegan, and my husband and my son admitted that they actually really don't like turkey. And I thought, why do we have to do this?

And then I saw this amazing opportunity to do something different and have fun with it...

Here's what we decided: I asked each of my children to come up with a dish they really, really wanted to make as a family. It could be anything — something that we had all the time that they loved, something that we had had at a restaurant but never made ourselves, or something they had always wanted to try. At the time, my kids were two, five, and seven years old. My oldest son said sushi right away.

My daughter thought of a few great desserts that she wanted to eat and looked forward to them being dairy-free and gluten-free but still delicious. My youngest daughter just loved the bread buns they served in a playgroup we attended. My husband and I put on our thinking caps to tie all these foods together.

With a fresh perspective, I began to put together our own version of Thanksgiving. I was excited to learn how to make sushi, something I had always wanted to do. My husband suggested that he would love to make the miso soup we usually ordered at Japanese restaurants. The bread and desserts were a way to challenge what we knew about baking — which was nothing — and make some yummy alternative food. I had become quite accustomed to my usual salad so I decided to push myself on the salad front. All the sudden, we had this meal that everyone was looking forward to and that was nothing like a traditional picture.

Perhaps most importantly, we made a conscious decision not to get stressed out.

It started in the morning. We woke up and made the bread buns. We figured out how to make them gluten-free and dairy-free so that everybody could eat them. We enjoyed them with tea for a very late breakfast.

We called a few friends to join us and began prepping and rolling sushi. We took our time and didn't really have a plan. We were just having fun. It was one of the first times I thought the process of cooking with a group was fun! We ate the rolls that did not stay together. Even though we had already pretty much eaten half of the sushi, at some point we sat down and added the miso soup my husband made and a salad with dressing just like a Japanese restaurant.

After dinner, we decided to take a walk and get some fresh air. We took lanterns and walked through the forest in the dark. It was cold, beautiful, and a tradition we knew we wanted forever.

And what was left? Four amazing, somewhat "healthy" desserts for dinner! We had cheesecake, brownies, and ice cream made from almond milk. We lit a fire, ate and enjoyed some warm drinks.

I looked around and realized that day was better than anything I had ever dreamed about or seen in a magazine. It was anything but traditional, but we were happy and had eaten really well!

That was six years ago. Now every single year starting at about Halloween, everybody starts talking about what their Thanksgiving dish will be. Every year the menu changes. Word traveled through our friend group, and every year different people join us for Thanksgiving.

Holidays are what you make them. You can follow a cookie cutter picture or you can follow your gut and make new traditions.

Usually our gut does not lead us to overwhelm and exhaustion. That only happens when we follow.

Of course, as you know, after Thanksgiving comes Christmas.

I realized I could make Christmas what I wanted. We could be joyous. We could be sparkly. We could be quiet.

After Thanksgiving had been such a success, I decided that we would do Christmas our own way too, as a family, and that meant beyond just the food. It certainly doesn't have to be chaotic. I always felt that Christmas was so busy, and it didn't have to be. Even as a child, I remember Christmas being a bustling time, and as a parent, I often feel overwhelmed to accomplish all the things needed to perpetuate the magic.

By the time Christmas rolled around, I was confident that I was on the right food path and we could create our own traditions. I had already learned some great tools, and created some healthy rituals that I was practicing daily. I really didn't want the obligation of over-indulging at Christmas to ruin my efforts. I thought it was best to keep the celebrations simple.

I grew up with an advent calendar. I cherished the act of counting down the days until Christmas by unwrapping a small treat each day. Today there are different variations on this concept, with or without chocolate. During this first year of simplifying our holidays, I took that concept and reworked it to support our new mission to stay sane and healthy. It has grown into what I call the Countdown Calendar.

COUNTDOWN CALENDAR STRATEGY

We often over commit ourselves during the months of November and December. Holiday parties, school events, work celebrations, family visiting, presents, church ceremonies, and most of all, the obligation to create the "holiday magic" for everyone else makes a time that is supposed to be a vacation very stressful.

That is where the Countdown Calendar comes in. If you celebrate Christmas, you can create an experience that starts on December first and goes through Christmas. If you don't do Christmas, you can countdown to the New Year. The idea is that you write a thought for each day and number them. Every morning or evening, the kids open a thought. You can pin the envelopes to a tree, a string, a wreath, or put them in a box. You can also purchase a wall hanging with pockets and do it that way.

The important task is to figure out what each thought says.

To do this, you first need to decide how you want to feel. If the holidays usually feel lonely, maybe you want to feel connected. Or if the holidays usually feel overwhelming, then you may want to express calm or ease.

The next step is to write out your holiday "to-do list." Write out everything. What you always do, what you need to do, what you want to do. Then go back through the list with the lens of how you want to feel during those particular times. Are you overbooked? What does not serve you anymore? What do you need to say no to and maybe change?

If a holiday dinner stresses you out, look at why. Do you have to make too much food? Can you delegate, or prep it in advance? Or is it about the people? You may not be able to un-invite Aunt Sally, but maybe you can invite your closest friend who will make the evening fun for you. What can you take away from your list or chunk into smaller things? What can you add that feels relaxing? Maybe a game night, a day reading by the fire, family back rub night, sleepover at Grandma's (for the kids only).

Then put it all in a calendar. Make sure there is only one thing per day, and that you feel good about most of the days. If something is overwhelming, at least you can sandwich it between two self-care days. If you have to go to your hubby's office party with the kids, maybe the night before you all take bubble baths, and on the way you all eat apples and donate some clothes to a shelter. That way, by the time you get to the party your tummy is primed to make good choices, and your mind is set on doing good. It turns that party around!

{For a full worksheet go to www.plansimplemeals.com/hub}

Weave everything into your plan that NEEDS to happen and let the rest go. Maybe one day the kids make ornaments — one for the tree and one for a neighbor. You can weave in gifts for friends, teachers and grandparents. Though you might have just done these things anyway, it's helpful to focus on them first thing in the morning and fold them into the rhythm of your day. Some days you may plan a special event, like going to the Nutcracker ballet or to see some Christmas trains, but because you have made a plan, you can construct the time around that outing. The piece of paper in your countdown calendar might say, "Pajama morning! Enjoy Papa's pancakes, and then read by the fire. After lunch, get dressed in something sparkly because we are going to the Nutcracker!" See how that makes your day seem easier and less stressful?

Of course, you have to stick to it! But if you plan mindfully, you've already factored in time for self-care — a yoga class, a quiet cup of tea, or a brisk walk. You can then do the same for your partner. By the time you go to the Nutcracker, you are both happy and emotionally fulfilled.

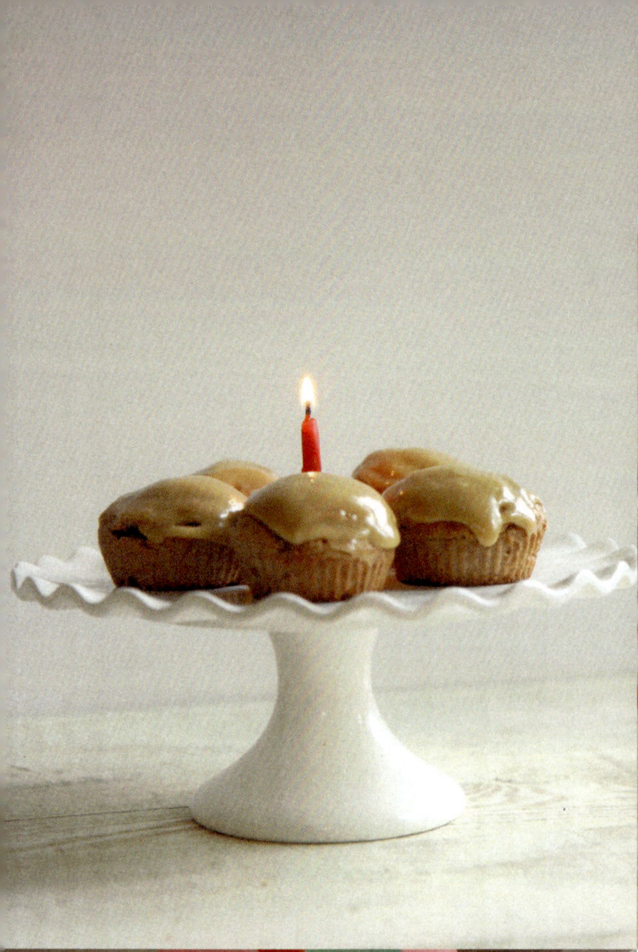
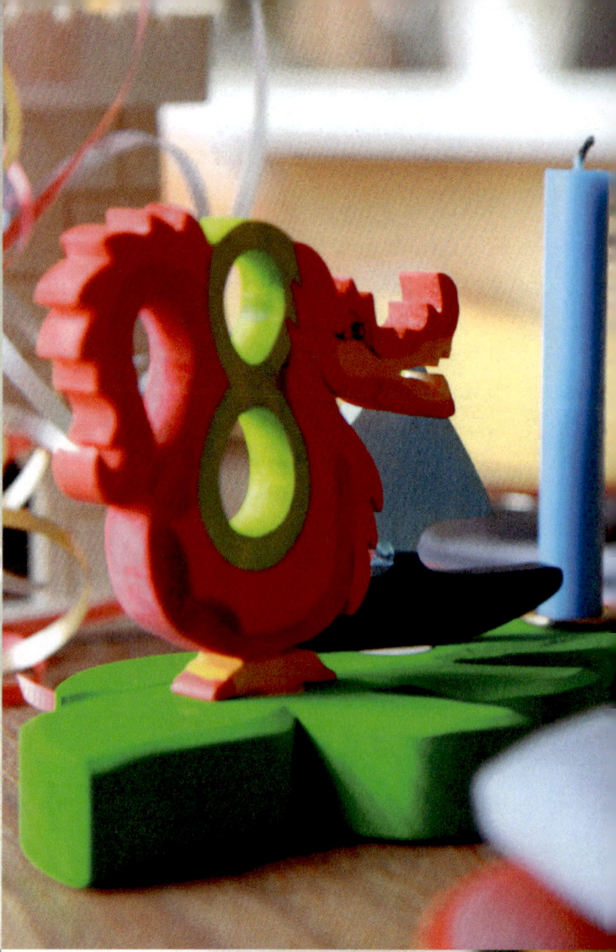
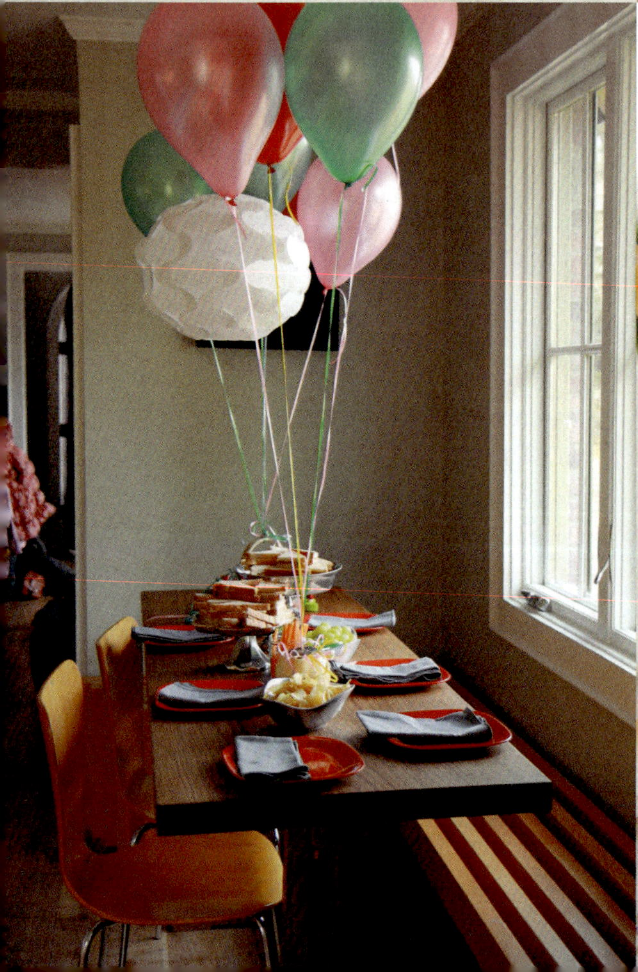
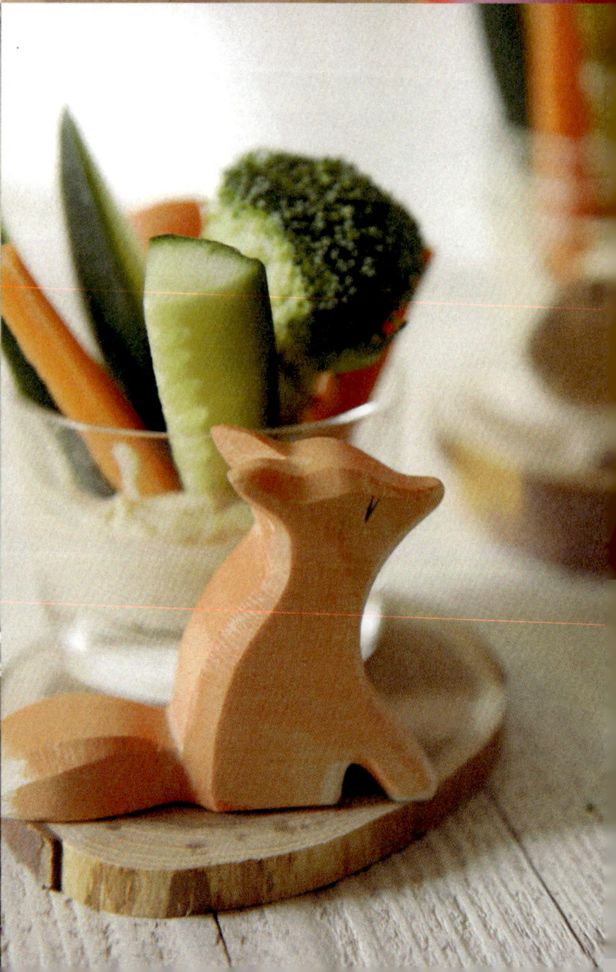

BIRTHDAYS

Once a year we circle the sun and celebrate another year. In a family, this adds up to a lot of celebrations! What do birthdays look like in your house? Do you enjoy them? It's really a personal matter—I look forward to and love mine, but my husband is not such a fan of his. Everyone is slightly different in their celebration — even kids. Birthdays are an opportunity to REALLY pay attention to the wants and needs of the person being celebrated. I've found with young kids this takes more observation than listening.

My third daughter has a "go with the flow" personality, and like most youngsters, gets attached to things quickly. She celebrated two parties for her schoolmates at a kid's venue that featured huge trampolines. Of course, she was sold. For months, a party at the "jumping place" was all she wanted her birthday. But here's is the thing — when she attended those parties, she spent the first 30 minutes attached to my leg. Then she went out and exerted herself to the max, ate lots of sugar, and was home sick two days later. I watched this happen on two separate occasions before her own birthday. The combination of lots of people, lots of activity, and lots of junk food just taxed her system. It was probably the worst way to celebrate her.

Now my other daughter loves people and is more in tune with starting and stopping, and actually can't eat a lot of party food because of her allergies. So she probably would do great with a birthday at the jumping place, and I could easily just switch up the food part to include veggies and hummus, fruit skewers and a yummy gluten-free, dairy-free cake, and all would be well.

This is why it is so important for parents to take the driver's seat and create situations where our kids can thrive, especially on their birthdays.

List of questions to consider when planning your child's party:

How many kids should attend?

What works for you and your child?

How much do you want to spend?

Can you have a party in your home or yard?

What time of the day will you have the party?

Do you want a theme?

What food will you serve?

What cake will you have?

Do you want to do a craft?

Where are you being wasteful? How can you shift that?

Do you need a party every year?

I highly recommend that everyone make a commitment to cook their own food for parties instead of buying store-made and that you challenge yourself to serve fruits and veggies.

Fruit and veggies can be put on skewers or in colorful Dixie cups. You can put hummus at the bottom of a veggie cup or pass it around for dipping. Making a cake is so fun if you reserve enough time to really enjoy it.

In our house, birthdays have run the gamut. We've gone on treasure hunts. We've gone on walks. We've gone ice skating on a pond. We always incorporate healthy, yummy food. On occasion, I have been inspired to prepare a dinner to serve to both happy children and their parents.

Our son always has a theme in mind, so we have honored the Native Americans, gone back to a time of knights and dragons, and celebrated Egypt. A theme can help frame the activity, the food, and the goody bag if you are inclined to have one.

It's amazing for everyone to come together and enjoy healthy food. Sure, there are going to be guests who might be wondering where the pizza is, or asking for juice boxes. That's okay. Remember that it's your family's moment and celebration. Don't be afraid to be creative, think outside the box and serve your own healthy menu.

Birthday cakes provide such a great opportunity to learn how to bake with healthy ingredients, and to share nutritious sweet treats with others. It also makes the cake really feel like yours, like something you are proud of and happy to share. You can tell all the children while they are enjoying it what it means to bake a cake and know where all the ingredients came from. That's huge. Consider that for your next birthday party as an alternative to a processed grocery store version.

There's a recipe here for our favorite birthday cupcakes that are allergy friendly, but there are so many online resources if you are looking for something specific. You can also find many ideas for party favors if you'd like to include those at your event as well. Just remember to keep it simple and thoughtful, and that kids and parents will be cool with no candy!

Parties might not be your thing, and that's totally okay. Figure out which part of the birthday celebration you look forward to, whether it's the cooking or the decorating or the music and focus on that. If you need to get out of the house, have the party somewhere else and bring healthy food along. Or skip food—just make the party short and sweet. If it's really stressing you out to throw a party every year, then don't. I know parents who do it every other year or wait until their kids are ten years old. There is no rule book and no birthday party police. Do what suits you and your family — keeping it simple, healthy and fun!

Don't forget that all holidays change over time.

Remember that rituals are nice because they create a rhythm to your year, but some of them will change over time. We used to always have a party with the whole class for my son, with decadent themes and dinner for all the families. It happens at a time of year when I crave that connection, so it was fun for us. But eventually, he just wanted boys, and recently, he has decided to just invite one friend on a day-long adventure. Be flexible and do what works for you.

Don't forget the small moments.

Technically, each time you sit down together as a family is a celebration. Use dinnertime as a way to connect, inspire, and educate.

This could mean you tell more stories. Tell stories of your children when they were smaller so they can connect to those moments. Tell stories about you and your spouse when you were younger so that they can really get to know you better — same with grandparents and your siblings. Maybe you had to solve some of the same problems that your kids are having to solve now with each other or in school. It's amazing how much children can learn and grow just through listening to shared experiences.

Whenever we have people at the table that aren't part of our family, I love to ask a bunch of questions and listen to the stories they tell. I always ask our guests about their fondest memories about food, because it's such a powerful thing to share.

Another way to celebrate food daily at the dinner table is to start each meal with gratitude. Some families have a tradition of saying grace at the table. You don't have to be religious for this to resonate. You can just simply say thank you to the earth, to the farmers, and to the people who sell the food you are eating together. When you begin to say your thank-yous, you notice that there are so many people who are responsible for the food getting to your table — mom or dad, store clerks, grocers, farmers, pickers, truck drivers, etc., who made it possible for you to be fed today. It's so powerful to express gratitude for each one of them.

An alternative to a spoken start to dinner is a moment of silence. If you're a family that often struggles with loud meals and whiny transitions, a moment of silence is a great way set the tone for the whole meal, and get everyone grounded.

Again, just find what works for you. There's no need to set expectations on celebrations. Celebrations, big and small, should feel good to you and good for you.

MEDIA WITH MEDIA

We have picked up many of our bad habits from media. So good media is a great way to share this notion of healthy kids with schools. Two movies we love for schools are *The Kids Menu* and *Forks over Knives* — not to mention a wealth of amazing videos coming out by health advocates through Ted Talks and on Youtube. Share such media with parents in your school and community, and start a dialouge in the hallways or in your living room.

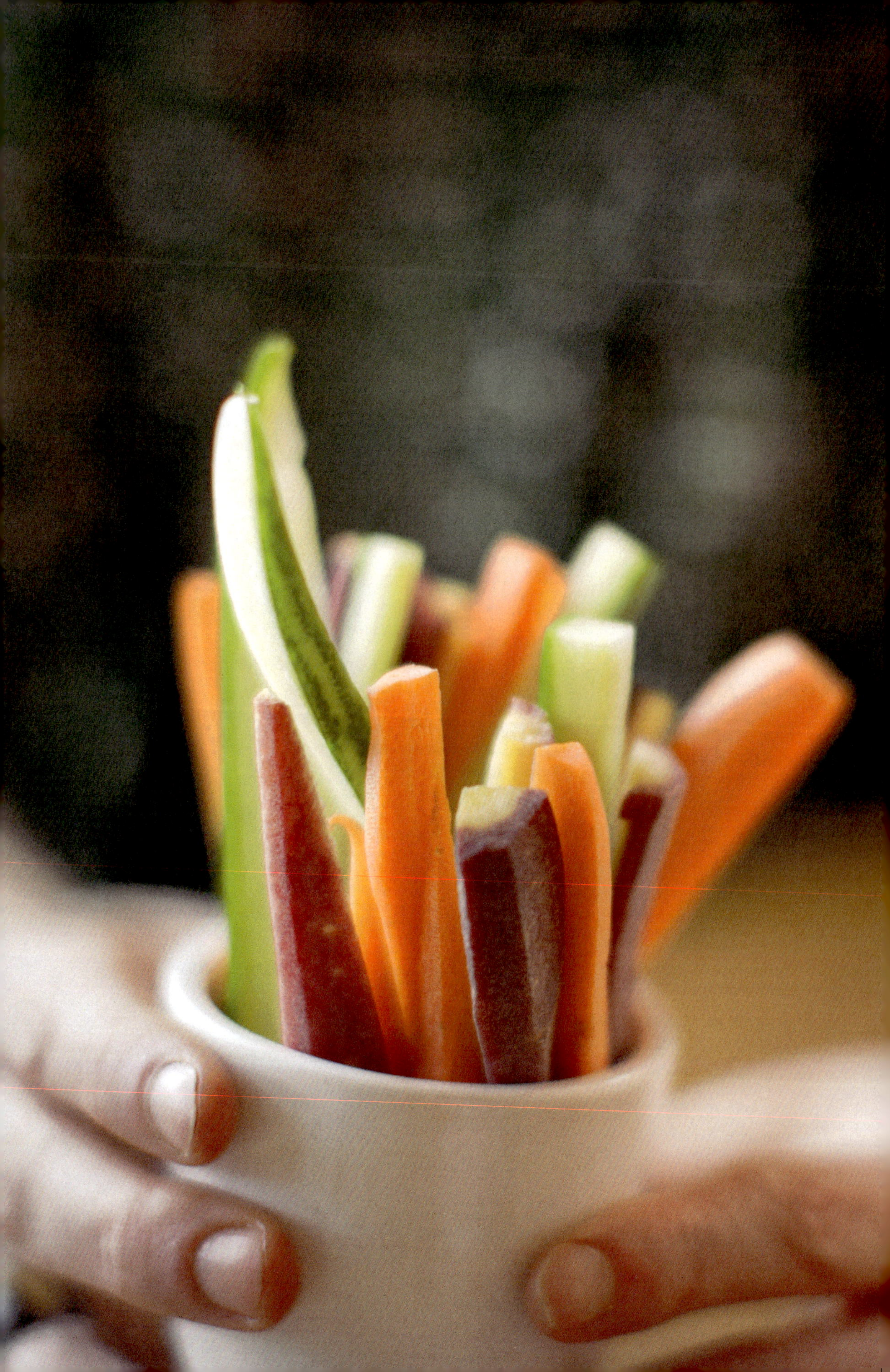

Food: Snacks

"Teach your kids to snack on carrots and celery and fruit and hummus and guacamole — things made from fruits and vegetables and beans and grains. Offer these things all the time."

— Mark Bittman

What are you eating for snacks? Snacks have the potential to be both good and bad. On one hand, if you prepare healthy snacks, you are more likely to make good choices at meals, and always have an option if you accidentally get too hungry. On the other hand, if we are constantly eating, we miss out on the feeling of hunger, something that's actually beneficial to experience.

There is something about lots of small meals that has served me over the years, but the flip side of that might be losing sight of "actual hunger." I am not sure many of us know when we are really hungry — especially our kids. There are snacks at school, at sports, at playdates, at birthday parties — and as grown-ups, we are always offering our kids food to make sure they eat.

If you have a child with allergies or food sensitivities, all the snacks at extra-curricular events is a tough obstacle! If you choose not to eat pizza and donuts, you may feel like the whining mom who is always complaining. And if you have a kid who never eats full meals, this may be why — they are full! So sometimes snacks work against us in that way. On the other hand, if you are out and about, having healthy snacks on hand is such a bonus, as it is hard to find food that serves us in a pinch.

With all that in mind, let's focus on packing good snacks. It's much better to bring your own than to depend on the outside world to supply you with good choices. Especially if you need them to be gluten and dairy-free. Below, I've developed seven groupings for snacks that you might find useful.

FRUIT

Fruit makes a wonderful snack! It is very portable and full of vitamins, minerals and water. It is also naturally sweet and delicious. It makes a hearty snack that is enough on its own if you stay mindful of your hunger cues.

If we saw more fruit at sports games, schools, and birthday parties, I can guarantee we would experience different children. Many fruits are delicious whole, and it is a gift to enjoy them in their natural state.

It is also fun to be creative with fruit! You can skewer it, put it in fun containers, make melon balls, or shapes like apple stars. You can eat dried fruit. If you are industrious, you can even dry your own.

Notice how many colors fruit comes in. Pay attention to all the colors you serve your kids. Teach them to want to eat a rainbow. Let them LOVE fruit.

A FEW FRUIT STRATEGIES:

- Invest in stainless containers to pack snack-sized portions.
- Get kids looking for a new fruit to try at the market.
- Make "Salad People." This is an idea from the Moosewood Cookbook where you cut up a variety of fruits (or veggies) and kids make people. Use the shapes of the fruit for body parts — you may have a pear upper body, kiwi head, melon skirt, with cashew cream hair for dipping.
- Always have fruit out on display in your kitchen.
- Pay attention to how you cut it and serve fruit — have fun with it!

DIRTY DOZEN AND CLEAN FIFTEEN

When your budget allows, it is always best to buy organic, but Environmental Working Group (EWG) has put together a list to help us make choices when organic isn't available or doesn't fit your budget. The "Dirty Dozen" are foods you should always buy organic because they are the most susceptible to pesticides and toxic sprays. The Clean 15 are items that are OK to enjoy conventionally.

Be sure to visit the Environmental Working Group for more info on their report.

DIRTY DOZEN

Apples
Peaches
Nectarines
Strawberries
Grapes
Celery
Spinach
Sweet bell peppers
Cucumbers
Cherry tomatoes
Snap peas – imported
Potatoes

CLEAN FIFTEEN

Avocados
Sweet corn
Pineapples
Cabbage
Sweet peas – frozen
Onions
Asparagus
Mangoes
Papayas
Kiwi
Eggplant
Grapefruit
Cantaloupe
Cauliflower
Sweet potatoes

DIPS

We love dips. On days when it doesn't go to school for lunch, dips make a great snack. And I love them even more since I realized the world is so much bigger than hummus — beans, nuts, and seeds all make beautiful dips, and they can all taste very different. Dips are a great way to introduce plant-based protein in your snacking regime and are an easy way to create something "creamy" within a dairy-free lifestyle. You can dip vegetables in them or healthy crackers. (Dip recipes on pages 119-123)

CRUNCHY VEGGIES TO CHOMP ON:

Carrots
Cucumber
Celery
Broccoli
Cauliflower
Snap peas
Green beans
Radishes
Romaine lettuce leaves
Fennel

OUR FAVORITE CRACKERS:

Any brown rice cracker, particularly plain, sesame and tamari

Mary's Gone Crackers

Most raw vegan brands

SMOOTHIES

Smoothies are one of my favorite snacks, and one of my favorite habits to help busy mom cultivate. Smoothies are a great way to overcome sugar dependencies and dairy cravings — and they're easy to make and naturally gluten-free. Hopefully, you start the day with your green smoothie, but there is an amazing world of milkshake-like smoothies that are dairy-free and processed-sugar-free that make a fabulous snack for all.

In order to make a smoothie creamy, you can start adding nuts and avocado, instead of milk and yogurt — water or coconut water could be your base. You can blend fruits with kale and add superfoods. To make them heartier, consider nuts, seeds, and coconut. If you have a sweet tooth, dates are an awesome substitute for processed sugar.

Some of our favorite combos! In many of them, nut milks can be switched for other nut milks, fruits can be changed up, and greens can be added.

SMOOTHIE TIPS

- ` When using any nut butter, read the label and make sure that organic nuts are the only ingredient — no added oil or sugar.

- Buy extra bananas every week to freeze. Frozen bananas create a "milkshake" consistency.

- Hemp is a great source of protein. Add it to any smoothie, and it's particularly great with chocolate.

- I am a big lover of JuicePlus Complete — a plant-based, yummy protein powder. Contact the PlanSimple Meals team, or someone you know who takes JuicePlus to get your hands on this gem.

- The blender really does make the smoothie. I sometimes feel like I owe my health to Vitamix.

- Add and subtract different fruits from the smoothies on the following pages. They are meant to show how to make smoothies sweet and creamy, but try peaches instead of strawberries, or blackberries instead of cherries — play!

BANANA SHAKE

INGREDIENTS

3 cups coconut milk

4 bananas

5 dates

1 tablespoon vanilla extract

2 tablespoons almond butter

DIRECTIONS

Blend until smooth.

MANGO LASSI

INGREDIENTS

1 cup mango

1 ½ cups almond milk

1 ½ teaspoons raw honey

DIRECTIONS

Blend in high-speed blender.

SIMPLE STRAWBERRY

INGREDIENTS

1 cup frozen organic strawberries

1 frozen banana

1 pitted date

1½ cups almond milk

DIRECTIONS

Blend in high-speed blender.

PB+C SMOOTHIE

INGREDIENTS
3 frozen bananas
1½ cups water
½ cup + 2 tablespoons peanut butter
2 tablespoons raw cacao
1 tablespoon maple syrup

DIRECTIONS
Blend in high-speed blender.

CHERRY BLISS

INGREDIENTS

2 cups frozen cherries
2 cups almond milk
½ cup gluten-free oats
5 dates, pitted
½ teaspoon vanilla

DIRECTIONS

Blend in high-speed blender.

VANILLA SHAKE

INGREDIENTS

1½ cups cashews
8 dates
2 tablespoons vanilla
3 cups water
2 cups ice

DIRECTIONS

1. Soak cashews for 30 minutes to an hour.
2. Blend everything in a high-speed blender.

ORANGE CREAMSICLE

INGREDIENTS

4 oranges (or 9 clementines)
2 frozen bananas
1 cup cucumber, peeled
2 cups almond milk
1 tablespoon honey
1 teaspoon vanilla
1 cup ice

DIRECTIONS

Blend all ingredients in a high-speed blender.

CARROT CAKE SMOOTHIE

INGREDIENTS

1 cup carrot juice
1 cup water
2 tablespoons walnut butter
3 medjool dates
½ teaspoon cardamom
1 teaspoon cinnamon
1 tablespoon vanilla
Pinch sea salt

DIRECTIONS

Blend all ingredients well in high-speed blender.

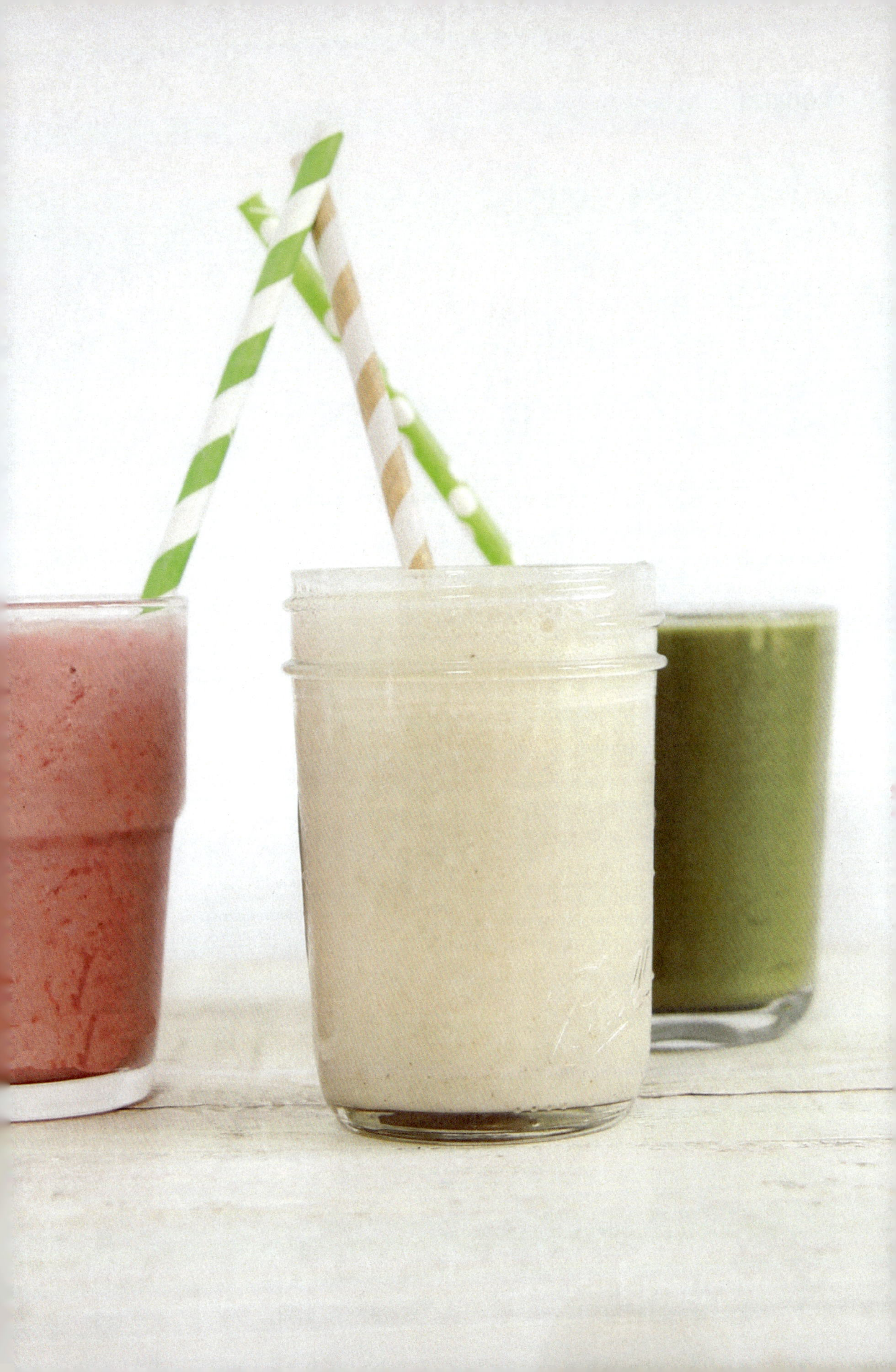

COOKIES

Whether at parties or school, cookies are such a welcomed treat, however, they're traditionally filled with sugar and dairy. With a few alterations, cookies can be packed with nutritious ingredients, and keep you in celebration mode without the negative impact on your body.

Baking healthy cookies together teaches kids that they can control what's in their food. It empowers them to make good choices. It also shows that baked treats are pretty quick to make, and can provide a much better experience than just popping open a box. They can even still taste amazing with healthy ingredients. I love them for a teaching tool and also as a way not to feel deprived if you're still getting used to healthy foods.

CHOCOLATE CHIP COOKIES

INGREDIENTS

2 cups gluten-free oats
¼ cup gluten-free, dairy-free chocolate chips
¼ cup coconut oil, melted
½ cup maple syrup
¼ cup coconut flour
4 dates
3 tablespoons almond butter
½ teaspoon sea salt

DIRECTIONS

1. Melt coconut oil by placing the glass jar in hot water.
2. Blend oil, maple syrup, dates, almond butter and salt in a blender.
3. Put oats and coconut flour in a bowl and stir in blended mixture.
4. Once mixed, fold in chocolate chips.
5. Make into 1" rounds. Shape them like the cookie form you want because they stay true to shape.
6. Bake at 200° for 45 minutes (you can also dehydrate these overnight at 108°).

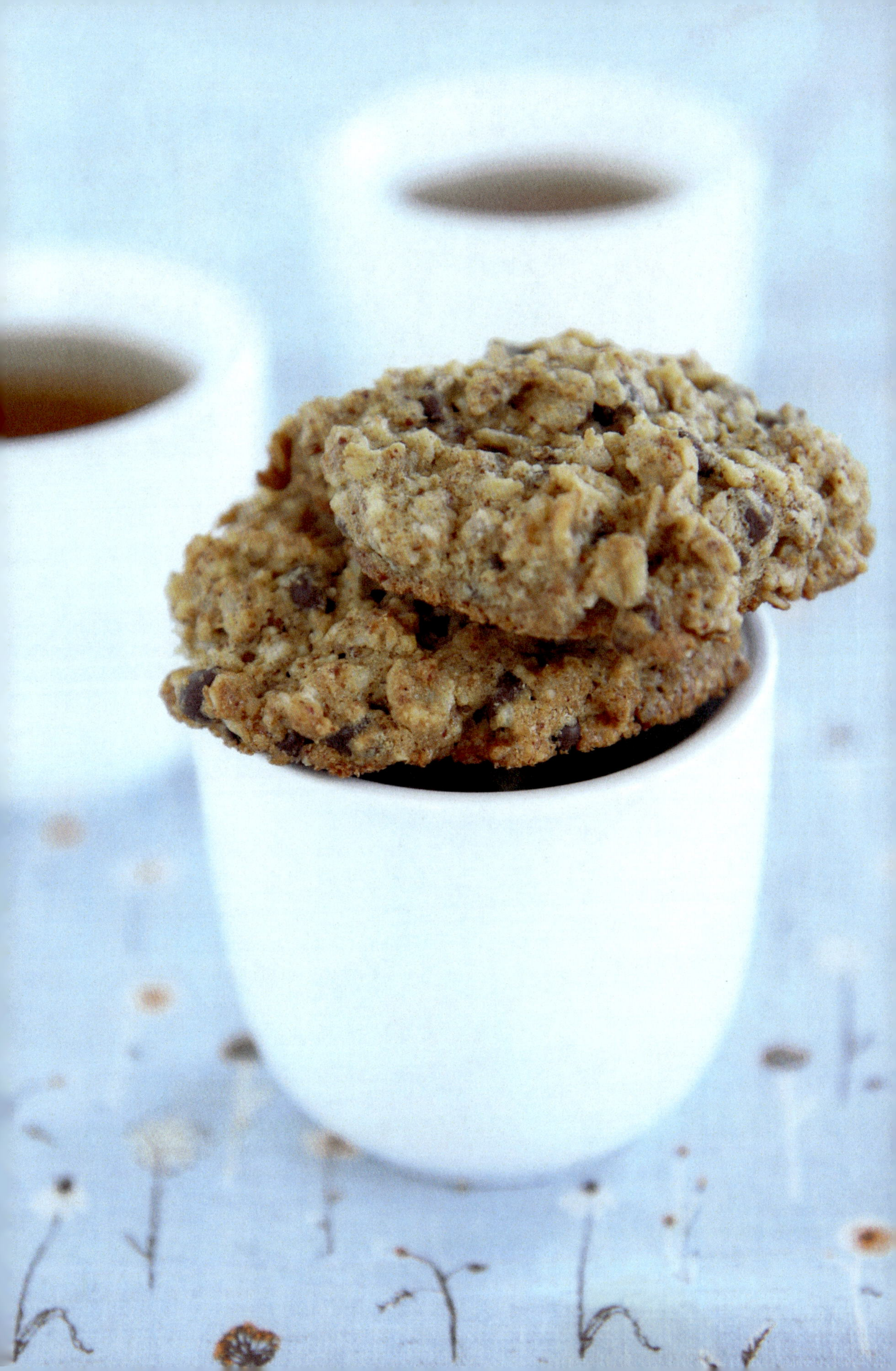

ALMOND BUTTER COOKIES

INGREDIENTS

1 cup almond flour
¼ tsp baking soda
Pinch of sea salt
½ cup almond butter
¼ cup maple syrup

DIRECTIONS

1. Put the dry ingredients in a bowl.
2. Blend almond butter and maple syrup in your blender.
3. Add the wet mixture to the dry ingredients and mix with a rubber spatula.
4. Bake at 275° for 8 minutes.

OATMEAL RAISIN COOKIES

INGREDIENTS

2 cups gluten-free oats
¼ cup coconut oil
½ cup maple syrup
¼ cup coconut flour
½ cup raisins
3 tablespoons almond butter
1 teaspoon sea salt

DIRECTIONS

1. Melt coconut oil by placing the glass jar in hot water.
2. Blend oil, maple syrup, almond butter and salt in a blender, add raisins and blend so there are still small chunks of raisins.
3. Put oats and coconut flour in a bowl and stir in blended mixture.
4. Make into 1" rounds. Shape them like the cookie form you want because they stay true to shape.
5. Bake at 200° for 35 minutes, or 350° for 10 minutes (the 10-minute version will be crumblier).

SUN DOUGHNUTS

INGREDIENTS

1 cup sunflower seeds
1¼ cups raisins
3 tablespoons sunflower seed butter
1 tablespoon maple syrup
1 tablespoon cinnamon
Pinch of sea salt
Coconut flour to coat

DIRECTIONS

1. Process all ingredients in a food processor. Keep processing until dough forms.
2. Form into small bite-sized balls.
3. Roll some of the balls in coconut flour.

MACAROONS

INGREDIENTS

3 cups raw coconut flakes
1 cup raw cacao powder
¾ cup raw agave
Pinch of sea salt
1 teaspoon vanilla

DIRECTIONS

1. Put all ingredients in a bowl. Mix with hands until well integrated.
2. Make bite-sized balls (Refrigerate for an hour if mixture is too soft to make into balls).

Keep in refrigerator for up to a week.

* You can also make these with almond meal instead of cacao.

VEGGIES

Vegetables are often overlooked at snack time. A lot of people immediately think sweet when craving a snack, but today I enjoy chomping on crisp carrots and cucumbers as an alternative treat. You can dip the veggies into your healthy dips, but try them plain every now and again — and teach your kids the same. You can combine lots of leftover veggies to make soup, which makes such a good snack on cold days.

NUTS, SEEDS AND DRIED FRUIT

Nuts, seeds and dried fruit can be eaten separately or thrown together to make a trail mix—a fun thing to do with kids. There are so many new and exciting ways to create a healthy, easy trail mix to take along to school or picnic.

ENJOY DRIED

Blueberries
Cherries
Coconut
Cranberries
Goji berries
Golden berries
Dates
Figs
Mangoes
Mulberries
Raisins

ENJOY UNSALTED

Almonds
Brazil nuts
Cashews
Pumpkin seeds
Sunflower seeds
Pistachios
Pecans
Walnuts

CHOCOLATE

Cacao nibs
Dairy-free chocolate chips

Make sure to get unsulphered, unsweetened fruit. It will be brown in color but better for your body.

PUDDING

Pudding is another loved snack in our household, and a clever way to transform something that's ordinarily unhealthy. In the following recipes, you'll learn how to use a blender to make pudding using chia, cashews, tofu, and avocado. You have to try them to believe them! Here are a few variations to serve you.

BLUEBERRY "JELL-O"

INGREDIENTS

3 cups blueberries, fresh or frozen
7 medjool dates, seeded
¼ cup coconut water

DIRECTIONS

Blend in high-speed blender until smooth.

I sometimes add a ¼ cup of soaked cashews to make it creamy.

Refrigerate for an hour before serving. Blueberries have pectin in them which causes them to turn solid like Jell-O.

You can pour in individual ramekins, pour into a pie crust, or pour into popsicle molds.

MAPLE CHIA PUDDING

INGREDIENTS

¼ cup chia seeds

1 cup cashews, soaked

3 cups water

4 tablespoons maple syrup

1 tablespoon cinnamon

DIRECTIONS

1. Mix everything but the chia seeds in your blender.
2. Put chia in a 4-cup Ball jar.
3. Pour in the liquid.
4. Seal jar and shake until chia is not sticking to sides.
5. Refrigerate.

Ready to eat after 2 hours, and keeps well for a few days in the refrigerator.

CHOCOLATE PUDDING

INGREDIENTS

2 ripe avocados, halved and peeled

1/3 cup cacao powder

¼ cup raw agave nectar or maple syrup

1 teaspoon vanilla extract

Pinch of sea salt

DIRECTIONS

1. Place the ingredients in a Vitamix or food processor and blend until smooth, using a plunger or adding a small amount of coconut milk if necessary.
2. Sprinkle with walnut, hemp seeds or cashew cream — or a little of each!

Good for 2-3 days in the fridge.

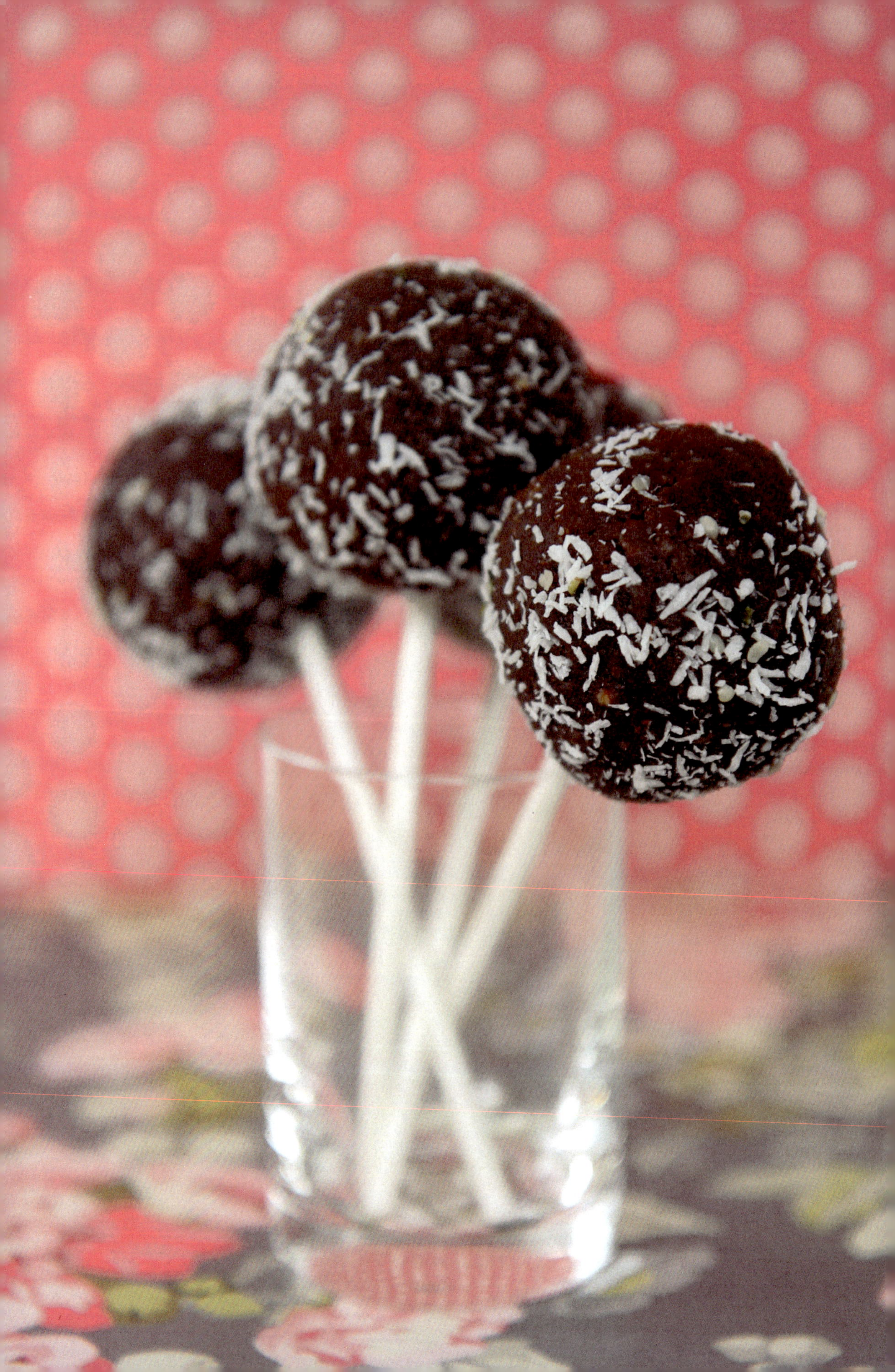

BIRTHDAY TREATS

CHOCOLATE POPS

INGREDIENTS

1 cup cashews (soaked for an hour)
1 cup cacao
1 cup Brazil nuts
1 cup maple syrup
Unsweetened coconut flakes for topping

DIRECTIONS

1. Process all ingredients in food processor to form a dough.
2. Place bowl in refrigerator for at least 30 minutes.
3. Roll dough into balls for cake pops or roll out the dough and use a cookie cutter to make shapes or just make organic cookie shapes with your hands — let the kids help!
4. Roll them in coconut flakes.

   You can freeze these and enjoy them cold; dehydrate them for 12 hours; or bake at 250° for 10 minutes.

   Store in airtight container.

BLACK BEAN BROWNIES

INGREDIENTS

2½ tablespoons flaxseed + 6 tablespoons water
¾ cup cocoa powder*
1 ¾ cups black beans
1 cup maple syrup
1 tablespoon vanilla
½ teaspoon salt
1½ teaspoon baking powder
½ cup gluten-free oats
3 tablespoons peanut butter
1 tablespoon safflower oil

*Read the label to make sure there is no added sugar or dairy.

DIRECTIONS

1. Blend flaxseed and water and let sit for 5 minutes.
2. Add the rest of the ingredients to the blender and blend until smooth.
3. Pour into silicone cupcake molds or a greased cupcake pan.
4. Bake at 350° for 20–25 minutes.

GLUTEN-FREE AND VEGAN BANANA MUFFINS

INGREDIENTS

1 cup brown rice flour
¼ cup hazelnut flour
¾ teaspoon salt
½ teaspoon baking soda
¼ teaspoon baking powder
1 ¾ cup mashed banana
5 ½ tablespoons coconut oil
¼ cup maple syrup

DIRECTIONS

1. Mix dry ingredients in a bowl.
2. Mix banana, coconut oil and maple syrup in a blender. Add mixture to dry ingredients.
3. Pour in cupcake tins greased with coconut oil. (I like mini cupcakes.)
4. Bake for 45 to 50 minutes at 350°.

CHOCOLATE VARIATION

Same recipe, but add half a cup of cacao powder to the dry mix. If you want them extra chocolatey, add a half of cup of grain sweetened chocolate chips to the batter.

FROST WITH A THICK CASHEW CREAM

For those of you who make cashew cream regularly, this will have less liquid.

INGREDIENTS

3 cups soaked cashews
½ cup coconut water
    (Start with less and add as needed)
¼ cup raw honey or maple syrup
1-2 tablespoons of vanilla

DIRECTIONS

Blend in Vitamix. (Or a food processor if nuts are very soft.)

You can add natural food colorings to make the frosting colors. The frosting on these chocolate cupcakes was colored by putting some pieces of cooked beet in the frosting. The caramel color on the following page is the natural color of the cashew cream.

250 PLAN SIMPLE MEALS: GET MORE ENERGY, RAISE HEALTHY KIDS AND ENJOY FAMILY DINNER

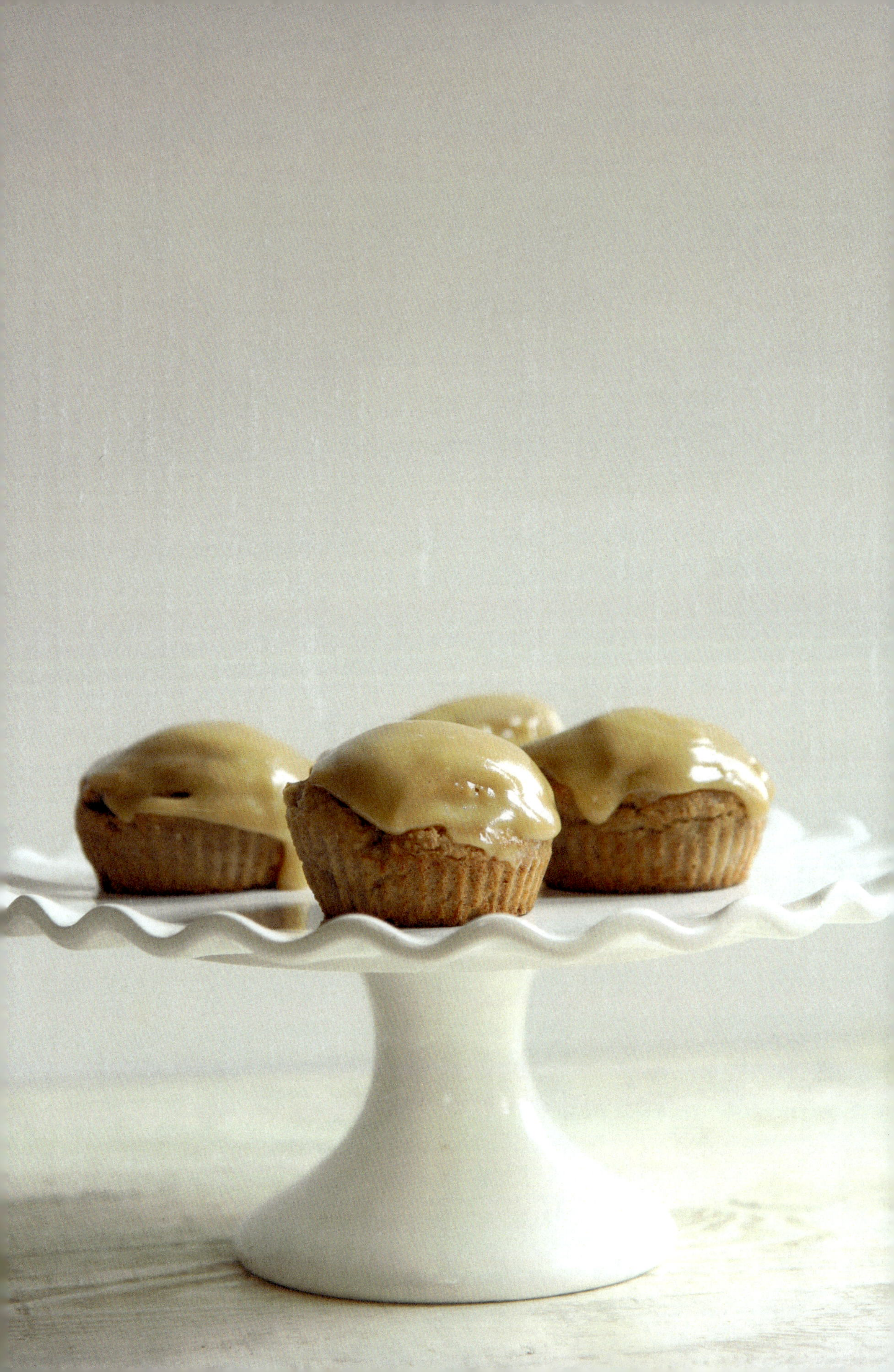

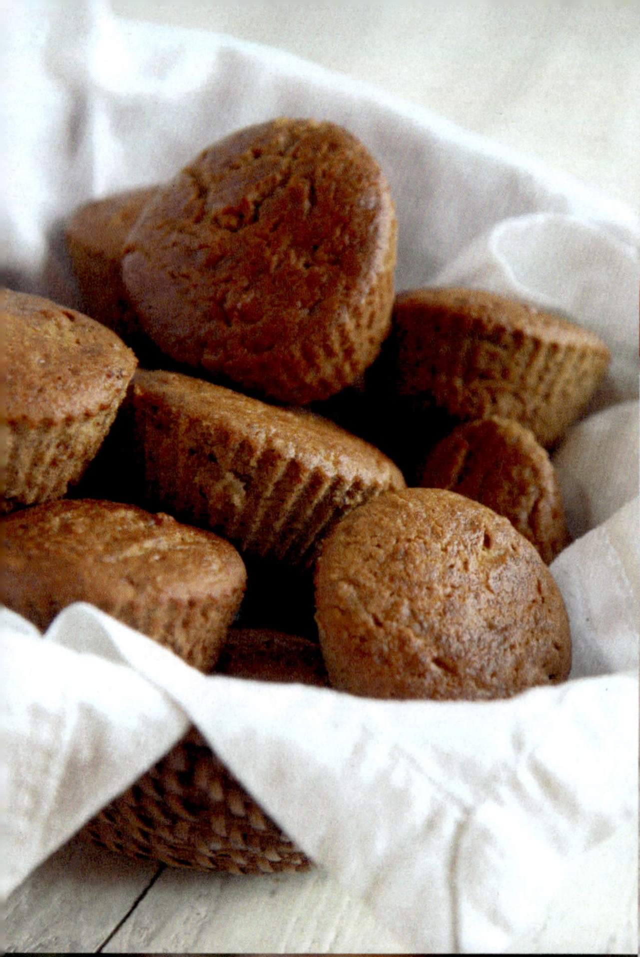
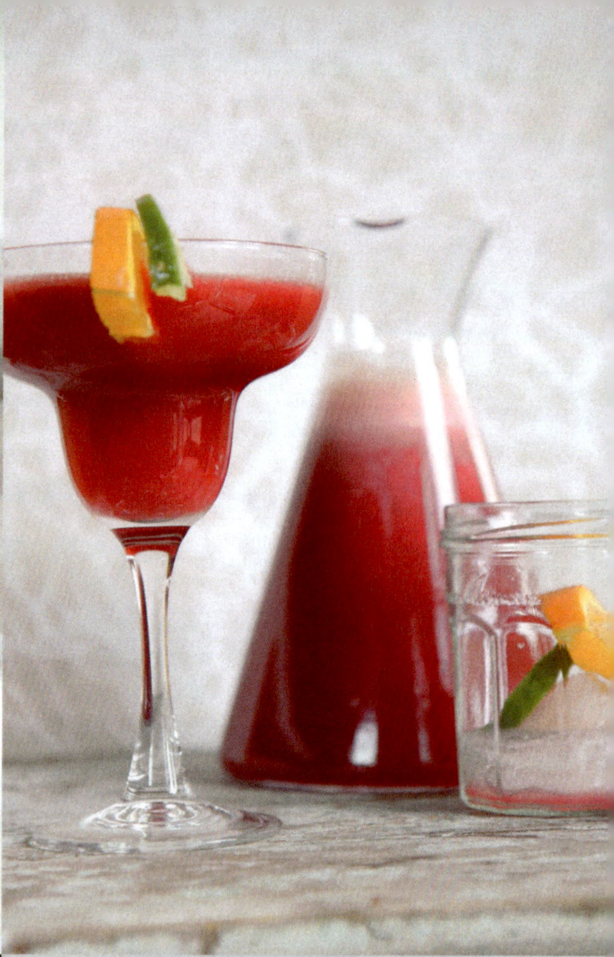
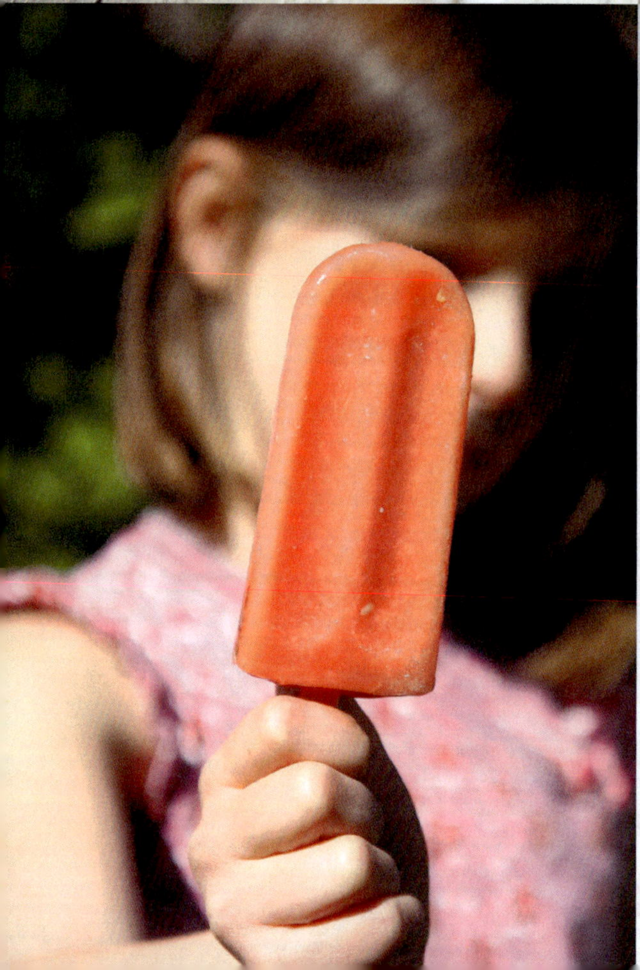
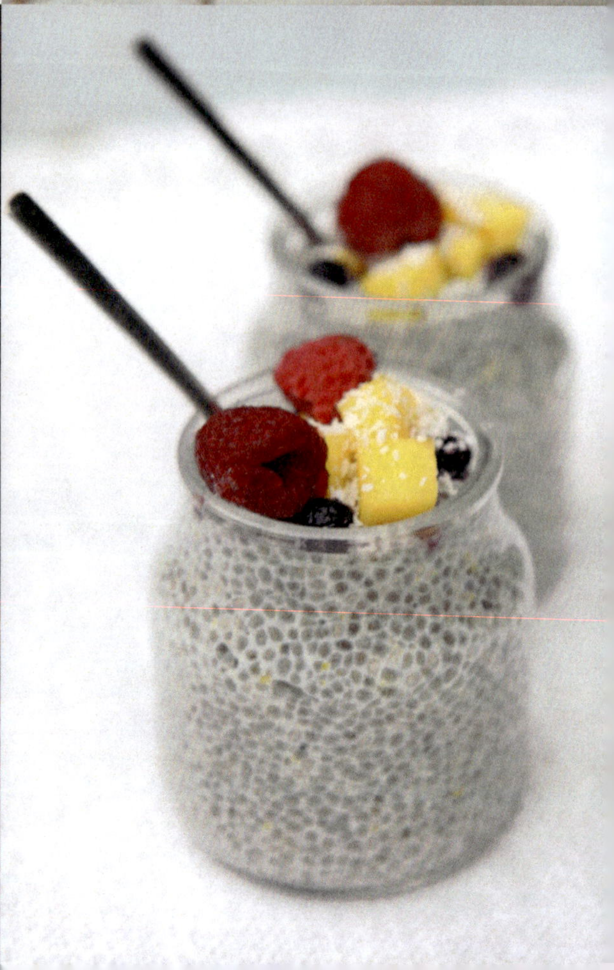

Doable Changes

Here are some doable changes inspired by this chapter. Choose one, and commit to experimenting with it this week.

1. Make a list of ten restaurants that you know have healthy options.
2. Celebrate even the smallest wins.
3. Craft your ideal holidays.
4. Tell the grandparents about your ideal holiday.
5. Drink Kombucha at the next event instead of wine.
6. Make popsicles with your kids instead of buying them so they are free of processed sugar.
7. Try chia pudding for a much-loved dairy-free, gluten-free snack.
8. Learn how to make healthy sweet treats.
9. When dining out, ask a chef to cook you his favorite gluten-free and vegan dish. It will be amazing!
10. Create a list of the foods you don't want your kids to eat and a list of the foods you would love them to eat. Communicate with them.
11. Arrange cut veggies and hummus out on the table at a time when kids come searching for snacks.
12. Bake healthy treats on Sundays.
13. Replace cookies and other boxed treats with homemade goodies.
14. Remove the packaging when you put the food away. Use glass jars instead.

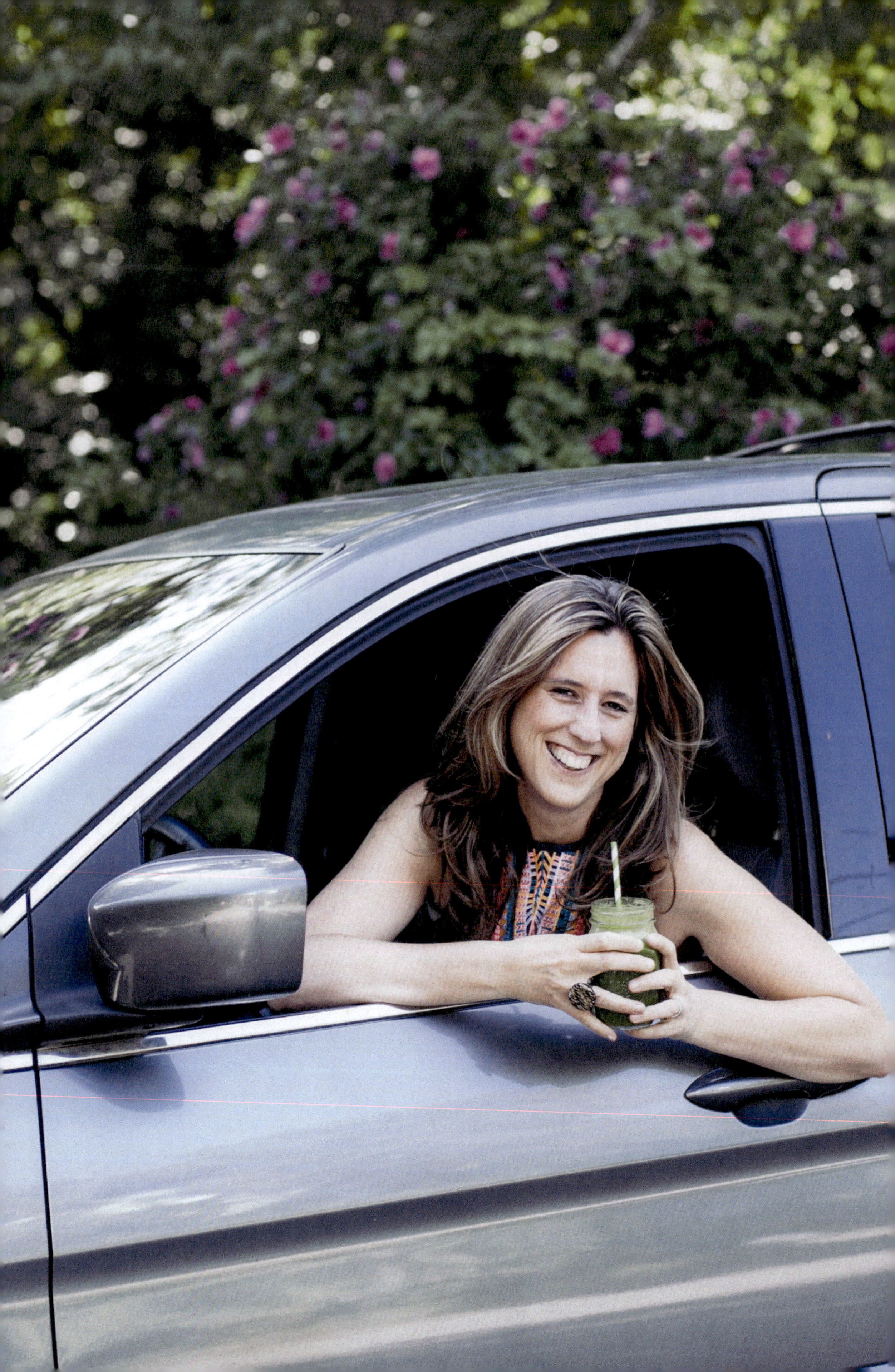

STEP SEVEN
Tell your Story

> "Be the change that you wish to see in the world."
> — Mahatma Gandhi

Our journey as eaters, teachers and storytellers does not have an end destination. It's a constant unfolding of seasons, growing of kids and making of meals that only get fuller and richer as time passes. What is the story that you will tell? What is the impact you will leave?

I often tell my story of losing 65 pounds to others as a source of inspiration, but really, that is only the beginning of my journey that is still unfolding today. Through those humble beginnings of weight loss, I learned how to cook to serve my daughter better. Once I was aware of the healing powers of food, I brought home-cooked meals to our family table. You've read how our holidays have changed, and how food has been a building block in our wellness. It's amazing how all these steps have changed both my family and myself over the years.

It's fascinating to watch how kids can show up in the world when they're not high on processed foods. And even if they may eat those foods occasionally through the course of their childhoods, they approach them with a different and enlightened perspective. Teaching healthy habits early on is a way to empower our families to make beneficial choices for their whole lives as eaters.

There's a turning point when all the changes are bigger than you. I hope you start to see this for yourself. Eventually, all these doable changes you've linked together, all these rhythms, rituals, daily healthy choices you make as an individual and as a family, begin to impact the broader conversation of healthy eating.

The role of a parent may feel inconsequential at times, but in taking care of our bodies, raising healthy children, and sharing food with those around us, we are changing the world, one meal at a time. I hope that idea empowers you to tell your story. Tell your story to others with love because that will inspire the change you wish to see in the world.

No other method is moving fast enough. Food laws are notoriously slow to change. Some schools are innovating but not at a mass level. McDonald's is not going away. The idea of food as convenience is crucial to many billion-dollar companies.

But we can start at home and our changes will have a ripple effect. I want to encourage everyone to intentionally start telling food stories. Share what you're eating and how it makes you feel.

When I see my children making healthy choices about food, I'm encouraged that what I've taught them is being seen or heard. I have met enough health-conscious high schoolers to know that good habits can be passed down.

My daughter came home recently and said, "Mama, Spanish class was crazy! No one could listen because the teacher gave us cupcakes." She is ten. They get it. They want to listen. They want to sit still. But for many of them, the food they are eating is not supporting this.

I am so far from perfect. Sometimes I yell. Sometimes I forget my green smoothie. I don't consider myself very patient. Sometimes I ignore my own advice and treat my kids to something from a bakery. This is not about perfection.

It is about treating our bodies and our planet with as much respect as we can each day.

With so much discourse going back and forth around food today—let's stop all the arguing. Instead, let's make happy, healthy choices for ourselves and celebrate them every day.

Doesn't that sound better?

It's less about demanding that our kids eat their veggies and more about inspiring them. It's less about whining at PTA meetings that lunches are bad for our kids, and more about bringing food, helping to plant a school garden or sharing our food with others.

Through all the resistance and negativity that can arise from healthy food, let's focus on the happy positives. The stories, the togetherness, the daily meals that piece together a lifetime.

Let's raise the bar everywhere we go. Let's change the ideas that have been ingrained in our minds and start anew. If enough of us start asking for sliced oranges instead of donuts at soccer practice, things are going to shift.

I invite you to join this movement.

Lead by your glowing example. By being fit. By having tons of energy. By gathering around the table for dinner every night. By appreciating every day and being grateful for the positive life around you. By watching your children grow into healthy adults and having their own children. All these things around you are evidence of your positive, healthy change.

It begins with you. You have the power, the tools, and the knowledge like never before. So really the only question is, what is your next doable step?

What is your next doable step?

I WANT TO HEAR... COME TELL ME!

INSTAGRAM @plansimplemeals
TWITTER @plansimplemeals
FACEBOOK @plansimplemeals

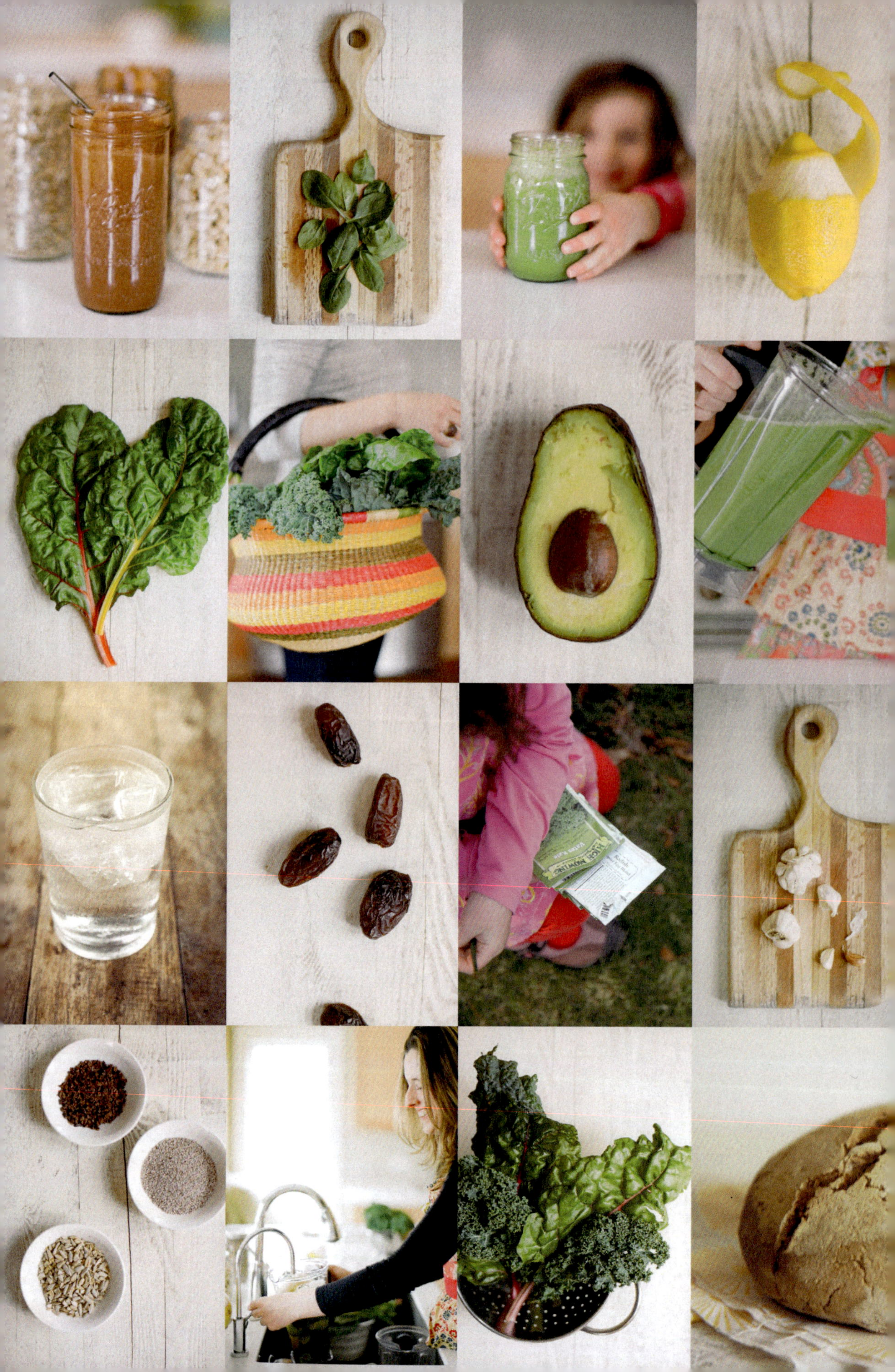

Doable Changes 2.0

Got it all down? I find there is a next step at every level. Keep going. Keep spreading your light — one doable change at a time. Together we will create a healthy future.

1. Plant a garden or a pot of herbs so your kids understand where food comes from and how to take care of it.
2. Think of how cleaning supplies, toothpaste, cream, and make-up could be cleaner. Use EWG.org as a resource.
3. Try a 30-day detox.
4. Invest in a Tower Garden and grow veggies all year (link in resources).
5. Try living one whole month off a farm share.
6. Train for a marathon.
7. Buy only organic.
8. Give up animal protein for one month.
9. Try 30 days with no processed foods whatsoever.
10. Make your own gluten-free bread.
11. Revamp your medicine cabinet. Think essential oils.
12. Drink more water.
13. Find a way that you can help spread the word about healthy eating.
14. Choose a new doable change every week — experiment.

THANK YOU! THANK YOU!

I want to deeply acknowledge all those who helped me write this book. It takes a village to raise a healthy family and the same is very much true to make a book happen.

I want to first and foremost thank my amazing husband for showing me, way before I was ready to listen, that food plays a big role in how I feel. Thank you Panch, for not saying I told you so, but patiently sticking by my side while I figured out the food, and then even more patiently being there as I created a career around it. This book would never have happened without your support.

I also want to thank my kids. Felix, Orly and Perla; you patiently sat through photoshoots and put up with your mama working longer than usual hours. More importantly, you all are part of this life that I depict on these pages and inspire me every day to show up as my best self. Felix, you were very often the voice of reason that this project really needed. Perla, you were always eager to help me in the kitchen. Orly, you are the reason I wrote this book. You are such a strong and kind girl, and it is so amazing to see you thrive as we get clear on your food allergies and sensitivities.

Thank you mom and dad for always putting family dinner first. It clearly had a big impact on me. Thank you for all the weekends you lovingly took the kids so I could write, not to mention the financial support you gave me to make this project a reality. I am so lucky to be your daughter.

Thank you Morgan, Jon and Jeremy for all your cheerleading from the sidelines that came with PR advice and logo designs. I think you all now have a Vitamix, so I feel like my job as big sister is done... Big smile.

Thank you Gene and Tamia for all the energy you bring to your kitchens. Until I met you, I did not realize how fun cooking could be. You continue to inspire me and I hope everyone who reads this book is seriously excited about green sauce!

Thank you Leah. You so beautifully took my children into your classroom and showed me how amazing a rhythm can be — it is surely the most important step presented here.

Thank you Jen Mazer, Amy Groome, Kelley Grimes, Kelsey Ramsden, Kim Deyoung, Patty Lennon, Dolores Hirschmann and Lanie Love for seeing my highest potential and gently nudging me to keep moving forward at different parts in this process. Fabienne Fredrickson, thank you for planting the seed of this book in our day together. Kate Tirone, thank you for being there on all the ups and downs of this journey and literally helping me get my thoughts from my head to paper. Taylor Wells and Nina Manolson, thank you for all you gave me at the beginning of my journey — I literally would not have gotten to this point with out those first baby steps.

Thank you Marina, you not only played a big role in the Kickstarter, but also planted the seeds to some key components that became this book —Simplicity Parenting, Waldorf and going gluten-free were all initially introduced to me by you.

Alex, I contacted you knowing only that you run an amazing business and drink smoothies. I thank you for having faith in my project. Ted gave you a chance, you gave me a chance, and now I get to pay it forward. Thank you.

All the folks at Best Selling Publishing, you were an amazing team to work with. I knew when I first met you that you would be able to help me with the parts that were not my strengths while I rolled with the design — so worth it! I can't wait for your help getting this book out in the world.

To all the amazing Kickstarter Funders. This book literally could not have happened without you. I hope it serves you and your families well as you tackle healthy eating one doable change at a time.

Three photographers played a big role in taking the shots that I could not take. Thank you Tom, Heidi, and Cristina for making the experience of being on the other side of a camera fun!

Tom Kates (http://www.tomkates.com)
Heidi (http://whiteloftstudio.com)
Cristina Llerena (http://www.crisllerena.com/)

I had this crazy idea that we needed some water colors! Thank you for making them so fabulous, Pam! The 5 illustrations were done by Pam Lostracco (http://pamlostracco.com).

THE PODCAST

Every week Mia interviews some amazing people who are on their healthy journeys too. Make sure to tune in to Plan Simple Meals on iTunes.

RESOURCES

Please visit plansimplemeals.com to see the latest promotions on the products mentioned throughout the book.

VITAMIX

If you need a Vitamix, we love getting you free shipping and great deals. Our favorite deal is the 5200 refurbished model. You can link to it from PlanSimpleMeals.com, or call Vitamix and give them the referral number 06-008764. We do get an affiliate commission, which helps us get you great recipes each week.

JUICE PLUS

If you are interested in Juice Plus — the juice supplements, vegan protein powder, or tower garden growing system mentioned throughout the book — Mia and her team of wellness warriors can hook you up.

Email mia@plansimplemeals.com and put "Juice Plus" in the subject line.

(If you know some one who distributes Juice Plus, please reach out to them first.)

CLASSES — ONLINE AND IN PERSON

There is nothing Mia loves more than teaching other busy mamas about cooking, wellness and family systems. Mia has invested in her own education along her journey, and understands the benefits of demonstrations and accountability. Please email mia@plansimplemeals.com with the subject "doable change" and she will set up a free 15 minute call to talk through your next doable change and talk through any offerings — free and paid — she may have to support you.

ACCOUNTABILITY

Please go to healthymomsmeetup.com to request access to our free forum, and meet other mamas on this journey.

We have created free worksheets that go with the exercises explained throughout the book. Please go to **www.PlanSimpleMealsBook.com/hub** to get your free printables.

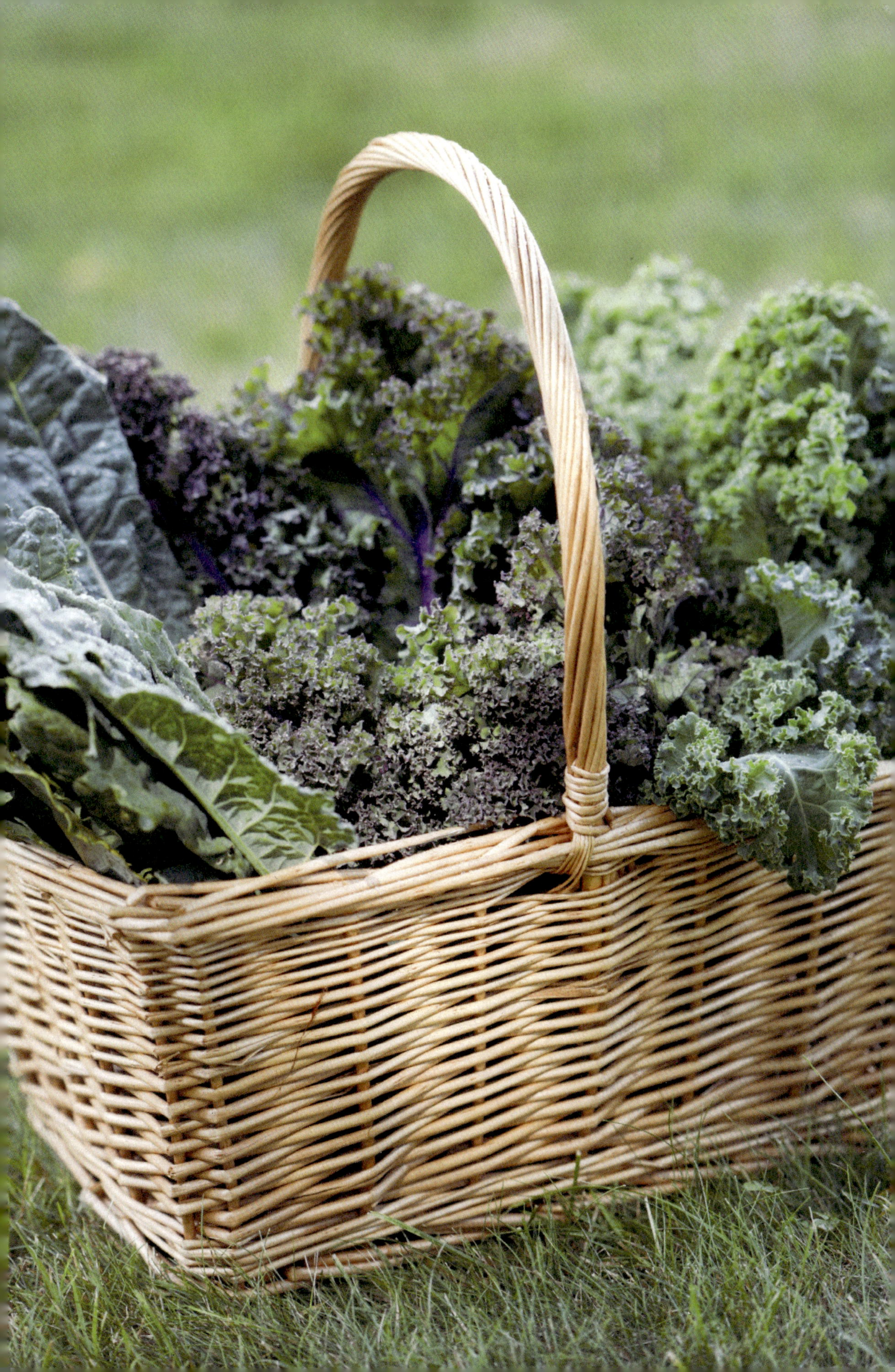

Copyright © 2016 Mia Moran.

All rights reserved. No part of this book may be used or reproduced in any manner whatsoever without prior written consent of the authors, except as provided by the United States of America copyright law.

Published by Best Seller Publishing®, Pasadena, CA

Best Seller Publishing® is a registered trademark.

ISBN-13: 978-1533490643
ISBN-10: 1533490643

Printed in the United States of America.

This publication is designed to provide accurate and authoritative information with regard to the subject matter covered. It is sold with the understanding that the publisher is not engaged in rendering legal, accounting, or other professional advice. If legal advice or other expert assistance is required, the services of a competent professional should be sought. The opinions expressed by the authors in this book are not endorsed by Best Seller Publishing® and are the sole responsibility of the author rendering the opinion.

Most Best Seller Publishing® titles are available at special quantity discounts for bulk purchases for sales promotions, premiums, fundraising, and educational use. Special versions or book excerpts can also be created to fit specific needs.

For more information, please write:
Best Seller Publishing®
1346 Walnut Street, #205
Pasadena, CA 91106

or call 1(626) 765 9750
Toll Free: 1(844) 850-3500

Visit us online at:
www.BestSellerPublishing.org.

Made in the USA
Columbia, SC
18 July 2017